What Should I Tell the Kids?

What Should I Tell the Kids?

A PARENT'S GUIDE TO REAL
PROBLEMS IN THE REAL WORLD

Ava L. Siegler, Ph.D.

A DUTTON BOOK

DUTTON
Published by the Penguin Group
Penguin Books USA Inc., 375 Hudson Street,
New York, New York 10014, U.S.A.
Penguin Books Ltd, 27 Wrights Lane,
London W8 5TZ, England
Penguin Books Australia Ltd, Ringwood, Victoria, Australia
Penguin Books Canada Ltd, 10 Alcorn Avenue, Toronto, Ontario, Canada M4V 3B2
Penguin Books (N.Z) Ltd, 182–190 Wairau Road, Auckland 10, New Zealand

Penguin Books Ltd, Registered Offices:
Harmondsworth, Middlesex, England

First published by Dutton, an imprint of Dutton Signet,
a division of Penguin Books USA Inc.
Distributed in Canada by McClelland & Stewart Inc.

First Printing, November, 1993
10 9 8 7 6 5 4 3

LIBRARY OF CONGRESS CATALOGING-IN-PUBLICATION DATA:
Siegler, Ava L.
     What should I tell the kids? : a parent's guide to real problems
in the real world / Ava L. Siegler.
         p. cm.
     Includes index.
     ISBN 0-525-93648-3
     1. Child rearing. 2. Parenting. I. Title.
HQ772.S495 1993
649'.1—dc20   93-13413
                                                 CIP

Printed in the United States of America
Set in Century Expanded
Designed by Eve Kirch

To my husband, Bob Siegler,
whose abiding love has made
all things possible,
and
for our sons, Dan and Jess

CONTENTS

ACKNOWLEDGMENTS

Acknowledgments tell a special story all their own—how things began and what happened along the way—so it is a great pleasure to thank all the people who have meant so much to me.

Though my parents, Charlotte and Phillip Heyman, did not live to read this book, I hope their wisdom is very much alive in its pages. I want to thank them both for creating the kind of family in which love, respect, and support were constant. I thank my sisters, too, Saida Baxt, M.D., and Adria S. Hillman, Esq., for their affection, intelligence, and endless generosity. Ed and Florence Brown, dear friends, played a supportive role in this, as in so many other important parts of my life.

Arnold Dolin, Associate Publisher of Dutton, has my deepest gratitude for his unflagging support from the very beginning to the very end of this project. I have also been fortunate to have wonderful editors—Deborah Brody, whose enthusiasm always buoyed my spirits, and Alexia Dorszynski, whose sensitive commentary helped bring this book to its final shape. I am particularly indebted to James Levine, my literary agent, who has championed me with such thoughtful and impressive professionalism.

My sincere thanks go to Rose Marie Horvath, my invaluable assistant, who deciphered my handwritten drafts with patience and persistence. I also want to acknowledge the tremendous debt I owe to psychoanalytic theory, and to all my patients, who helped me to learn about the pain and pleasures of family life. Last, I thank my husband, Bob Siegler, whose rare sensibilities and wit have sustained me throughout this year and all our years together.

Ava L. Siegler, Ph.D.
New York
1993

Introduction

As parents we have a peculiar job. We spend years devoting ourselves to the care of our children in order to help them to leave us! It takes us a very long time to do this job well—as much as twenty years, longer than any other creature on earth. And even then, our children only become relatively independent from us. Most of them keep their connection to us once they are grown and will miss us when we die—just as we miss our parents. This persistent attachment between parents and children produces much of the pain and pleasure in human affairs. It informs our myths and religions, influences our literature and art, and defines our destiny.

When we first begin the job of being parents we all work overtime. Remember all those sleepless nights! But as our children grow, we're able to move to part-time work, and eventually we semi-retire from our job as parents, as our kids become adults and move away from our home. We realize that we will not be required to be child-bound forever, and this promise of eventual freedom helps us to make the enormous personal sacrifices that are a necessary part of every parent's job: We feed the baby, so that he will one day know how to feed himself; dress him so that he will one day dress himself; wash him so that he will one day wash himself; speak to him so that he will one day speak; soothe him so that he will one day soothe himself; and love him so that he will be able to love himself and others. This is an extraordinarily complicated and demanding job, but most of us accomplish it day after day, without any special training. Though most of us become parents, few schools prepare students for that eventuality; the information we need wasn't tucked into our schedule between algebra and earth science!

In the past twenty years I have worked with thousands of parents and children in all kinds of settings—in my office, in mental health clinics, in public and private schools, in social agencies, and in the courts.

I have seen happy families, where a child was adopted after years of trying to conceive; bewildered families, where a child had run away from home; mortified families, where a child was expelled from school; stunned families, where a child was diagnosed with leukemia; bitter families torn apart by divorce; grief-stricken families, where death had claimed a parent; shocked families, where a child was sexually molested; exhausted families, where alcohol addiction had taken its toll. I have seen sixteen-year-old mothers struggling to raise a child alone without support. I have seen forty-seven-year-old mothers struggling to raise a child with a husband and a great deal of support. I have also become a wife and a mother myself and raised two children. In that amazing transformation, I have had the chance to learn firsthand about the pain and pleasure of parenthood. I have become convinced that it is very hard to be a parent; it is even harder to become a good one—the kind of parent we would all like to be.

Why is being a parent such a hard job? For one thing, *a parent's psychological job never ends.* We all become only relatively independent from the people who first loved us and took care of us. Even when we are physically independent and raising our own families, the image and influence of our original family stays with us and echoes throughout our lives and within the lives of our children.

For another, *parents must continually sacrifice their own desires for those of their children.* A parent cannot leave a feverish child alone in the house in order to catch a late movie, or decide to hitchhike cross-country in the middle of the school year, or fly to Africa to participate in an archaelogical dig without consequences for her children.

Third, *the life of a parent is also the life of a gambler.* In the face of uncertainty, so many things can happen, and so few of them are of our choosing or under our control. Life makes unexpected claims on parents again and again: an unplanned pregnancy, a sudden illness, a separation that comes as a shock, a death in the family. Our children also share our fate. We are hard-pressed ourselves to understand life's twistings and turnings, but it is even more difficult to explain these unpredictable and devastating events to children.

And last, but hardly least, *our modern world is dramatically different from that of any previous generation.* Social and family structures have drastically changed, as have the politics and economy of the world around us. All of this means that today's parents are faced with the challenges of managing new problems with their children that they may never have expected—stepparenting, AIDS, drug abuse, and more.

It is hard enough to move from being someone's child to being someone's parent, but it is even harder when we can barely see any resemblance between the world we grew up in and the world we have created for our own children. Today's parents must learn to walk a thin line between the *exposure* of their children to life's possibilities and the *protection* of their children from life's burdens. This is not easy to manage when we feel flooded by images of destruction in our world and confused by feelings of helplessness in ourselves. The most frequent question I have been asked by *all* parents I have seen in *all* the different circumstances in which they have sought my help has been *"What should I tell the kids?"* The topics I have chosen to explore are the same topics parents have most frequently asked me about. The ways I suggest you talk to kids are the ways that have worked with the kids and parents I've known.

There will be times when you don't agree with something I say in one of these chapters. You may come from a culture where the things I mention are not a problem; your religion, your grandmother, or your doctor may have given you a different way of thinking about the issue I am discussing. This is a book about *your choices* as a parent, not about *my* conclusions as a professional. It is a book to help you understand what to tell your kids, and why they need to be told, and how, and when. It is *not* a book about right and wrong. My hope is that this book will help you to get your bearings as a parent, as you and your child set out together, and to give you some new ways of seeing, some new ways of understanding, and some new ways of speaking.

There's an old saying, "If you can get through life, you can get through anything." I hope this book will help you get through your life as a parent. If you get through that, the rest should be easy!

1

Protective Parenting

We all want to raise our children to make their way in the world without us. That's a parent's job. But it's not so easy to accomplish—particularly in today's world where our children are exposed to so much, so soon. It may be that our world has changed more in just one generation than at any previous time. But no matter how nostalgic we may feel for "the good old days"—and our preoccupation with old styles, old movies, old sitcoms, and old music indicates that we all retain a strong emotional connection to our past—change is inevitable in human affairs. And parents today are already adapting their lives to meet the challenges of these times. If a father's income alone can no longer support the family, then mothers must also work, necessitating leaving a child in the care of others. If one out of two marriages end in divorce, then single parents (raising their children on their own) must double their efforts (emotional and financial) to provide for their children. If economic and political and environmental changes will leave our children with shrinking or depleted resources in the future, then we must prepare them to manage their lives with less than we have, rather than more. And we will need to adapt to our new world in psychological ways as well.

All of the changes that I have been describing in our world contribute to what I call the "betrayal of childhood." These

changes have made it harder for children to simply feel secure; they have made it harder for parents to keep their children safe; and they have made it harder for all of us to be
protected from daily intrusions. These changes have also made
it harder for our teachers to educate our kids, for our law en-
forcement officers to police our streets, and for our doctors to
treat our problems.

We have already begun to see the results of some of these
inevitable changes on children—in the increase in learning disabilities, in the rise of juvenile violence, in early drug and alcohol abuse, and in the increased incidence of childhood
depression and suicide. Today's children, exposed so early to
the temptations of modern life, are less able than ever to "just
say no"—to drugs, to alcohol, to sex, to crime. We have seen
some of the results of these changes on parents, too—in the
rise in job dissatisfaction, in the increase in family violence, in
drug and alcohol addiction, in the statistics on divorce, in the
spread of stress-related diseases, and in the increased incidence of parental child abuse, both physical and sexual.

There is a special pressure on parents to try to find a way
to establish and maintain the safety of their children particularly at the time that the child begins to move outside of the
family circle and begins to wonder and to worry about the
world—three to twelve years of age. These are the years
when a child's character will take root and begin to establish
itself; this is the time when both thinking and feeling begin to
crystallize; these are the years when kids will ask those hard
questions. When they do, we may feel as if we're being asked
to manage problems with our children that we may never
have envisioned, let alone encountered when we were growing
up! On the one hand, we want our children to be stimulated by
experiences that will enhance their growth, but on the other,
we also want our children to be shielded from experiences
that might compromise their development. How can we find
the right balance?

In order for our kids to grow up and grow away from us we
need to help them overcome their fears. Of course, all children
have fears (all adults, too!). But often it seems as if our kids'
ordinary fears have been heightened by today's extraordinary

pressures, at the same time that our abilities as parents to protect our children seem considerably diminished. We work outside the home at demanding jobs, our children are supervised by caregivers or sent to preschool and play groups early in their lives, and they are inevitably exposed to the pervasive influence of television. All of these factors draw our children away from the family circle more quickly. But even if none of these outside influences existed, there would still be the possibility of unpredictable events that can happen within our families. Parents can separate, shattering family life; a depressed father can become an alcoholic, or a young mother can suddenly fall ill; a home can burn to the ground; a brother can go out sailing and drown; a child can be mugged in the park. When things like this happen, we all feel uncertain about how to help. What should we tell our kids?

Fortunately, there is a powerful weapon against adversity easily available to us—*plain talk*, the kind of talk that I believe will help you become a *protective parent*, a parent who can help your kids to thrive in the face of adversity. In order to become this kind of parent, you'll need to understand how kids grow and develop, you'll need to know how times have changed and how to change with them, you'll need to find out what fears your children face, and you'll need to learn how to talk to your kids about tough topics.

At the beginning of a child's life, we make many choices about his survival because without proper attention to food, clothing, sleep, and safety, a baby will not thrive. (The thousands of baby care books that are written for new parents are proof of how difficult even these most basic decisions can be in the first years of a baby's life.) But as the baby grows and becomes a child, our choices are no longer limited to these basic needs. Now we must address ourselves to the kind of child we want to raise and the kind of life we want our kind of child to have. Now we need to make more subtle and complicated decisions. Should I let her continue to suck her thumb or make her stop? Should I send him to nursery school, or is he too young? Should I warn her about strangers, or will it only frighten her? Should I let him cross the street alone? Is it all right for her to watch that horror movie if all her friends do?

Should I tell my eight-year-old about homosexuality? What should I tell him?

We make these decisions all the time—instinctively. Many of them involve important judgments about whether to expose our child to a new experience that could be helpful or to protect him from some new experience that could be harmful. We make these decisions without knowing where we developed our parental "instincts." Sometimes we feel that a particular decision is easy; it just takes "common sense." Sometimes the decision seems very hard. Most of the time when we make these decisions as parents we are acting out of our own personal history, either identifying with those aspects of our own relationship with our parents that we liked—"I loved the times my Dad let me work with him in the garden. He was so patient with me, even though I was a klutzy kid"—or reacting against those aspects of our parents that we disliked—"I promised myself I would never, ever make my kids finish everything on their plates like my Mom did!"

It is not unusual for some of our good intentions to backfire—"I swore no daughter of mine would ever have to get dressed up in frills or wear her hair in corkscrew curls like I did, and now all she wants are these awful pink party dresses and curled hair!" or "We never let him play with aggressive toys of any kind, not even water pistols. We wouldn't even let him dress up as a soldier on Halloween, and now all he reads about is World War II." And sometimes, no matter how hard we try, we can't seem to stop ourselves from taking after our own parents: "My mother smacked me across the face if I was fresh to her, and now when my daughter sasses me, I can barely stop myself from smacking her, even though I remember how much I hated it." This means that we not only need to protect our kids against harsh aspects of the world, we need to protect them against harsh aspects of ourselves as well.

As their children grow, wise parents try to do less and less, permitting their kids to take on more and more responsibility for their own existence. The better we manage this lessening of our influence—a sort of built-in job obsolescence—the more capable and confident our child is likely to feel about stepping outside of the family circle and facing the world. We also realize that as our kids grow, we have in fact less and less control over their circumstances and choices. When a child is very little, we feel we can still define her world. If anything goes wrong, Mommy can usually "kiss it and make it all better." But soon our child begins to encounter people, events, and situations that Mommy or Daddy can no longer solve. As our children begin to move out of our arms and into the world, we begin to feel less powerful as parents. Sometimes this makes us offer more protection than the child really needs.

If a child is overprotected, parents can prevent the very growth and maturity that they wish for their child; she may have little or no motivation or skill for facing the challenges of life. We call these kids "infantile," or "immature," or sometimes "spoiled." We see them as ill prepared to cope with real life and overly dependent on their parents, or anyone they can get to serve as parents. They can feel uncertain and insecure about themselves and require constant adult attention. They can become hypochondriacal, exhibiting every little ache and pain for adult examination, or they can suffer from a Peter Pan syndrome, always looking for a "mum" like Wendy to take care of them so they can stay children forever, and never, ever grow up. Here's an example of an overprotective parent at the park whom we can all recognize. Her own caution undermines her son's confidence:

DAN: Look at me, Mommy, look at me! I'm a monkey! *(climbing higher on the jungle gym)*

MOM: Stop, Dan! Don't move! That's too high. You're going to fall and hurt yourself. I'm coming right over to take you down. How many times have I told you it's dangerous to climb so high!

Here's another way this mom could respond so that her anxieties don't undermine her son's achievements:

DAN: Look at me, Mommy, look at me! I'm a monkey! *(climbing higher on the jungle gym)*

MOM: I see you, Dan! You really are a monkey up there so high. Hold on tight! I'm going to come over there to see you in your jungle. If you need some help coming down, Mr. Monkey, let me know.

Sometimes, in contrast, parents feel that the sooner their children learn about the real world the better off they'll be, and they try to expose them as early as possible to adult experience. But if a child is overexposed, a parent may actually prevent the very growth and maturity she wishes, because her child's limited psychological resources are called upon prematurely. At the time, these kids may seem to manage perfectly well, but they often pay a high price for this effort later on in life. When I was a young teacher in an inner city school system, I remember being extremely impressed by the strength and maturity of one little ten-year-old girl whose mother had recently died. Ellen seemed to be managing well, but she never seemed to hand in her homework. When I asked to speak with her after school, she became frantic. I learned that she was responsible for the care of her four-year-old sister (whom she collected from a daycare center each day), an infant brother (whom she picked up from a neighbor's home by 5 P.M.), and her bedridden father (who was ill but desperately trying to keep the family together and the children from being sent into foster care). This little girl was sole caretaker, cook, and nurse for her entire family, a job she performed valiantly—but in the process, her childhood was completely eclipsed.

We call kids like Ellen "pseudo-mature," or "overly grown-up," or "parentified" children. We see them as kids who are at risk for later psychological problems because they've been pushed beyond their psychological endurance, just as kids who are pushed beyond their endurance physically may be at risk in their lives for physical problems. Sometimes they may suffer from what I call the "Superman/Clark Kent" syndrome: On the outside these kids look strong and powerful like Superman, but inside they feel weak and vulnerable like Clark Kent, the mild-mannered reporter. This discrepancy is painful to the child. He may feel he's a "phony" or a "fake"; he may believe that he's fooling everyone by "putting up a good front," or by "putting on a happy face," and feel that no one knows his true self.

All of us, then, with each of our children, must find the right balance between exposure and protection. The nature of this balance will vary because each child's development, temperament, cultural background, and destiny are unique. The balance also varies because each parent's development, temperament, cultural background, and destiny are unique, too. One parent may encourage a child to be fearless and adventurous, because she felt fearful and inhibited as a child, while another, faced with a temperamentally bold and active child, may attempt to restrain the child because her culture rewards more sedate behavior in girls. A third child's fate may move him from one country to another, as he and his family follow in his father's occupational wake, while a fourth child's mother may need months of hospitalization because of an accident, compelling her to relinquish parental control to others.

A parent could well strive for a different balance between exposure and protection for different children in the same family or for the same child at different points in his life. However, regardless of the child's temperament, the family's culture, or the parent's destiny, we all continuously participate in decisions regarding the exposure or the protection of our kids. This is what the job requires; this is what being a parent means.

Creating a Cushion of Safety for Your Kids

When you first learn how to drive a car, your instructor teaches you to leave a *cushion of safety* between yourself and the car ahead of you. In case of an unexpected move by the other driver, this cushion of safety will leave you enough room to think and to take action to protect yourself. In these times, parents, too, need to think of creating an emotional cushion of safety for their kids. I call this cushioning "protective parenting." Protective parenting means helping kids to establish psychological room to bounce back from the unexpected assaults of modern life—a bitter divorce, an uncle with AIDS, the suicide of a friend's mother. Protective parenting enables you and your child to meet the special demands of modern life with more strength and more resources. It is based on four ideas:

- *Avoiding Overexposure:* Today's children see and hear too much, too soon.

- *Avoiding Underprotection:* Today's parents spend a limited amount of time with their kids, so they have less ability to safeguard their kids and to maintain the developmental sanctuary of childhood.

- *Talking About Tough Topics:* Today's parents need to explicitly address the specific psychological needs of their children to combat today's special pressures.

- *Providing a Cushion of Safety:* Addressing these psychological needs directly enhances your child's development and strengthens her reserves to deal with her destiny.

Psychological resources are similar to financial resources. When you are a protective parent, you help your child to build up an "emotional bank account" as she grows, upon which she can draw in hard times.

Let's take a parent we mentioned before, the mother who was smacked as a child for being fresh and now feels like hitting her daughter for the same behavior. This mother is still reacting now to being hit when she was a child. As a child, she was the victim of her mother's temper, but she also felt that her mom wouldn't be hitting her if it wasn't her fault. Consequently, she blamed herself. Now, when her own daughter is fresh to her, she is torn: If she remembers how she felt as a child, she will want her daughter to "get away with it" without being punished—indeed, she may encourage her daughter to be fresh without realizing it! But if she identifies with her own mother now that she's a mother and no longer the child, she is no longer a victim. Now she's the aggressor and in control. In this case, she will be compelled to punish her bad daughter (and also punish the old, bad part of herself). She will not want to protect her daughter, but rather to *expose* her to exactly what she was exposed to as a child. When this happens, the mother switches roles, like an actor switching parts, and she winds up with an irresistible impulse to smack her daughter's face! If you find yourself in this same psychological spot, you can help yourself to understand what's going on by *remembering* rather than reacting. To help you remember, and gain more control over yourself, you need to ask yourself questions like:

- Why does my daughter's sassiness bother me so much?
- Was I fresh as a child, or was any other member of my family?
- How did my daughter get so fresh, anyway?
- How did my own mother handle it when I was fresh?
- Do I feel my mother was right or wrong?
- Do I want my daughter to feel toward me the way I felt toward my mother?

Your answers to these questions ("I wasn't fresh, but my kid brother was, and boy, did he get into hot water with his big mouth!") will help you to remember the trouble spot in your own past, revive the feelings you once experienced, and reevaluate your behavior in the present.

Fast Forward: Changes in Our World, Changes in Ourselves

Children need to feel secure about themselves and their lives in order to meet the demands of ongoing development without resisting or retreating from the challenges they face. And it's up to us as parents to provide our kids with this security. The British pediatrician turned child analyst Donald Winnicott called this kind of parental care "good-enough mothering." This kind of parenting helps the child feel safe and comfortable; it provides her with a foundation for further growth.

But even when a child has a good-enough parent, her safety can always be subverted—a mother unexpectedly called out of town by her job, a harsh and humiliating teacher, a father who's a compulsive gambler, the accidental death of a play-mate, a home destroyed by floodwaters can all interrupt the child's development. Any of these events could happen to any of us at any time, but if we are lucky, not many of them do, or at least not all at the same time. When difficult things happen to us we call it stress; when a lot of difficult things happen to us at once, we call it cumulative stress. We know that there are profound, long-term effects on both our minds and our bodies from cumulative stress: It can break down our physical immunological system, which defends our bodies from physical illness. It can also break down our psychological immunological system, which defends our minds from psychological ill-ness.

As our world changes, as we change with it, and as our children are born into these changing times, the potential in-terruptions of our lives become more pervasive and more per-sistent. Many of us live in cities, where the pace of life and the stimulation of the ordinary sights and sounds of our days are intense and often overwhelming: We are confronted by home-less men sunken in doorways, drug peddlers hustling in parks, sirens screaming in the distance. Our children have to learn how to become street-wise, adept at negotiating their way through their city world. They must develop thick skins to protect them from the painful part of what they see and hear. They learn to keep their doors locked and their keys around their necks, not to walk down dark streets, to keep "street rent" in their pockets and their real money in their socks in case they're mugged. Sometimes this makes them appear cal-lous; they are trying to deal with the stress of their ordinary city lives.

But even in the relative quiet of small towns and villages, our children are exposed to more of life than ever before through the pervasive influence of television. It is hard to overestimate the impact that television has had on family life in this country, or on the education of our children. Most kids spend more hours of their day in front of a television set than in the company of adults. And many children are more familiar with the thoughts and feelings of characters in television shows than they are with the thoughts and feelings of their own friends and family. A two-year-old can click on the television with the remote control and flip through twenty channels. A four-year-old can take out any movie from her parents' collection and slip it into the VCR without any help or supervision.

TV OR NOT TV

Television is a pervasive and persuasive part of our lives; virtually every American household has at least one television set. Television shapes the popular culture that influences our children. But most television programming is not geared to the developmental needs of children; rather it is geared to the needs of advertisers and the entertainment of adults. Throughout each day a great deal of information and misinformation is continuously broadcast to our kids. The average child in our country spends almost five hours a day watching television! This fact alone dictates that television viewing be closely supervised by a protective parent. This supervision will be relatively easy when your child is very young, but it will become increasingly difficult as your child grows older and visits other homes, joins in sleepovers, and goes to parties. That's another reason why the early foundation you lay down with your kids is so very important. Your children need to hear about life from *you*, first, before the media takes over!

As a protective parent, you need to limit your child's exposure to adult television, just as you would limit his exposure to adult movies, particularly when he is most impressionable and the least able to understand these impressions—from ages two to five. You cannot build a cushion of safety into your child's development if you permit your child unsupervised access to television. A three-year-old who watches the news every night—with or without you—is learning in vivid color about all the horrible things that can happen in life. (That's what makes it news!) Not only the news but commercials, rock videos, movies, and even game shows often portray people in situations that distort, devalue, or damage the values and attitudes we want our children to see and absorb.

And don't forget about your VCR: That's television viewing, too. Be sure to keep your adult collection of videos separate from your child's collection. Young children are confused and overstimulated by explicit sexual scenes and can become anxious and frightened by scenes of violence.

Here are some televisions *do's* and *don'ts* to help guide you as you try to be a protective parent:

Do: Use the enormous educational resources of television programming to expose your child to more of the world than he could ever see before. Take advantage of children's shows created by the Children's Television Workshop, and nature, science, and news shows for kids, etc.

DON'T: Let your child watch shows you haven't seen and admired. Even some children's programs can distort and damage development, too. Watch those Saturday morning shows and make an informed decision.

Do: Limit the amount of time per day that you want your child to be sitting and watching television. Remember, no matter how good the program is, children still need to move and run and actively use their bodies!

DON'T: Use television as a babysitter or as a substitute for you. It can't hug or talk to your child.

Do: Make sure anyone who cares for your child when you're not there understands and supports your view about television.

DON'T: Let your child hang around watching just any show that an adult has selected to watch. Don't let her keep the adult company if the adult is watching something inappropriate for her.

Do: Resist your child's attempts at peer pressure ("Mommy, everybody watches *Friday the 13th!*").

Don't: Take an extreme or rigid position that doesn't take into account your child's need to be a part of his own generation and its culture.

Remember, television, early education, and substitute caregivers may occupy most of the day for a child as young as two. This often means that even if a parent wants to offer her kids protection against the intrusions of modern life, she may have absolutely no idea what her child has been exposed to on any given day. She may not know what has disrupted her child's life, or what stress he has suffered.

This book is about helping you become protective parents. It's about knowing how and when to talk to kids; it's about finding out where you developed your parental instincts. It's about helping you build in a cushion of safety for your kids by understanding their fears and talking to them about tough topics. And finally, it's about how to exercise the kind of "good-enough" parental judgment that advances your kid's psychological growth and prepares her to take her place in the real world.

In many of the chapters of this book, there will be a section for parents called *"What Should I Ask Myself?"* In these special sections I will try to help you explore your own history as a child, so that you can see how and why you are encountering difficulties in your job as a parent. Usually when parents become entangled or frustrated with themselves and their kids, it's because they've come up against an obstacle that they were never able to work out when they were children with their own parents.

Now let's look at the basic fears that form part of every child's approach and reaction to the changing challenges of life.

2

The Five Basic Fears

An Ordinary Child's Life

We are all afraid at times. Only over time do we learn to become brave, and even then we can never learn to be completely brave—there is always someone or something that can make us feel apprehensive. Being afraid at times is a normal part of being human. Fear reflects the power of our senses, our consciousness, our intelligence, and our imagination. Being afraid is also crucial to our survival: fear is an emotional warning signal, just as fever is a physical warning signal. Our fears tell us that what we are doing, or thinking about doing, could be dangerous; fear keeps us alert and alive. Fear teaches us to think before we act.

Children are afraid of the world with good reason. No animal on earth is as helpless for as long a period of time as a human baby. It cannot walk; it cannot talk; it cannot feed itself. It is wholly dependent on the care of an interested and devoted adult for its survival and remains more or less dependent on that adult for many years.

Children's fears are shaped by their lives. Being left in the care of strangers, seeing blood ooze out of a tiny cut, losing consciousness while falling asleep, seeing giant shadows moving in the dark are things that young children fear—and rightly so, since all of these warning signs could indicate a more serious danger. A young child cannot yet understand that Mommy will soon return, or that bleeding will stop, or that he will wake up alive and conscious in the morning, or that nothing fearful lurks in the dark. The child's mind is still developing, his body is small and vulnerable, and his imagination is easily stirred.

In addition, a young child has an undeveloped sense of time and space, of cause and effect, and of action and consequence. She does not understand how long two hours is or how far away California is. He thinks that because he wet the bed Daddy divorced Mommy, or that the new baby got sick because he wished it would. Young children must be taught not to touch a flame, so they won't get burned, and that they cannot lean out a window, because they'll fall.

At first, young children see their parents as masters of their destiny. They believe that their parents can control all the events of their life, and this is reassuring. But quickly they learn otherwise. It frightens children to learn that accidents, disease, and death fall outside of their control and yours; it frightens parents, too. Parents must accept the fact that there will be many problems they cannot solve for their children no matter how hard they try: a friend is diagnosed with cancer, a grandfather dies, a teacher is mugged, a house is burglarized, a plane crashes. Some fears and anxieties may never go away, but rather ebb and flow, like our fears of illness and death. Some fears and anxieties help alert us to experiences that could be dangerous, like a fear of the dark or a fear of heights. And some fears and anxieties are even helpful, like the anxiety that helps an actor prepare for a role or a child prepare for a test.

Throughout the course of our lives, we may call our fears by many names: worry, nervousness, apprehension, anxiety, dread, horror, terror, panic. But I believe that five basic fears actually underlie many of our other feelings: fear of the *unknown*, fear of *being alone*, fears about *the body*, fear of the voice of *conscience*, and fears about *the self*. Our capacity to feel these fears is a vital part of our conscious understanding of ourselves and our world. In this respect, *fear is a develop-*

mental accomplishment. Indeed, these fears do ordinarily appear in a developmental sequence, with fears of the unknown appearing early in the life of the child, fears of being alone appearing when the child becomes aware of his attachment to and separation from the parent, fears about the body emerging as the child begins to separate from the mother's orbit and approach the world on his own, fears of the voice of conscience occurring as the child internalizes parental and social prohibitions, and fears about the self evolving as the personality of the child crystallizes.

Once established, however, in one form or another, the five basic fears remain with us throughout our lives. An important part of our job as parents is to recognize, differentiate, and describe the five basic fears for our children.

Every time you try to develop a cushion of safety to smooth over the rough spots in your child's life, every time you help him master a developmental hurdle, and every time you try to understand the impact of real problems in the real world, you will be dealing with—and helping your child deal with—some version of the five basic fears. That is why I will be highlighting their formation and transformation throughout the chapters of this book. If you understand the five basic fears, you will be able to translate your understanding of your child into the language of protective parenting—parenting that helps your children grow strong enough to embrace life's satisfactions and endure life's sorrows.

The First Basic Fear: Fear of the Unknown

Even though a child's fears are exaggerated and our child's judgments about the reality of these fears are poor, we can still understand the basis for his fear. To a great degree the child is a stranger in our adult world. Much that we take for granted is brand-new to him: light and dark, wind and rain, thunder and lightning, cold and hot. The tiniest baby responds to the warmth of his mother's arms; a four-year-old is still reassured by a light in the dark; and even a ten-year-old can still be filled with terror by the power of a storm.

Our first fears reflect the helplessness of our beginnings—the deep and primitive fears of the unknown. When we are very young, we do not even know the name for what we see, what we feel, or what we think. We rely on the familiar in order to feel safe. First, a familiar face, then a familiar toy, a familiar blanket, a familiar food, a familiar room. Anything unfamiliar—the voice of a stranger, a shiny jack-in-the-box, a paisley bedspread that looks like cat's eyes—can fill a child with fear. The child's first feelings of confidence come from being able to master the fears of the unknown. The more things stay familiar, the less these embryonic feelings of mastery are challenged. The more things become unfamiliar—if he is left in the unpredictable care of strangers, for example, or moves from apartment to apartment, or changes schools—the harder it is for the child to develop that psychological cushion of safety which buoys him against the ebb and flow of life. This is why children need the security of predictable routines, people, and places.

While the mind is capable of absorbing all kinds of new experiences—indeed, even thrives on stimulation—too much, too soon can heighten the child's fears of the unknown and prevent the child from developing a sense of security in himself and his world. Protective parenting, which gives the child an ongoing sense of safety, helps the child to absorb and digest new experiences. Some children may have heightened appetites for life. They seem to relish a great deal of experience; they open their mouths and swallow the world. Others are picky eaters and often turn their heads away; they need to be continuously tempted to taste life's experiences. By knowing what each particular child can take, parents can help to modulate their child's experiences and make unbearable events more bearable.

While we all remain, for all our lives, afraid of what we do not know, we also have an extraordinary human characteristic that mitigates against our fears: curiosity. This characteristic is so pervasive in human affairs that we are constantly warned against it in our myths, fairy tales, and proverbs. Curiosity is a powerful motivating force. It is present in the very first Bible story we learn: the story of Adam and Eve, where a woman's curiosity results in our knowledge of the world, as well as our expulsion from the Garden of Eden. It is also reflected in the Greek myth of Pandora's Box, where once again a curious woman draws us away from paradise and into the real world.

While there is no doubt that a child's fears of the unknown can draw him away from the world, curiosity plays a powerful part in pulling the child back toward it. Because curiosity is so useful to us in our lives and is at the source of much of what we call culture, it is important for parents to foster its appearance. On the other hand, parents must constantly be alerted to the dangers that curiosity may create—the interesting knobs on the gas stove, the pretty bottles of cleaning fluids under the sink, the holes in the sidewalk gratings. Protective parenting, then, means finding the right balance not only between exposure and protection of your child from stimulation, but also finding the right balance between your child's natural fears of the unknown and your child's bold curiosity.

The Second Basic Fear: Fear of Being Alone

Sometimes our fears have less to do with the world and more to do with ourselves. These kinds of fears are also called anxieties. We all know what it feels like to be anxious—that sense of dread the moment when the mind goes blank; the quavering voice and sweaty palms; those butterflies in the stomach. Our anxieties begin inside of us. At first, a young child will protest vigorously at any separation from those who love and care for him; this protest signals what professionals call separation anxiety. He will cry when you leave him in the morning to go to work, or worry about your safety when you go to the movies, or protest when you take a vacation without him. This protest is proof of your child's unique attachment to you. It demonstrates your child's recognition of your importance in his life. It expresses his fear that he might be left alone in the world without you. Adults, too, often feel like "a motherless child" when things go wrong. This fear echoes throughout our lives and plays an important part in all our relationships. It reaches back into our earliest experiences, and it testifies to our absolute dependence on our parents— particularly our mothers—for life itself. The intensity of our fear of being left alone testifies to the intensity of our earliest need for attachment.

While parents are extremely gratified when they are needed, the intensity or desperation with which the child attaches can be bewildering or can even trigger anger. A mother who has just spent all weekend with her six-year-old son can lose patience when he makes a scene about going to school on Monday morning. A father who has worked and saved to send his seven-year-old daughter to camp can feel exasperated when she calls each night begging to come home.

Parents may be unable to know when to insist that the child take the leap from attachment to separation, and when severing the tie that binds parent and child is premature or precipitous and will create more problems than it will solve. The most important thing to remember is that the transformation of an infant into an individual is a long process. The human condition often requires twenty or thirty years for this process to be completed. Even then, everyone cries at weddings, not only for happiness, but also for the sad realization that the intense attachment once felt by this young bride and groom for their parents is now being transferred onto the strangers they will marry.

In the beginning, your toddler may cry when you turn your attention away for even a phone call. He must be taught to let go of his profound attachment to you, bit by bit. You help your child to accomplish this by teaching him to be by himself for longer and longer periods of time. At first, your child will protest when you leave the room; he'll cry when his father goes to work; he'll cry when it's bedtime and he must let go of everything at once to go to sleep. But gradually, his protests will diminish. The pleasures of the freedom accompanying separation begin to outweigh the pain.

All the small separations of infancy help pave the way for the more substantial separations of childhood, where children first learn to spend large portions of their days apart from their parents. A school child, whose emotional needs are still quite considerable, may spend no more than two or three hours a day in the presence and under the care and supervision of a parent. No wonder that children protest so vigorously when their parents go out at night, as well. No matter how devoted a parent may be, modern life, with its social and economic and political realities—the need for both mother's and father's income to support the family, or the challenge and interest of career opportunities—increasingly separates us from our children, and these necessary separations are occurring earlier and earlier in the lives of our children.

Some parents, aware of the nature of the life that lies ahead, try to prepare their child by encouraging or even compelling precocious independence. This tactic usually backfires, producing not a secure and confident child but an anxious and clinging one, always afraid that his moments of attachment will be wrested away from him. Other parents, afraid to limit any attachment, hold their child too close, interfering with the child's growing need to become an individual in his own right. They make it impossible for the child to distinguish between being alone and being lonely.

As your child grows, his fears change. After babyhood, his earliest fears of the unknown are diminished by his attachment to his powerful parents, who can strengthen and soothe him. Freud tells a charming story about a little boy, afraid of the dark, who calls for his aunt to speak to him. When his aunt replies, "What good would that do? You can't see me," the little boy, smart enough to know the truth about attachment, replies, "That doesn't matter. If anyone speaks, it gets light."

Once this new capacity for love and attachment is in place, it is understandable that the child most fears its disruption. As the child begins to focus on a sense of his separate self in the world, the vulnerability of his position—increasingly detached from the powerful parents who protect him—is heightened. Two- to four-year-old children may now begin to experience the whole range of fears which are so much a part of early childhood: the biting and devouring animals (vampire bats, spiders, snakes, and crocodiles) that lie in wait behind the closet doors; the witches and monsters who devote themselves to luring and destroying unsuspecting children; the robbers, the kidnappers, and murderers they fear will steal, imprison, and kill them. These are all ordinary personifications of the passionate need for attachment and the equally passionate wish for autonomy all young children feel.

As parents, we are aware of how much our children depend on us. But we need to be equally alert to our children's emerging needs for independence. These needs ("Mommy, let me do it myself!") reach a crescendo between one and a half and three years and cause the familiar "push-pull" conflicts of will between parents and toddlers. Your toddler has a dilemma. As he begins to harbor wishes to separate and stand on his own, he also becomes increasingly resentful about his dependence on you. But how can you get angry with the very people you need? Now, your child becomes afraid of the consequences of his wishes for autonomy. By projecting his normal anger toward his real parents onto imaginary monsters and witches, the child both protects his parents from his hostility, and in the bargain, through his fearfulness, gets them to keep him attached to them.

The Third Basic Fear: Fears About the Body

Your child's own body provides him with the basis for the third fear. Children are aware of how small and helpless they are in the real world, and they are often afraid that their bodies will be hurt. In addition, their ability to distinguish between what's real and what's unreal is not yet consolidated. Young children (ages two to five) can feel confused by the blurred distinction between reality and fantasy presented by cartoons, movies, and television programs. Because they do not yet have the advantage of understanding how the body works, young children observe the world about them and come to their own conclusions. Toys break, so they think that they can break apart, too. They see men without arms and legs on the street or television, so they fear that they too can lose their precious body parts. They see that there are people with penises (boys) and people without penises (girls), so they think that penises can be taken away, can be put back, or sprout from nothing. As adults, we're all surprised by the ter-ror that a young child can feel at just a tiny cut, or their anx-iety about seeing an adult missing an arm or leg. We've all been amused by the confusion young children display about the anatomical distinctions between the sexes. The three-year-old daughter of a colleague remained convinced that her penis had broken off when she was a baby, despite her moth-er's attempts to convince her otherwise, and often embar-rassed her professional mother by asking her in public to please sew it back on!

Parents and kids can only learn about the strengths and weaknesses of their bodies through experience, through trial and error, through testing their bodies' limits. But children differ in temperament, just as they differ in height and weight. Some children are physically cautious and never place themselves in situations that they can't handle. Other children are physically bold and always seem to reach beyond what they can comfortably manage.

It takes a long time for your child to absorb more realistic ideas about his body. Some of that time, he is frightened. Dur-ing some of that time you will be frightened, too—if your child falls and breaks his wrist; if he runs into the ocean and a wave pulls him under; if he isn't at school when you go to pick him up. A parent cannot save a child's body all the time. Children can get hurt; children can even die.

We call our sense of self our ego, and we call a child's sense of his body his *body ego*. This body ego takes shape early in childhood. It grows along with your child and reflects the sum of all the courage, confidence, and pleasure that your child feels about the use of his body in the world, as well as the ef-fects of any limitations, illnesses, and pain that have fallen his way.

Many of the most bewildering scenes in childhood between parents and kids reveal underlying fears about the body. Without understanding these fears, a parent has little hope of calming a child. For example, most parents are completely be-wildered by the fuss kids typically make over a haircut, un-aware that to a young child, the scissors, the white coat of the barber, and the draping of their bodies with cloth and plastic are frightening. Think of the strange spectacle in a barber's shop, where grown men with soapy faces are being shaved. Children sit immobilized in strange chairs while men snip at their hair, which falls to the ground in sad little piles. A barber shop can seem ominous to a child, not unlike the doctor's office, another place where men in strange white coats with shiny instruments and strange chairs and tables do things that hurt. Besides the fearfulness of this association, children also see their hair as part of their body. They are filled with dread at the idea that a part of the body can be cut, fall to the floor, and be swept away beneath their feet. What appears to the parent as an ordinary visit to the barber can appear to a two- or three-year-old as his worst nightmare. The first time I took my little son to a barber for a haircut, he told me, "Please tell the man to stop cutting, Mommy; when I see the scissors, my penis gets scared."

Similarly, many kids are terrified of the toilet and cringe and cry when they must sit on it or flush it. Again to the child, urine or bowel movements are parts of the body—inside parts. A child is concerned about losing anything that was once inside of his body. This is why flushing BM's down the toilet, with its loud rushing noises, can be so scary for kids. This is also why bleeding can be so frightening to a child: What belongs inside is coming out. As one little girl I knew told me when she cut her finger, "I'm leaking, Dr. Siegler. Stop it, or I'll get all dry, and I won't be juicy anymore."

Older children may have a more realistic understanding of their bodies, but this understanding does not necessarily obliterate their fears. Even ten- and twelve-year-olds can get queasy at seeing blood or hearing about an operation. Repeated viewings of horror films, with their exaggerated blood and gore, are used by some older kids as a kind of self-imposed desensitization experience. These children have chosen to handle their fearfulness about body damage by exposing themselves to violence over and over again, until the experience gets blunted and loses its terror for them.

And even if an older child is able to negotiate the years between ten and twelve relatively smoothly, as he nears adolescence, the bodily transformations of puberty will inevitably heighten his anxieties, exposing him to a new level of fearfulness ("Am I normal? Am I ugly? When will I get taller? Why can't I control my body?").

The Fourth Basic Fear:
Fear of the Voice of Conscience

Some fears and anxieties are connected to the first stirrings of conscience. Conscience, too, must be taught by parents and learned by children. In fact, the child's conscience is really an internalized version of the parent's voice. When it is properly embedded within the child, he will not do things that the parent would disapprove of, even in the parent's absence. We learn to listen to our parents' voices when we are very young. It's a way of keeping our parents within us all the time, and it helps us to combat the fear of being left alone without our parents' love. In a young child this internalized voice still operates quite imperfectly, but an older child will respond quite well to that inner voice of conscience. This is because disobeying one's conscience produces a very unpleasant sort of fear, a feeling that we call guilt. Guilt is linked to the child's fear of the loss of the love of the parent; it also stimulates the earlier fear of being left alone.

You can easily understand the developmental differences that occur as the voice of the conscience matures and is consolidated. Picture a two-year-old, a four-year-old, and a seven-year-old left in an empty room with a jar full of cookies. The mother of each admonishes, "Don't eat the cookies!" as she leaves the room. The two-year-old, after waiting a bit, will happily consume the cookies, as the adult prohibition, carrying little weight, quickly fades from his memory. The four-year-old can be overheard saying out loud, "No, no, don't eat the cookies," but after a while, though still verbalizing the prohibition (and perhaps even looking worried), he will probably still eat some cookies. The seven-year-old, however, is already capable of listening to the voice of his conscience, and even a bite of a forbidden cookie will elicit guilt, the underlying fear of the adult's disapproval and punishment.

One of the most difficult jobs a parent has is to get children to want to do what they have to do. The internal development of the voice of conscience helps parents accomplish this, and guilt helps enforce the parental voice. The trick is to accomplish this while still preserving the child's spirit, will, and autonomy. Guilt is a necessary part of our social life, but too much guilt can cripple your child's spirit, and too little can leave him unable to tell right from wrong.

The Fifth Basic Fear: Fears About the Self

As your child becomes seven, eight, and nine years old, the earlier fears of unknown forces, of being left alone in the world, and of bodily harm will recede into the background to reappear only under specific stress—during a walk in the woods when it's dark, while he's feeling homesick on the first night at camp, when he suffers a mysterious and worrisome stomach pain. By the time your child is school age, the most significant fears he feels will have to do with his sense of self—the self he has created and now hopes the world will welcome.

This self has accumulated in layers over all the years that your child has lived—and even before his birth, because the bottom layer is your child's genetic inheritance, his biological beginnings. We know that children bring certain temperamental characteristics with them into the world. There are calm, placid babies, restless, sensitive babies, alert, active babies. As parents react and respond to their baby's temperament, they shape and are shaped by their baby's emerging personality. This then becomes the next layer of the self: the interactive experiences of parent and child. Your baby begins to perform for your approval and applause. He begins to display his characteristic behaviors in consistent ways, and you can soon tell when your baby is "acting like himself" and when "he's not himself."

As your baby becomes a child, this sense of self continues to crystallize. The self is anchored in a wide array of behaviors which characterize your child's way of being in the world. With the emergence of a continuous sense of self, *self-esteem* (good feelings about the self), *self-doubt* (uncertain feelings about the self), and *self-contempt* (bad feelings about the self) are possible. Self-esteem regulation—the ability to keep up good feelings about your self even when bad things are happening to you—now becomes a crucial developmental objective.

When your child's good feelings are compromised—by striking out at a ballgame, for example, or failing a spelling test, or fighting with his best friend—fears about the self get raised. "I'm such a loser," he may think, "Boy, am I dumb," or "Nobody likes me." Such fears come and go throughout our lives. We feel the same sense of shame, dread, and despair in our teens when we can't pass algebra, or when we're first married and we overcook the veal for our in-laws, or later in life when we lose an important case in court, or get passed over for a promotion, or discover a husband's affair.

This fifth basic fear, fears about the self, will always be with us—more or less. It's the "more or less" that protective parents try to negotiate as they and their kids develop.

These five fears mark out the boundaries of what it means to be human. They define our perceptions, stimulate our senses, guide our judgments, and testify to our shared experience in the family of man. A child raised with too much fear will cower and cringe before life's demands, but one raised with too little fear may never survive to live at all. By understanding the five basic fears, you can help your kids to strengthen and grow. By *talking* to your kids about their fears, you can become a protective parent.

Let's see how.

3

Why, When, and How
to Talk to Kids

Even before a baby is born, as she still lies nestled in the womb, we begin to talk to her. We tell her who we are and how we came to be. We tell her about the world she is about to enter and all the things we have done to prepare for her arrival. Sometimes we even sing to her or make her promises about what her life will be like. Sometimes this is a silent conversation, but often we talk aloud, hoping our baby will hear.

Once the baby is born we continue our conversation. Now we can call her by name and talk about her: "What a pretty girl. Look at those tiny toes!"—"Good morning, sweetie pie. Ready for breakfast?" The helplessness of our little baby makes us want to shield her and comfort her. Her absolute dependence on us for her survival brings out the best in us. We are beginning to become protective parents. But soon, the baby will be able to help us to do our job, because as we talk, the baby listens, and as the baby listens, she learns our language. She becomes familiar with the different sounds of our voices, and she learns how to use those voices to help her wait, to feel safe, or to go to sleep.

After a while, through imitating the sounds we make, the baby begins to be able to communicate her own newly emerging thoughts and feelings. The very first sounds a baby makes bring joy and recognition to her parents ("I think she just said

Dada, honey"). They open the way into the baby's inner world. Now you and your baby share the same vocabulary.

Talk: The Great Connector

Talking bridges the gap between you and your child. It is one of the most important ways that we come to know ourselves, each other, and the world around us. If the two of you can establish an open, honest, ongoing dialogue, you will be able to find a way to become a protective parent—one who creates a cushion of safety for your children that permits the all-important feeling of safety and security that we discussed in chapter 1. You will be able to avoid both overprotecting your child by not talking enough to her and leaving her at the mercy of her own imagination and overexposing your child by talking too much about information she is not able to manage or understand. In this chapter, I will show you why, when, and how to talk to your kids.

What We Don't Know *Can* Hurt Us

Sometimes, when parents are faced with an upsetting change or a disturbing event in their lives, they don't want to talk about it; they particularly dread telling their kids about it. They hope to save themselves and their children emotional pain by avoiding the whole issue. These parents believe that they can shield their children from traumatic events by not addressing them directly. They believe that what you don't know can't hurt you.

But this is rarely the case. Children are inherently curious and inquisitive. They find things out—particularly hidden things, particularly things you don't want to talk about. Further, by the time a child is two years old, she has a well-developed imagination. A child's imagination can easily run wild, especially if she is deprived of appropriate knowledge or excluded from vital information. When children don't know enough, they tend to imagine the worst. This means that a parent who sets out to protect his child by not telling her about certain realities can wind up exposing the child to her own half-glimpsed, fragmentary, and often distorted version of reality.

If your child has been damaged by a painful experience—whether as simple as a fight with a friend or as devastating as the death of a grandparent—and you don't talk to her about it, your child will attempt to repair the damage as best as she can, but she is limited by her own immature resources. She may not be able to even understand what happened much less how to deal with it, and her attempts at repair may result in emotional scars that disturb or inhibit her further development.

Parents often ask, "Why not leave well enough alone? Won't she get over it on her own? Can't she outgrow it?" Let's see how this idea stands up. Imagine a traumatic physical event instead of a psychological one. For example, suppose that your child has fractured a small bone in her hand. Would we say, "Why not leave well enough alone? Won't she get over it on her own? Can't she outgrow it?" Most of us would never expect a broken bone to heal by itself. We would ask the child about the pain, examine the situation (X-ray the fracture), consult a specialist to make sure the bone was placed in the right position (set the fracture), and offer special support for the bone's subsequent growth (put a cast on the fracture). Further, while the fracture was mending, we would watch over the child to make sure that her activities did not interfere with the bone's healing.

A child's mind benefits from this kind of attention as well. When a painful emotional event takes place, it may similarly require that we ask the child about the source of pain, examine the situation, possibly consult a specialist, and certainly offer special support to the child in order to ensure the mind's healing and encourage subsequent growth. This book is about enabling you to watch over your child and to offer your child a special kind of support. Unfortunately, we are seldom as aware of the mind's internal fractures as we are of the body's physical fractures. This is what makes a parent's job so difficult. But we have a capacity that makes our job easier—*we*

can talk to our kids. Good talk is a way to cushion the inevitable pain your child will feel as she goes through life. It also
helps us to locate the pain, to name it, to transform it, and to
support our child so she can bear it.

Inevitably, we must all be hurt in life, but protective parents realize that often what we don't know *can* hurt us—what
we don't know about ourselves, what we don't know about
other people, and what we don't know about the ways of the
world.

Speaking the Unspeakable

Most of us talk to our kids all the time. We ask them about
their days; we offer them reassuring words at night. We rejoice
in their good news, and we instinctively comfort them when bad
things happen. But there are certain problems in life that are inherently difficult to talk about with children. Illness, with its potential threat to our existence, is one such problem. Death, with
its strange rituals, unknown dimensions, and final losses, is another. And there are other unspeakable aspects of family life as
well—passion, hatred, envy, deceit, betrayal. Every family has
its dangerous or embarrassing or shameful or guilty secrets. Every family has its unspeakable stories: for one family, it might be
Momma's previous marriage or a daughter's secret abortion; for
another, a father's drinking problem or the loss of a job; for a
third, a family feud or a hidden crime.

Children have unspeakable thoughts and feelings in their
lives, too—they wish that the new baby would go back inside
Mommy's tummy and stay there, or they feel that they hate
Daddy and wish he were dead when he yells at them, or they
feel ashamed about playing doctor with their cousin, or they're
guilty about stealing a dollar from Mommy's pocketbook to
buy candy. Often these unspeakable thoughts and feelings are
invisible to both you and your child.

But invisible feelings, which hide in all the secret places in
our minds, have a way of visibly disrupting our behavior. A
child who is struggling with emotional problems, who is sad or
anxious or angry, often shows confused and conflicted behav-

iors that bewilder the people who love her. She may be restless and impulsive, or moody and irritable, or listless and sad. She may be unable to attend or concentrate in school, or unable to sleep or eat or play. One of the first tasks you will face as a parent is to make these underlying invisible feelings visible to you and your child. To do this you must first locate and name the feelings.

The Power of Names

We all know the fairy tale of Rumpelstiltskin, in which a wicked dwarf is prevented from taking the Queen's baby because she finally guesses his name. In this story, naming the dwarf takes away his magical power. The fairy tale emphasizes the importance of naming in human affairs. Naming is the first step we take to define our experiences. It points the way to understanding, modifying, and even controlling the experience. It helps us to defy the unknown by making it known. Naming gives you the power over the things that trouble you, just as naming Rumpelstiltskin gave the queen power over the dwarf. This is particularly true when we are dealing with threats to our welfare. Any parent who has stayed up all night with a child who has a high fever will recognize the relief with which they hear the doctor pronounce, "It's only a virus." Any parent who has seen her four-year-old rip apart her baby brother's teddy bear will recognize the relief of realizing that, "it's only sibling rivalry."

We actually begin our job as parents, before the baby is ever born, by naming her, and this name announces her presence in the world. Later, we name aspects of the child's world, over and over again, until she learns the names of things and can say them. But our naming job does not end with naming what's visible to the child.

As protective parents we have another important task— naming what is invisible to your child: the underlying thoughts and feelings that are troubling her as she grows. You may say, "I know that you're *worried* about Grandma. We're all worried. We love her very much and she's very sick. The doctors don't know whether she'll be all right. But they're trying very hard to help her." Or: "I think you don't want to see your best friend right now because you feel *jealous* of her. She's started to play with other kids, and you wish she would only play with you." Sometimes, talking about painful experiences involves explaining things to a child that we ourselves may not understand. Then we just have to try our best: "I guess it's called a *heart attack* because suddenly your heart can't work well. Nobody attacks you; it's not that kind of attack; it's more like your heart gets sick, and that's bad because your body needs your heart to be healthy in order to live."

Here are some examples of naming emotional experiences for a child who is suffering and may not be able to locate the pain:

ANGER:

"I know you've been *angry* at us since Billy was born and we have to spend so much time taking care of him because he's such a little baby."

FEAR:

"I think you've been *frightened* because Mommy and Daddy have been fighting so much, and you've heard us talking about getting a divorce."

GUILT:

"My pocketbook was open yesterday and I think you took money out of it to buy all those new stickers. Maybe you feel *guilty* today."

ENVY/JEALOUSY:

"I think you feel *jealous** of Michael. He seems to get everything you'd like to have for yourself."

---

*While we're really talking about *envy* here, not *jealousy*, popular usage has blurred the distinction between the two words. Children use and understand *jealousy* as the word that covers both states of mind. They are often unfamiliar with the more correctly used term *envy*, or *enviousness*.

Keeping the Dialogue Going: Using the Four C's

If you want to talk to your children and you want your children to talk to you, you must make it possible for a real dialogue to take place and keep going. Remember, in a dialogue we want two people to respond to each other. We try to encourage a back-and-forth, give-and-take interaction that allows both participants to feel they've had their say. Often when we talk to our kids we're actually lecturing them. We're engaged in a monologue to which no answer is expected (or given).

Following is an example of a monologue, where the parent is only talking to herself:

MOM: You've spent every single night this week glued to the TV. I haven't seen you do one stitch of homework! I'm sick and tired of your laziness. You're never going to amount to anything if you don't develop some good work habits, young man.

Here's an example of a true dialogue between a mother and daughter:

MOM: You know, I was noticing that you haven't had as much homework lately as you usually do. Are you finishing it before you get home, or is your teacher giving you a break?

JENNIFER: Ms. Horvath's been out sick this week, and the substitute teacher decided she wouldn't give us homework because Ms. Horvath is giving us a big social studies test when she gets back. So we're supposed to spend the week studying for it.

To avoid a monologue and to encourage a dialogue, try to remember what I call the "four C's"—*compassion, communication, comprehension,* and *competence.*

Compassion

Compassion is a powerful human capacity and has been used for centuries by all healers. Parents are healers, too; in fact, they are probably the most powerful healers of all, because their children endow them with great powers. Young children believe that their parents are magically omnipotent, like the giants and queens and wizards who perform such wonders in the fairy tales they read. Compassion, or empathy, is different from pity, or sympathy. When you are compassionate or empathic, you don't *feel sorry for* the other person, taking a superior position. Instead, you *feel for* them, from an equal position—you try to put yourself in their place. By being compassionate, you are able to understand the person's plight without being so drawn into it that you're suffering at the same level that they are. This amount of psychological distance is critical if you're going to be able to help them. Think of it this way: If someone is drowning, and you want to save them, it's better to stand on the shore and throw them a lifeline than to jump in the waves with them and take the chance that you will both be swamped.

Here are some examples of compassionate responses to events in a child's life that a protective parent could make to help create the cushion of safety that permits emotional growth:

"Oh boy, that scraped knee must really sting."

"I bet you must feel a little scared to be trying out for the soccer team."

"You must feel sad about that big fight you had with your brother."

"I know it doesn't feel good to know you cheated."

These responses, in which the parent puts himself in his child's position, add compassion to the first step we've already taken to locate and name the visible and invisible pain.

Communication

When you're compassionate, your child will be more willing to talk to you, setting the stage for real communication between the two of you. Through this communication you will begin to comprehend your child's distress. Watch for body language that indicates your child's worry or fear (moodiness, tension, a "hangdog" slump that looks as if she's carrying the world on her shoulders). And trust yourself to get the message. If you've been spending time with your kid and paying attention to her, and you sense she isn't "fine," go with your parental instinct, no matter what she says.

Keeping the channels open between you and your child requires a real commitment on your part. Many kids are not born talkers. They have to be coaxed and teased and drawn out. They need your encouragement, your attention, and your support to share their thoughts with you. Some openings that help "jump start" a conversation include, "I've been thinking about your problem with . . ." or "Remember the time that . . ." or "You know that idea we were talking about. . . ." Communication enables you to enter your child's inner world and to find out what is troubling her. Communication gives you an opportunity to find out and offer information. You can also confirm important realities for your child. ("Yes, Aunt Millie is very sick" or "You're right, Daddy's been worried about losing his job" or "I think you're having trouble eating dinner because you're really worried about the math test.")

Comprehension

Compassion and communication get things going between parents and kids. They set up the structures of the dialogue. But without comprehension, a parent has no clues about where to go with the dialogue, and no opportunity to address the emotional crisis the child is experiencing. Comprehension is the contribution you make as a protective parent to understanding the dimensions of the situation. It's not enough to be compassionate and to open up lines of communication between you and your child—you also have to understand what your child is telling you so you can deal with the problem competently.

Here's an example of a parent who doesn't get it. He can't comprehend what his eight-year-old daughter is trying to convey to him.

DAD: When's Mrs. Gilbert's piano concert this year?

HILLARY: I don't know, but I'm not going to play in it anyway. Concerts are stupid!

DAD: Piano lessons are a waste of my good time and money if you're never going to get up there and play for an audience.

HILLARY: Oh, Daddy. You just don't understand!

Here's another response this parent could make that helps him comprehend his daughter's plight:

DAD: When's Mrs. Gilbert's piano concert this year?

HILLARY: I don't know, but I'm not going to play in it anyway. Concerts are stupid!

DAD: It sounds like you don't feel so good about performing. Do you think you're feeling so negative now because you're really worried about how you'll do?

HILLARY: I was really nervous last year and I made two mistakes.

DAD: I remember, but they were tiny mistakes and everyone enjoyed hearing you. Even concert pianists miss a few notes when they play.

In this example, the father refuses to take what his daughter says at face value ("Concerts are stupid") and listens instead for the hidden fears beneath her response (fears about the self). Then he draws upon his knowledge of the experience to help her ("Everyone enjoyed hearing you"), and normalizes her apprehension ("Even concert pianists miss a few notes"). Sometimes it will also be important to correct misinformation, modify distortions, or absolve a child of responsibility in troubling events. Here's an example of a dialogue in which all three of these things happen. This mother is discussing her husband's brief hospitalization for chest pains with her six-year-old son—with some surprising results.

MOM: I saw Daddy today and he's doing just fine. The doctors are almost finished with his checkup.

ALEX: It's all my fault. *(He bursts into tears)* I made Daddy's heart attack him.

MOM: Alex, what are you talking about? Of course you didn't make Daddy get sick.

ALEX: Yes, I did. I hid in Daddy's closet and scared him and he told me I gave him a heart attack and then I heard you talking to Aunt Lily and you said so. *(cries)*

MOM: Wow! It's a good thing we got a chance to talk about this. You must have been so scared all day today! Now listen carefully. First of all, Daddy didn't have a heart attack, I told Aunt Lily the doctors were testing to *see* if Daddy had a heart attack. Hospitals always test your heart if you have chest pains. Daddy's chest pains were just gas pains from a stomach ache. He's coming home tomorrow morning. Secondly, a child can't cause someone to have a heart attack. You just scared Daddy and he probably said, "Oh boy, Alex, you almost gave me a heart attack!" to let you know that he was really surprised. That's just an expression grown-ups use.

By paying thoughtful attention to her son's experience, this mother was able both to correct his misinformation and to absolve him of responsibility in these events. Protective parents draw on their knowledge about themselves as well as their knowledge about the world to help their kids face hard times.

Competence

Ultimately, we really want to feel competent to deal with our children's problems, to help them deal with their problems and become competent themselves. This means encouraging our kids to think through a crisis and develop strategies—and showing them how. It means using our skills as protective parents to help our kids build resources they can bank on later in their lives. When we help our kids to work out a resolution to a real problem in the real world, we also help them grow, to become stronger, and to feel hope for the future. So, protective parents need to use all four C's when they talk to their kids: compassion, communication, comprehension, and competence.

Here are some examples of statements that demonstrate each of the four C's:

COMPASSION

"You know, vampires aren't real; but they're still scary to think about."

"You seem sad today, even though it's your birthday."

"It's really hard to go to school the first day! You look worried."

COMMUNICATION

"What were you imagining about vampires?"

"You must have been thinking about something that makes you unhappy."

"Sometimes it helps to talk about what you expect will happen."

COMPREHENSION

"Maybe when you're afraid to go to sleep at night, it's because you're worrying about vampires getting you."

"I think you're really upset because Daddy wasn't here on your birthday, and he didn't call you or send you a card."

"Maybe you're worried that you won't know what to do in school once you get there."

COMPETENCE

"You know, when I was little, I was afraid of witches in my closet, and I was sure I could see the witch's cape. But then I realized it was only my own clothes hanging there. Kids often imagine bad things at night when they're alone with their own thoughts. Witches are only 'pretend.' I'll give you a special flashlight and if you get scared, just turn on the light and it will chase all your bad thoughts away."

"Maybe we can write Daddy a letter telling him how upset you felt that he forgot your birthday, and you can get your angry feelings out. You know that Daddy sometimes forgets things that we think are important, but he still loves you. He just needs us to remind him."

"Maybe we can make a list of all the bad things you're worried about and all the good things that could happen today, too. I remember being so nervous for the first day of school that I forgot my lunch, but all the kids in the class gave me part of *their* lunch, so I got four desserts!"

Missing the Boat

Here is an example of a dialogue between a parent and an eleven-year-old child where the conversation goes nowhere and nothing goes well:

JONATHAN: I don't want to go to school tomorrow. I hate school! My teacher's mean and no one likes me.

MOM: Don't be silly! You have to go to school unless you're sick, and you're not sick. Besides, your teacher's very nice and you have lots of friends. I'm sick and tired of hearing your constant complaining. Don't make such a big deal about nothing. (no COMPASSION, no COMPREHENSION)

JONATHAN: Never mind. There's no use talking to you. You never understand. (no COMMUNICATION, therefore, no COMPETENCE for parent or child)

This parent is not making use of the four C's. She has not offered the child compassion nor has she encouraged communication. As a result, she cannot comprehend her child's distress, and she is not able to deal with the crisis competently.

Getting It!

Here's another, more effective response to the same situation, where using the four C's leads to more protective parenting:

JONATHAN: I don't want to go to school tomorrow. I hate school! My teacher's mean and no one likes me.

DAD: You sound really upset. (COMPASSION) Did something happen in school today that's making you feel so bad about your teacher and all the kids in the class? Do you think you could tell me about it? (COMMUNICATION)

JONATHAN: Well, today we got back our science test and I got a 72, and Jamie and Susannah both got good grades. Jamie called me a dope right in front of Susannah.

DAD: Oh boy, I understand why you wouldn't want to go to school tomorrow. (more COMPASSION) You feel upset about how you did on the test and you must be really angry with Jamie for embarrassing you like that. (COMPREHENSION)

JONATHAN: I hate him and I hate school.

DAD: I know just how you feel (more COMPASSION). But you and Jamie are really good friends most of the time. Remember how much fun you had last summer? I think he was just showing off, like sometimes you do with him. He was making himself feel *big* by making you feel *small*—kids do that sometimes. (more COMPREHENSION) Maybe you can think of something you could say to Jamie, rather than staying home and avoiding him and everything else. And now that I know about the trouble with the science test, maybe we could make a plan to help you do better next time. What do you think? (COMPETENCE)

This parent is telling his child a story in this response. It's a story to help smooth the way over a rocky spot in his child's life; *it's a story to help heal hard times.*

In the next section, I will describe these special kinds of stories that I believe protective parents can use to create that important cushion of safety—to repair the ruptures that will inevitably appear in your child's life. I call these stories *reparative narratives*. Learning how to construct them will help you and your child to face the unexpected contingencies of ordinary life.

The Reparative Narrative: Helping Kids Heal Hard Times

We live by stories. Our myths, our religion, even our sciences are stories—about how the world began, and why the sun rises in the east and sets in the west, about the births of the gods and goddesses. Stories are one of the most important ways that we make sense of ourselves and our world. Stories tell us the beginnings, the middle, and sometimes, the end of things that we are interested about.

When a child is born, we construct a narrative: the story of his birth and the dangers he faced to come into the world. ("It was snowing very hard and Daddy couldn't get the car started, but we knew you were coming, so we called Mr. Warren next door, and he drove us to the hospital. But he was so worried that he drove very, very slowly, and I thought you'd be born in the back of his car. But we made it just in time. And then you were born!") And we die with stories—our obituaries and our eulogies, stories about how we lived and what our lives meant to others. Even the epitaph on our graves tells a story: "Here lies Charlotte Heyman, beloved wife, mother, and grandmother."—"Here lies Michael Flanagan, a sailor, and a brave man."

Parents have known for centuries that stories are an important way to teach children what they need to know. That is why every culture has its special stories, stories about little ones who outwit giants, or loyal children who save their parents' lives, or clever children who trick evil wizards, or greedy children who get their just rewards, or curious children who cause trouble. Stories are popular in all their forms in all cultures because human beings need narratives as a way of organizing, understanding, and transforming their lives.

Narrative thought is a particularly important kind of thinking in childhood. It helps children to learn about the ways of the world, how to get along in the world, and how to get along with the people in the world. Sometimes a story will convey important information to your child; sometimes it may bridge a gap between your child's fantasy and a different reality; sometimes the story may help your child rehearse for an upcoming experience; and sometimes the story might help to repair a wound your child has suffered.

No matter how protective of our kids we try to be, we can't control their experiences, but we *can* have some control over the way our kids understand their experiences. Remember, words can heal as well as hurt. By using words to construct reparative narratives—narratives to help heal tough times— you can help your kids deal with many of the problems of today. These special stories can explain the ways of the world to your child as she grows, and they can interpret her experiences after she has them. What makes a narrative reparative is that it helps place a child's experience within that cushion of safety. By telling our kids stories about events—stories with a beginning, a middle, and an end—we can help them find meaning in their lives and heal the unavoidable hurts.

Putting It All Together

When we put together the four C's, compassion, communication, comprehension, and competence—in any order that makes sense—we can begin to construct a reparative narrative. This reparative narrative can then be used to help you and your child to cope with real problems in the real world. Here's how a reparative narrative would finally look, and what its reparative elements would be:

MIRANDA (age three): Mommy, I can't go to sleep. I'm scared.

NARRATIVE	REPARATIVE ELEMENTS
MOM: What are you thinking about, honey? Sometimes bad thoughts can keep us awake.	COMMUNICATION: This mother is trying to get the conversation going with her child. She's obtaining information and confirming the child's reality.
MIRANDA: I'm afraid of vampires.	
MOM: No wonder! Vampires are really scary to think about! Anybody would be afraid. That's why you've been having such trouble lately falling asleep. You're afraid vampires will get you, even though vampires are only make-believe and not real at all.	COMPASSION: Now, the mother offers her child empathy about her feelings. COMPREHENSION: Here, the mother expresses her underlying understanding of the meaning(s) of her child's experience.
MIRANDA: Can't I sleep with you, Mommy?	
MOM: It would feel safer if you had some company. But you need to know how to feel safe in your own room and in your own bed.	More COMPASSION: The mother makes another empathic statement.

NARRATIVE	REPARATIVE ELEMENTS
You know, when I was little I was was afraid of alligators hiding under under my bed.	More COMPREHENSION: By using her own experiences, this mother expands her child's understanding of her situation.
Kids often imagine bad things like vampires when they're alone with their own thoughts, particularly if they've been angry or upset about something during the day. We can talk about what's on your mind, and if you get scared at night, we can turn on your night light and it will chase all your bad thoughts away.	COMPETENCE: Now, this mother uses her understanding and experience to help her child come to a resolution of her problem. She also suggests a possible outcome or solution that offers hope for the future.

Notice that the mother's solution functions like the ending of a story. By using the four C's, the mother has created a reparative narrative.

Because this is a book about trying things out—new ways of thinking, new ways of understanding, and new ways of *speaking*—I have used lots of examples of actual dialogue between parents and children. I hope that these exchanges will help you develop your own voice as a parent and help you to know why, when, and how to talk to your kids.

4

Love and Sex—A Family Affair

A New Look at Old Desires

All families teach their children how to love. Our earliest loving experiences are at the hands of our parents, who stroke, squeeze, hold, clean, dress, kiss, and soothe us. These early experiences provide the foundation for adult love and sexuality. Without these first intimate experiences of pleasure, we would be unable to go on to feel love or find love in our lives.

Everything we know about how we grow up in our world tells us that love between a parent and a child is incredibly persistent. It reverberates throughout the course of our life. No other animal on the face of our earth lives in such profound and prolonged attachment to its parents. But just as *attachment* to you is necessary for your child's normal development, *separation* from you is also essential for your child to live an independent life. This separation begins the moment your baby is born and the umbilical cord is cut. At each point along the way, protective parents will try to strike a healthy balance between attachment and separation. But this is easier said than done.

Too much attachment, too late, will make it difficult for your child to grow away from you when it is time for him to take his place in the world. He will be unable to relinquish his ties to you, learn to love a stranger, and eventually leave to form his own family. Too much separation, too soon, however, can also cripple your child's ability to love. He may spend his life trying, directly or indirectly, to get from you what he still needs, being unable to look for love beyond his family circle.

Parents need to get it just right. But how? Luckily, love and sexuality are integrated in childhood during the years between ages two and six. We call this integration the *Oedipus Complex*. Freud borrowed from the Greek myth of Oedipus to illustrate this family romance. Oedipus, you remember, was banished by his father at birth and, returning to his homeland as a grown man, unwittingly fell in love with his own mother and committed incest. (This same oedipal theme was given a humorous modern twist in the film *Back to the Future*, where the hero's mother as an adolescent falls in love with the teenager who, in the future, will be her son!) The Oedipus Complex is a special story about family life—a romantic drama that offers you and your child a unique developmental opportunity. The healthy resolution of this "family romance" will help your child grow up, and, eventually, grow *away* from you, enabling him to lead a life of his own.

The Family Romance: Its Uses and Abuses

From the time a baby is born until he is about two years old, we care for him directly, conveying messages of love and pleasure to the baby through attention to his body. Even a little baby soon begins to realize that his body is a source of many good feelings, including the sexual feelings that touching his genitals provides. He has varied opportunities for sexual pleasure during the normal caretaking routines—the wiping and washing and powdering of his body by his parents. As he grows, he has greater control over his fingers and hands and uses them to explore his own body. Masturbation in childhood is not only normal, it's an important way your child learns about his body. And sexual curiosity is like a spark that will go on to ignite curiosity about other kinds of learning as well, such as learning to read, learning how things work, learning about the world.

As the baby grows, his own feelings of sexual pleasure and his feelings of love for his parents will merge and deepen. By the time he begins to speak, he will begin to use language to express this love directly. The romantic nature of a child's loving feelings for his parents is easily detected, particularly toward the parent of the opposite sex (if there is both a male and a female parent) or toward the "other," if there is a mother and an "other" (as is the case for single parents* or gay parents).

Sometimes parents are astounded and dismayed by the blatant sexual and bodily nature of their children's feelings ("Daddy, I want to sleep with you and feel your fuzzy hair"—"Mommy, I love to touch your soft skin"). But it is normal for children to have these feelings for their parents; in experiencing these feelings, children begin to set down the structures of love. In infancy, the mother is most often the recipient of this love (if she is the primary caregiver), but as the child approaches two or three years old, gender differences begin to be displayed—girls will begin to take their fathers as the object of this special romantic feeling, and boys their mothers.

Without a little knowledge—and a sense of humor—the parent who is *not* the object of the child's romantic yearnings can begin to feel excluded and even betrayed by the child. Your child may not just begin to express a preference for one parent; he may express envy, rivalry, and outright hostility toward the other parent as well. A boy may say: "Daddy, when you die, I'll live with Mommy." Or a girl may say: "Mommy, why don't you go live in another house, and then I can sleep in Daddy's bed."

It is important to understand that your child's competitive feelings toward you are as natural as his romantic feelings. It makes sense to him to turn to you for romantic love as he becomes capable of feeling this love. And it makes sense, too, that he might wish to eliminate any rivals for this special love.

---

*The special problems of raising a child alone are discussed in chapter 8, "Single Parents, Double Efforts."

Both the passion and the provocation in this phase of development can be hard to take. But these loving and hating feelings signal an important developmental milestone. Your child is coming to realize that you and your partner engage in a special sexual relationship from which he is excluded. This exclusion is important. It defines the boundaries between the generations and enables your child to develop a sense of a separate self. But it's also a difficult boundary for your child to accept. Children feel hurt and angry by this exclusion and will try to get themselves included in your nights by disrupting them—by being unable to go to sleep, waking up and slipping into your bed, asking for lots of special attention in the evening, and so on. This is why bedtimes are so problematic for many kids and parents.

As protective parents, we need to keep our lives at night separate from our children's intrusions. Unless we do, we cannot help our children to accept the normal "oedipal limits" which encourage them to relinquish their earlier, infantile reliance on us. Your refusal to fulfill your child's romantic/sexual wishes ("No honey, you can't touch Mommy's breasts, or kiss her on the lips") while continuing to offer your child parental affection helps him to turn away from his parents for satisfaction—and to turn toward the outside world. This turning toward the world will begin to characterize the school-age child and help make it possible for him to reach out to others for love and satisfaction. Nevertheless, sometimes parents ask, "Why do I have to limit my child's desires? What's wrong with encouraging my child to continue to love me in this romantic way? It's so cute!"

If we continue to encourage our children in their passionate feelings toward us, we cannot begin to protect them from the intense sexual excitement which is so obviously linked to these feelings. (You can clearly observe the sexual aspects of these feelings when your children wish to see your body, touch you, bathe with you, or sleep with you.) Fulfilling these wishes does not calm the child's feelings, as many parents hope; rather, it *excites* them. But the refusal to fulfill a child's wishes does not come easily to parents. All along, as your child has been developing, you have fulfilled his needs. When he was hungry, you fed him; when he was crying, you held him; when he needed encouragement, you applauded him. Now in this oedipal period, your role as a parent must change. You can no longer facilitate your child's desires; instead, you must gently deny them. In this developmental phase, your child wants to participate in a loving relationship with you that includes sexual feelings, and you must turn him away, so that later on in his life he will be able to find love and sexual satisfaction outside the family circle. How can we do this without hurting the child or making him feel rejected?

In order to help your young child negotiate this developmental hurdle, you must function as a protective parent: You must acknowledge your young child's romantic yearnings while clearly limiting his ability to fulfill them with you. To do this, we use empathy or compassion. We enumerated some of the uses of empathy/compassion in chapter 3; it's one of the elements that we use to construct reparative narratives with our kids. Empathy/compassion is always a powerful parental tool, because at any given moment it can help you to understand how your child is thinking and feeling.

Here is an example of a mother who is able to acknowledge her little five-year-old son's romantic feelings toward her, but is also able to limit his sexual expression in the present and direct his desires to the future. She is using empathy/compassion to help her act like a protective parent. Here's the reparative narrative she's constructed to encourage her son's healthy growth and separation from her:

BOBBY: Mommy, I want to sleep in your bed so I can kiss you all night and touch your soft skin. Daddy can sleep in my bed.

NARRATIVE	REPARATIVE ELEMENTS
MOTHER: I know that sometimes you get lonely and you'd like to sleep with Mommy, honey.	COMPASSION: This mother starts with empathy for her son's wish.

NARRATIVE	REPARATIVE ELEMENTS
But daddies and mommies need to sleep together at night.	COMMUNICATION: She offers her son information and gently confirms the reality.
When you grow up and you're a daddy, your wife will sleep with you all the time. Now you need to learn to sleep alone in your bed at night.	COMPREHENSION: She also expands her son's understanding of the situation and offers hope for the future.
I'll come in before you go to sleep for some hugs and kisses. Then I'll be reading in the living room until it's time for me to go to sleep.	COMPETENCE: She offers a resolution that maintains oedipal limits.

The following is an example of a parent who doesn't know how to thwart his child's normal oedipal wishes and doesn't realize how his inability to limit her desires fosters a continued attachment to him and a preoccupation with his body. He is abusing the family romance and interfering with his six-year-old daughter's healthy growth and separation from him:

TERESA: Daddy, can I take a shower with you again?

FATHER: Wasn't Mommy going to give you a bath tonight?

TERESA: Oh, please, Daddy? It's more fun with you. I love you and your penis, and I love when you wash my tushy.

FATHER: OK, just this once.

Sometimes, it's very hard for us to say no. Just as our children have passionate feelings toward us, so we, too, have passionate feelings toward them. And children are sensual. We love their cute, cuddly bodies and their uninhibited affection for us. We love to be caressed by their soft little fingers. In fact, all of the intimate things we do for our children when they are little have parallels in our later adult sexual experience—the strokes and caresses you give your baby now are transformed into petting in adult life, baby kisses and hugs will later become the actions of adult romance.

As protective parents, we realize that much of what we do to our infants in normal baby care would be *incestuous* with an older child. Only *we* can see and note the difference as the child grows; only *we* can maintain the boundaries appropriate and necessary for our child's growth. That's why it's so important for protective parents to set oedipal limits. If we stimulate our children's sexual feelings toward us, we keep alive their hope that we will let them participate with us in our sexual lives. The most extreme outcome of this kind of stimulation, of course, results in incest. Incest is the ultimate parental failure, when a parent uses the child's natural, loving feelings for his own sexual ends. Incest is at the extreme end of a broad continuum with normal, affectionate, protective parent–child relations at the other end.

How can we know where we are located on the continuum? Walking around naked in front of your two- to six-year-old children, permitting them free access to your bedroom and bathroom, letting them rub their body against yours for masturbatory purposes, giving or getting body massages can all stimulate incestuous feelings. The mother who calls her son "my little lover" and lets him sleep with her, the father that holds his little girl on his lap when he's naked, the parents who believe that children should learn about sexuality by watching them having intercourse are not functioning as protective parents; they have not taken the developmental necessity of separation into account, and they have not considered the developmental dangers of sexual overstimulation. Their actions take them too close to the incestuous edge of the continuum.

Children who are not protected from their normal oedipal desires by their parents may continue as adults to enact a *hidden*, incestuous drama. The young woman who grows up and repetitively falls in love with older, married men is an example of this enactment; so is the young man who remains a "mama's boy," and never leaves home. Only a protective parent can help a child to negotiate this oedipal phase and to observe the generational boundaries necessary to healthy development.

Beyond the Family Romance:
Sexual Stimulation in the World

We've been talking so far about how important (and how difficult) it is to set limits on sexual stimulation within the family. But what about the sexual stimulation your child will be exposed to in the world?

Young children today are exposed to sexuality in all of its diverse and potentially destructive forms. They see pornographic magazines on display at the neighborhood newspaper stand; they hear reports of rape and sexual harassment on the news; they learn about AIDS in school; they read stories about incest and sexual abuse in magazines and books; and they see explicit sexual scenes in the movies and on television. Because of this exposure, it is particularly crucial for modern parents to find a way to shield their youngsters and ensure that their child's healthy sexual development is not distorted or damaged. While we have no control over many of these influences, we do have a powerful tool at our disposal—*we can talk to our children openly and honestly about sex.* By doing this, we can provide them with that cushion of safety, early in their lives, which will help them absorb and evaluate experience later on.

In today's world, protective parents face more challenges than ever before in talking to their kids about love and sex. But your efforts will help you to use the years of childhood to lay down a foundation that will help your child to respect himself, his body, and his life.

What, When, and How to Talk to Your Kids
About Sex

When your child asks a question, start first by inviting your child to tell you what he already knows: "Have you heard anything about that? I bet you have some of your own ideas." Knowing what your child knows (or thinks he knows) lets you know what kind of an answer your child needs and gives you a chance to immediately correct any distortions he might be harboring.

Here's a conversation in which a sensitive mother seizes that opportunity:

TIMOTHY: How does a baby get born?

MOM: I bet you have some ideas about that. How do you think?

TIMOTHY: The mommy pushes the baby out like a BM.

MOM: That's an idea that would make sense, because you know there's an opening for a BM to come out, and the baby needs an opening, too. But mommies not only have an anus, which everyone has to be able to make BM; they also have another special opening for the baby called a *vagina*. The vagina is the special place that the baby comes out. It's a little opening that stretches to help the baby be born.

What to say *when* you talk to your kids about sex and *how* you say it, depends on three factors:

- *The age of your child:* Very young children need simple explanations in simple language that they can easily understand. Keep it short and sweet. Children under five years old have a limited attention span, only a rudimentary sense of cause and effect, and a poor grasp of time.

- *The personality of your child:* Some children are open to experience—they're curious about everything they see and hear, and they feel reassured by having lots of information at their disposal. They feel armed by knowledge. If your child is like this, you can feel free to elaborate on his questions, to give details and to expand on explanations. But other children may be sensitive to stimulation—they need to scan and screen their experiences; they need to take in information cautiously and carefully explore the consequences. As a protective parent, you want to match your responses to your child's personality. A child who thrives on elaborate details will be frustrated by a condensed reply, while a child who needs psychological time to absorb experiences will be overwhelmed by too much information.

- *The information you want to convey:* We all have our own values, our own beliefs, and our own level of comfort with sexuality. Before you can know how and when to talk to your kids about sex, you need to know what you want to say.

What Should I Ask Myself?

Teaching kids about sex doesn't only mean answering questions about where babies come from. That's the easiest part of the job! Teaching them also means helping them to know about people, about trust, about self-control, about relationships, about their bodies, about sexual roles and differences, about moral values, about emotional and physical dangers, and most important, about choices. How can we know what to tell our kids until we know what *we* think?

A good place to begin is to think about what your parents told you about sex and how you felt about it. Was it meaningful? pitiful? ridiculous? disgusting? Did they tell you too much or too little, too soon or too late? Think about what you would have wished they had told you. Then, think about what you would like your kids to know about sex. This is your chance to make a real difference—to improve on your parents' version, or to carry through their wisdom to the next generation.

It's also important to explore what you really feel about your own sex life. To answer this you will need to think about your body and all of its processes and potentials: menstruation, ejaculation, masturbation, foreplay, intercourse, homosexuality, heterosexuality, etc. This is not as easy as it sounds. Most of us still have a lot of conflicts about sex left over from our own childhoods. We may have feelings of envy or disparagement that need to be acknowledged and addressed. Women often complain bitterly about men, and men about women, but who raises these male and female children? We do! If you don't like the battle between the sexes, this is your chance to contribute to the cease-fire. You can try to raise girls who will grow up to be proud of being women and respectful of men, and boys who will grow up to be proud of being men and respectful of women.

Protective parents need to consciously examine their own attitudes toward sexuality, so that they can avoid unconsciously conveying attitudes to their kids which give them mixed or even mistaken messages. Be honest with yourself about your sexual feelings: Do you really enjoy sex? Does it leave you wondering what all the fuss is about? Do you dread it? If you are able to recognize and acknowledge your own fears, you may still be able to carefully plan to keep them out of your conversations with your child (just as a thoughtful parent will try to help her child to feel comfortable about climbing even though she herself may harbor a fear of heights). If this doesn't seem possible because your feelings and fears are too intrusive, then ask your spouse or a close friend or relative to help you talk to your kids, or use a good children's book as the basis for your sexual discussion. (Of course, it might be useful to seek out some counseling to understand more about your own sexual feelings. Why are you so unimpressed by sexuality? What happened to your passion? What do you really dread?)

Do you feel comfortable with your body or disappointed by it? Do you see masturbation as a normal part of sexual curiosity or as disgusting? Remembering that masturbation is normal in childhood (and in adulthood, too—do you know the old joke that 98 percent of adults masturbate and the remaining 2 percent lie about it?) may help you feel more comfortable with yourself and your body. Do you feel homosexuality is biologically determined, an individual developmental outcome, or a perversion? You will need to do some thinking about all of these matters way before you talk to your kids about sex, because if there's anything you feel uncomfortable about, you can be sure your children will ask you about it!

Young Children's Questions

Toddlers (two to four years old) will display curiousity about their bodies and their bodies' contents (blood, snot, spit, urine, feces), as well as about other people's bodies. Because life is so new to them, things that seem quite ordinary to you—breasts and genital hair for example—may seem extraordinary to them. Children at this age are filled with curiosity and they ask questions incessantly. They may be particularly interested in the sexual differences between boys' and girls' bodies and adults' and children's bodies. Typical questions might be: Will I grow a penis when I'm bigger? Will my penis fall off like Lila's did? Why does Daddy have hair on his penis? Will I grow breasts? Dissatisfaction with one's own gender and envy of the other is often expressed by *both* sexes. One three-year-old girl, when looking at her brother's penis, stated her preference clearly, sighing, "I'm so plain and he's so fancy," while a four-year-old boy, seeing some little girls taking off their bathing suits near him, observed, "Girls are so neat and boys are so dangly."

Be sure not to express any gender bias (even if you have some!) in talking with your children about their bodies. For example, in defining sexual differences many parents state that boys have penises and girls *don't*, indicating to their children that sexual identity is structured by the presence or absence of the male genital. Instead, emphasize to girls that they have a *vulva*, which has two parts, a *clitoris* and a *vagina*. (Many parents never even give the girl a name for her clitoris! No wonder she thinks it's insignificant. Remember the importance of naming.) And don't forget to mention a little boy's *testicles* to him, as well as his penis. Many boys have no idea of the function of these important body parts that link them to their potential roles as fathers.

Here's an example of how a protective parent might respond to a three- to five-year-old's inevitable question, "Where do babies come from?"

"Mommies and daddies make babies together. They love each other and hold each other very close. The daddy has a penis made to fit into the mommy's vagina so that the daddy's sperm can meet the mommy's egg and begin a baby. The baby is very little at first and then it grows and grows in a special place in the mommy's body called a womb. The womb stretches as the baby grows, and that's why you see pregnant ladies with big bellies. When it's time for the baby to be born, he comes out through the mommy's vagina, which also stretches to let the baby through, and then he's born, just like you."

School-age Children's Questions

Children who are five to eight years old have begun to be interested in what Mommy and Daddy do with each other that they don't do with them, including the mechanics of sexual intercourse. They may ask questions like, "How does the sperm get to marry the egg?" and "Does the egg get tired of waiting?" They need to have a clear idea about intercourse that includes the feelings adults have for each other.

Parents usually feel more comfortable talking about sex as a way to have babies than they do talking about sex as a way to have pleasure. You can explain to your child that sex is a way of getting as close to someone you love as you can and that men's penises and women's vaginas are made to fit together. People have sex or make love with each other because it feels really good and it's a way of getting pleasure yourself and giving pleasure to another person: "A mommy and daddy fit together in a special way to show each other love. The daddy puts his penis in the mommy's vagina." If you only link sex with making babies, you risk distorting your child's vision of the whole enterprise and limiting his understanding. One little girl, catching her parents caressing in bed, asked her mother, "Why are you kissing Daddy? We don't need another baby!"

Older Children's Questions

Older children, ages nine to twelve, exposed now to the world, are likely to bring up an entire range of sexual concerns, from rape to incest to AIDS. The older child has begun to be influenced by people other than his family, ideas other than his own, and experiences different from those he has had. Now, as he begins to be exposed to the varied influences of the world around him, his curiosity is stimulated by everything he sees and hears. More complex, more difficult questions may emerge. Your eight-year-old may ask you what oral intercourse is, or your ten-year-old may have heard sexual abuse campaigns on TV and ask about incest. At this age, children also begin to come home with questions about ugly words they've heard in school, or graffitti they've seen on the walls, or names they've been called, like "faggot" or "cunt." At this age it's not enough to say, "Those are bad words that bad kids use, and I never want to hear them in this house!" It's important to explain to your child: "People have a lot of mixed-up or bad ideas about sex, and so they use mixed-up or bad words to describe sexual experiences. These words can also be used when people get angry—they say 'fuck you.' Or they can be used to insult people, like calling someone a 'faggot,' which is an ugly word for a man who's homosexual, or 'cunt,' which is an ugly word for a woman's vagina."

By the time he's ten or eleven years old, there are already psychological and physical changes taking place in your child that are helping him to prepare for the profound developmental transformations of adolescence. Romance, fidelity, loyalty, and love are now important preoccupations for him. Children at this age are fascinated by how adults "fall in love." They may ask about how you met your partner, how you knew you were in love, and whether or not you had intercourse before you were married. They may also begin to talk and think about birth control and ask for specific information about various methods.

If you want your child to have an open, sensual, pleasurable feeling about sex, *you* need to convey this feeling to him. It is important for your older child also to understand that intercourse is not the only way that partners express their sexual feelings for each other. You might want to tell your pre-adolescent child something like this: "People show their love by hugging and kissing and touching. They use their fingers and their mouths on many private parts of their bodies, too.

Sometimes men and women experiment with getting close to each other or fitting together in new ways." This is the time when you need to begin to prepare your child to lead a responsible as well as a pleasurable sexual life. This is the time when *your values* about love and sex need to be conveyed. Remember, you transmit these values to your children every day, in every way—in your actions and in your reactions to a television show ("What a sexist show! I can't believe they put that on!"), a movie ("You know, that's the first time I really understood love between two men"), or even the news ("I'm so sick of hearing about all these older guys ditching their wives for young actresses").

THE PROTECTIVE PARENT'S GUIDE TO TALKING
ABOUT SEX WITH KIDS

Here are some general principles of protective parenting to keep in mind when you talk about sex with your kids:

Remember to match your answers to the age and the interest of your child. Don't make the mistake of one mom who, when her three-year-old asked, "Where do I come from?" launched into a detailed description of conception, pregnancy, and birth, only to have her daughter exasperatedly interrupt, "Do I come from New York or New Jersey?"

Answer your young child's questions when they come up. Don't evade or avoid them. Children have very little capacity for understanding delay and will certainly see your evasions as a rejection of them, or a signal that they shouldn't be asking these questions, or as evidence of your own anxiety, which can only increase theirs. If your child asks you about sex in a public place, tell him, "That's an important question, but it's private and I'll tell you all about it when we're alone (or at home)." If this isn't possible, draw your child aside and talk to him quietly, so he knows the information isn't for release to the general public.

Answer only what the child asks. Try not to expand your answer beyond their needs. Don't overwhelm your child with too much information or they'll be unable to absorb the answer.

However, try not to withhold information, either. An abortive answer can give your child the message that the subject is taboo and should be avoided. ("Dad, did you have sex with other girls before you met Mommy?" "I don't know. That was a long time ago; who remembers?")

Use words your child can understand. While it is important to give children the right names for everything they're asking about, use the names they are familiar with before you explain further. ("How do the fish in my wee-wee get to the mommy's egg?" "Your wee-wee is really called a penis. Men use their penises to help make babies because men have the sperm—those little things that look like fish—to meet the mommy's egg. The sperm comes out of the penis when the daddy puts it in the mommy's vagina. Then the sperm can swim up to meet the mommy's egg.")

Encourage your child to ask questions. If your child hasn't asked any questions by the time he's three years old, begin to encourage and create opportunities for questions to be asked. ("Did you know Adam's mommy is going to have a baby?" or "Did you know that when you grow up, you'll have hair near your penis like Daddy does?") Even if your child doesn't ask, you can be sure he's thinking about these matters and developing his own theories. Remaining silent on the topic may give your kids the message that they can't talk—and shouldn't ask—about sex. Your lack of conversation about this important experience may build up a wall of silence, which they're reluctant to break through.

Remember the five basic fears. Often your child's questions will reflect one or more of these fears (fear of the unknown, fear of being alone, fears about the body, fear of the voice of the conscience, or fears about the self). A five-year-old boy who asks, "Does the baby get lonely when he's inside you?" may actually be expressing his own fear of being alone. A protective parent might answer, "The baby doesn't get lonely like you might, because he's really not a separate person yet who thinks and feels. He's still connected to his mommy's body through the umbilical cord." The nine-year-old girl who asks, "Will the mommy rip apart when the baby comes out?" may be revealing her underlying fears about her own female body. Here, a protective parent might say, "A mommy's vagina is specially made to stretch when the baby is born, like a rubber band, to help the baby come out. Sometimes if the baby is very big or the mommy needs some help, the doctor can make a little cut called an episiotomy to give the baby more room to come out. Then the doctor sews the little cut up, and it heals quickly just like when you cut your finger." You can use the principles of protective parenting to address your child's fears and to empower him to master them and move on in development.

You can make use of your local library and the children's librarian to help you develop your approach to sex with your kids. Books can particularly help parents who don't feel comfortable talking about sexual matters. But make sure you read the book yourself first and that you're comfortable with the sexual ideas that are expressed in the book, before you share it with your child. That way, there are no awkward surprises for either of you.

5

Surviving Childhood: Facing Illness, Disease, and Death

Illness and death provide us with our darkest hours and draw upon our deepest fears. Our bodies house our selves. When we become ill, fears about the body as well as fears about the self are heightened. But if we can name and then treat and forget our illness, as happens with the flu, or hives, or a strep throat, our fears dissipate quickly because we know we will soon bounce back to health. Neither our body nor our sense of self is compromised. If it turns out that our illness will be chronic or life-threatening, however, then our sense of self as well as our body image will be altered. And if we cannot even name our illness, much less treat it or forget it, then fears of the unknown will add their weight to fears about the body and fears about the self, increasing our psychic burden.

Parents have a difficult time facing their own physical vulnerabilities, but it is even more painful to face physical vulnerabilities in your children. What should you say to a child with asthma who still wants to play baseball? How do you help a child with migraine headaches to feel in control of her life? What's the best way to handle the daily injections of a diabetic child?

This is where protective parents need to use the four C's to create that all-important cushion of safety for their children. This is where they need to chart a middle course between overexposure—giving your child more information about her condition than she can manage—and overprotection—not telling your child enough about her condition so that she can master her fears. Of course, charting this course can be quite complicated and a parent's decisions can produce some unexpected results. As an oldest child, I was often asked to submit to various medical procedures first, in order to demonstrate to my younger sister that "There's nothing to be afraid of!" I have often wondered what role these childhood lessons in the mastery of anxiety played in my later adult decision to become a psychologist and to help children master their anxieties! It can't be without meaning either that my younger sister (who got to scientifically observe my reactions while awaiting her turn) became a physician!

There are four kinds of physical crises that we may face with our kids:

- *Acute, short-lived episodes of illness* that are usually not life-threatening: bronchitis, chicken pox, diarrhea, etc.

- *Acute, unexpected illness* that can put our lives at risk: pneumonia, meningitis, severe allergic reactions, etc.

- *Chronic, treatment-controlled conditions* that may still compromise our lives: diabetes, epilepsy, colitis, etc.

- *Illnesses from which we are likely to die:* advanced cancer, AIDS, kidney failure, etc.

It is terrifying for us when our children fall ill. We feel powerless in the face of their discomfort and pain. We fear what might lie ahead. How can we help ourselves and our kids to face illness and disease? What should we tell them?

Facing Childhood Illness

Caring for a child who is ill without being able to offer relief is every parent's nightmare. Our child's cries cause us emotional pain, even as they suffer with physical pain. "Mommy, my ear hurts, take it away," or "Daddy, my throat can't swallow, make it better," they say. When your child falls ill and you know she will get better, you can be calm and comforting—and reassuring about the future: "It's only that old earache that you always get, honey. I know it hurts. We'll put some warm drops in your ear and give you some medicine, and the pain will go away soon," or "You have a sore throat, sweetie, but this warm tea with honey will help it."

But parents cannot be so calm and reassuring when they don't know if their child will get better, or even the name of their child's illness. Then your own anxiety and fear start to build as you begin to imagine all the dreadful possibilities. Your child is bound to become more fearful, too, not only because she picks up on your emotional message, but also because in your search for an answer, you may need to subject her to extensive medical examinations, tests, and procedures—all of which will raise her anxiety and some of which will cause her pain.

Parents are often tempted not to tell their children about medical procedures in the hope that their children won't be frightened. But it's *always* best to tell as much of the truth as you can to your child: "The doctors need to find out what's making you sick, so they are going to take pictures of your body and also to look at your blood to see what's happening inside." However, you don't need to tell her the whole truth. For instance, even though you may know about a procedure weeks in advance, there's no reason to tell your child until shortly before she has to undergo the procedure. For one thing, young children don't have a realistic concept of time, so telling them about something that will take place in two weeks is useless as well as unnecessarily alarming. For another, your child will begin to worry from the moment you tell her—we call this anticipatory anxiety, and we all feel it!—so you want the anticipation to be as short as possible. The same day for young children and one or two days' notice for an older child is probably all that's needed in most medical situations.

To be able to provide your child with that developmental cushion of safety, you need to talk to your doctor first about any procedure, so that you know exactly what's involved. That way you can at least help your child to know what to expect. Remember: A prepared child will be a less frightened child.

Here's a protective parent preparing her seven-year-old child to face an intravenous pyelogram (IVP) in order to discover whether she has kidney disease:

> "The doctor has to take a picture of your kidneys. She's going to give you a special colored injection in your arm, and you're going to lie very quietly for a while so she can follow the special color as it travels through your body on an X ray and see how your kidneys work. The only part that will sting just for a minute is when she puts the injection in your arm. None of the rest hurts, and even that only hurts a tiny bit. It hurts less than shots you've already gotten when we go to see Dr. Morris."

Any surgical procedure in which the body's boundaries are invaded, even the most routine, creates a potential for psychological trauma in your child. Surgery raises frightening fantasies for all of us, but particularly for young children, because of all the losses it entails: the loss of a part of one's body (through surgery), the loss of consciousness (through the anesthesia), and the loss of the mother or caregiver (through the separation and hospitalization). Surgery always stimulates the five basic fears—fear of the unknown, fear of being alone, fears about one's body, fear of the voice of conscience (because the child may imagine that the surgery is some kind of punishment for recent wrongdoing), and fears about the self. As a protective parent you will want to address as many of these five basic fears as you can before your child undergoes a surgical procedure. The more attention you can pay to your child's psychological preparedness, the less compromised your child's sense of self is likely to be, and the more easily she will be able to cope with the trauma.

Tonsillectomies are one of the most common operative procedures you and your child may face together. Here's the way one mother created a *reparative narrative* for her five-year-old son, Jess, who was going to have this operation:

JESS: Why do I have to have my tonsils out?

NARRATIVE	REPARATIVE ELEMENTS
MOTHER: Because Dr. Baxt told us that it's the only way we're going to help you get rid of those awful, painful ear infections. Tonsils are little parts in your throat that can get swollen and infected, and then they give you a sore throat and sore ears. Lots of kids need to get their tonsils taken out to help them feel better. I had mine taken out when I was little and so did Daddy. Your brother had his taken out when he was five, just like you.	COMMUNICATION: This parent is confirming the reality of the tonsillectomy and offering her child information geared to address her child's fears of the unknown and fears about the body.
JESS: Will it hurt?	
MOTHER: I know you're worried about all of this, but you won't feel anything during the operation because the doctor is going to put you to sleep while he takes out your tonsils.	COMPASSION: An empathic statement and more COMMUNICATION
JESS (crying): "I don't want to go. I promise I'll be good. Please let me stay home with you.	
MOTHER: It sounds like you think you're being punished. Getting your tonsils out has nothing to do with your being good or bad. It has to do with getting well and not being sick so much. I'll be staying with you in the hospital, and you're only staying overnight. Daddy will pick us up and take us home in the morning.	COMPREHENSION: Here, the parent is helping the child understand the situation and absolving him of responsibility. She's also addressing his fear of being alone and fear of the voice of conscience.

NARRATIVE	REPARATIVE ELEMENTS
JESS: Chiara said she ate ice cream when she had her tonsils out. She said ice cream helps.	
MOTHER: She's right. That's because your throat will feel sore at first. Cold things like ice cream will make it feel better. Then, pretty soon, you won't have sore throats or sore ears that wake you up at night.	MORE COMPREHENSION and COMPETENCE: Now, the parent is helping the child to understand the outcome of the operation. She's also offering hope for the future.

There are many good books about going to the hospital written for parents and children, and many hospitals will schedule a pre-operative visit for you and your child. Talking to other kids who've had surgery, playing doctor, or drawing about the experience will all help your child to anticipate and rehearse. Remember, the more you know about your child's fears, the more competently you can address them.

But no matter how well you prepare your child beforehand, don't be surprised if your child still shows a considerable psychic strain afterwards. This is quite normal. Children usually display three kinds of reactions in the aftermath of an illness or surgical procedure:

Regression: Your child may retreat to more babyish behavior because her illness has compelled her to relinquish her autonomy and the ongoing nursing necessary to an illness has encouraged her dependency on the adults who care for her.

Anxiety: Your child may be left with a legacy of heightened anxiety about her body because she may have been subjected to painful and frightening procedures over which she had no control.

Anger: Your child may appear irritable, cranky, hostile, or angry at you because she feels that you were unable to bring her relief from her pain and distress while she was suffering or blames you for subjecting her to painful procedures.

Parents have their own emotional reactions to illness and surgery, too. They may become overprotective of the child, taking total control of the child's body, infantilizing her, and increasing the child's sense of helplessness. They may become overidentified with the child's pain and distress, unable to bear the child's suffering or to help the child bear it, or they may become overburdened and feel exasperated at the demands of caring for a sick child.

Protective parents remember that even very sick children still need to exert as much self-control as they can over their minds and bodies. They try to control their own fears of the future when they are around their sick child and to focus instead on whatever comfort they can give in the present. It's important, as well, to realize that parents need to take time to take care of themselves when they care for a sick child. Your sick child needs you. If you're exhausted and depleted, both you *and* your child will suffer.

Because caring for a sick child is so demanding, relationships among members of the family can become strained and difficult too. Parents who care for a child who is acutely or chronically ill need to pull together and provide for each other's support. Too often, however, this does not happen. Under stress, parents pull apart from each other, turning away and withdrawing; conversely, they can pull each other apart, blaming and attacking each other in their anger and anxiety about the illness.

If you are a parent facing this dilemma, try to get some occasional childsitting help for your chronically ill child so that you and your spouse can spend some time together (even an hour or two will help!) or ask a relative or friend to make dinner one evening, so that you and your spouse can take a walk (or a nap!). Help the other children in the family take a break, too, by arranging play dates and childsitting coverage during particularly tense times. And anticipate that you're all going to feel drained and depleted after any physical or emotional crisis with your sick child, and that you will need time to help each other recuperate.

Protective parents try to remember the other children in the family, too. Healthy children's fears for themselves, as well as for their sick sibling, need to be addressed. They need to be given enough information to understand their sibling's condition and an explanation about what the future might bring:

"Your brother has a disease called cancer. It's a very serious disease, but you can't catch it. He's very sick now, but doctors know a lot about cancer and they can help kids get better. That's why we've taken him to the best hospital we know. We hope he's going to come home soon. Meanwhile, I know it's been hard on you because we're not around much and we're worried and tired a lot of the time. Remember that we always love you very, very much. We hope this hard time will be over for all of us soon."

Helping a Child with a Chronic Illness

Some of us are blessed with healthy, sturdy bodies right from the start. But many of us will have to consider that our body doesn't work the way we need it to work, even when we're young. If your young child suffers with allergies, or gets migraine headaches, or has periodic seizures, she must learn to live with the idea of physical limitation; she will be exposed early in her life to a significant alteration in her body ego and a subsequent alteration in her sense of self. She must also learn to accommodate to the episodic nature of her illness. Sometimes she will feel completely well, and other times she will be terribly sick. These ups and downs are normal for her, and you need to protect her against always remembering that she could get sick when she feels well, and forgetting that she will get well again when she feels sick. Through this protection, your child will be able to accommodate to the ordinary rhythms of her chronic illness and still lead a normal life.

It's important, too, for protective parents to try to place their child's illness in an ordinary context—to *normalize* it.

> When a child complains of feeling "different," for instance, you might say, "Everyone has something that they need to take care of in their body. Some people get stomachaches, and others have trouble with their eyes or their back. David has asthma and takes medicine to stop his wheezing. You get migraine headaches like I do, and Katie has diabetes and has to get an injection every day. It's hard to get headaches, but we're going to try to help the pain so you can sleep and feel better quickly. Dr. Gabriel said that the headaches will probably go away when you're a teenager, so we've just got to do the best we can now."

A reparative narrative that helps a child deal with chronic illness should include the information your child needs in order to understand and respond to her illness; it should explain that she has not been singled out or punished through her illness; it should help her express her anger and frustration at her bad luck; and it should eventually help her to gain perspective on her situation, neither dwelling on it (and placing her physical limitations at the center of her sense of self) nor denying it (and refusing to take responsibility for managing her life).

PHILIP (eight years old): Why do I have to have asthma? Nobody else on the team has it!

NARRATIVE	REPARATIVE ELEMENTS
FATHER: I don't blame you for feeling angry and frustrated. It's such a drag to have to worry about wheezing and losing your breath when you're playing a game.	COMPASSION: This parent is able to offer empathic support for his son's feelings.
PHILIP: I hate it! I look like a wimp when I wheeze. Why do I have to have asthma? What did I do?	

NARRATIVE	REPARATIVE ELEMENTS
FATHER: You're not only worried about how you feel, you're also worried about how you look and what the other kids think about you.	MORE COMPASSION
You know, we can't change the fact that you have asthma. You didn't do anything to get it; it's just the way things are. I have it, too, and so does your cousin Wendy. Asthma runs in our family.	COMPREHENSION: Here, the father tries to expand his son's understanding of the genetic factors in his illness in order to absolve him of responsibility.
PHILIP: Nobody's going to want me on the team! I can't play all the time.	
FATHER: I can see you're afraid the kids won't want you because sometimes you have to sit on the bench, but when you play, you're good. Some kids aren't any good with or without asthma! That's why they picked you to be in the league. You're a really good hitter and a good pitcher.	MORE COMPREHENSION: Now this father is trying to further expand his son's understanding of the situation by emphasizing that we all have different strengths and weaknesses.
PHILIP: But lots of times I can't run and they have to get a pinch-runner for me.	
FATHER: Even in the major leagues, when a player has an injury or just isn't fast enough, they use pinch-runners. That's no big deal. But we might be able to change the way you're managing your asthma. You think if you ignore it, it'll go away, so you wait to take your medicine until you're	COMPETENCE: This father uses his son's distress to open up the possibility of another outcome. Instead if criticizing ("You never take your medicine when you should!"), he offers his son the opportunity to rethink the way he's handling his chronic illness. This offers some hope for the future.

NARRATIVE	REPARATIVE ELEMENTS
really sick. But if you want to feel stronger and run better, you've got to use your spray the *minute* you feel your chest tighten. Then you'll be able to run more. You could try that new way to see if it helps.	

When a Child Is Dying

It is almost beyond our endurance to think about a child's death, yet some of us will have to endure this most devastating loss. When a child falls ill with a life-threatening illness, your most important job as a protective parent will be to provide her with your ongoing emotional and physical support throughout her ordeal. Often parents think they are protecting their child by trying to keep the knowledge of the severity of an illness from her, but children quickly pick up the anxiety in their parents' eyes, the grave tones of the doctors and nurses, the hidden fear in the voices of family members. Young children, in particular, have little understanding of the finality of death, so what is frightening to them is not death itself, but rather what death is about (triggering fear of the unknown), being hurt or suffering (triggering fears about the body), and facing death on their own (triggering fear of being alone). If your child is hospitalized, try to stay with her as much as you can. Make sure she's surrounded by familiar faces to combat and calm her fears of being left alone. A parent's ability to listen to a child's fears, without retreating or withdrawing from the painful realization of a grave prognosis, is a great comfort to a dying child. Here's a parent who is unable to help her five-year-old daughter face the diagnosis of leukemia because she's trying not to face a harsh reality.

ALEXIS: Why do I have to go to the doctor all the time? I hate blood tests. I hate pills.

MOTHER: The doctor helps you feel better.

ALEXIS: Am I very sick? Am I going to die?

MOTHER: Of course not! Don't say that. You're fine and you'll be all better soon.

This child's understanding of her illness has not been addressed (her mother has not shown comprehension) nor has her parent been able to hear her fears (they have not been able to communicate). Because of this, no realistic comfort (compassion) can be given to her.

Here's a protective parent trying to face the same situation. Because she doesn't let her own fears interfere with her ability to help her child, and she uses the four C's to construct a reparative narrative, the dialogue (though painful) offers the child the emotional comfort she needs at this point.

ALEXIS: Why do I have to go to the doctor all the time?

NARRATIVE	REPARATIVE ELEMENTS
MOTHER: Because you have a sickness called leukemia. It's a blood disease, so the doctor needs to see how your blood is doing so we can make sure you're getting the right medicine.	COMMUNICATION: Here the mother names and explains the illness, confirming the child's reality and offering important information.
ALEXIS: Will I die?	
MOTHER: Everyone worries about dying; I do, too. Some children who have leukemia do die, but lots and lots of children don't. They get better because now doctors have lots of new medicines to	COMPASSION: This parent is able to offer her child empathy for her situation.

NARRATIVE	REPARATIVE ELEMENTS
help them. That's why we go every few weeks to check your blood to make sure you're getting the right medicine.	COMPREHENSION: By touching on the idea of death but keeping up hope, this parent helps her child understand the situation.
ALEXIS: If I die, will you be with me?	
MOTHER: I'll always, always be with you whenever you need me.	COMPETENCE: Here, the parent offers her child a resolution that empathizes ongoing emotional support. She can address her child's worst fears about death—which turn out to be about being alone.

When a Parent Is Ill

While facing the serious illness of a child is unbearable for any of us, at least we are healthy and can bring our fullest resources, both physical and psychological, to the painful task. But what happens when a parent is facing a serious illness? How can a protective parent help her children to face her illness at the same time that she needs to mobilize all her own energies to get better? And how can children be prepared to see a parent in a hospital whose face or body may have been ravaged by illness?

Here's a mother trying to prepare her children (Terry, age eleven, Alan, age nine, and Dorothy, age six) to see their father after he's had a stroke.

MOTHER: We've all been very worried about Daddy, but the doctors have told me that he's out of danger now, and he's not going to die. I know you've been anxious to see him, and he's well enough now for you to visit, but he's going to look a lot different because when you have a stroke, a part of your brain gets hurt.

ALAN: Can Daddy talk to us?

MOTHER: Yes, he can, but one side of his face has been paralyzed, so he'll look and sound a little different now.

DOROTHY: I don't want to go. *(cries)*

MOTHER: You're worried about seeing Daddy, but even though he'll look a little strange, he's still the same Daddy.

TERRY: Will the paralysis ever go away?

MOTHER: Yes, Daddy is lucky. The doctor said it wasn't a bad stroke and he's going to get well. One side of his body is weaker now, and he'll have to have physical therapy all this year to get better.

Facing a Mental Illness

We all know that our minds as well as our bodies can get sick. But this idea is very hard to convey to children. And the experience of a beloved parent mysteriously transformed through mental illness to a withdrawn, silent depressive, an enraged, hallucinating psychotic, or a weird, wary paranoid is terrifying.

What can we say to help our kids understand this transformation? How can we encourage them to sustain their good feelings toward the mentally ill parent, while coping with the bizarre and frightening behavior mentally ill parents display? And what can we do to help our kids cope with the prolonged or repeated separations from a mentally ill parent?

One of the most disturbing cases I ever treated was a little five-year-old boy whose mother suffered with paranoid schizophrenia. Bright, loving, and devoted to him when she was lucid, in a paranoid episode, she would begin to hear commands from God to sacrifice her son. Once, in a terrible moment, she tried to strangle her little boy, but the child ran out to a neighbor's house.

This little boy loved his mother and, poignantly, missed her when she was hospitalized. I worked with the father to create the following reparative narrative for this child:

DYLAN: When is Mommy coming home, Daddy?

NARRATIVE	REPARATIVE ELEMENTS
DAD: Not for a while, honey. She's still sick and her mind is still too mixed up. Mommy doesn't realize what she's doing or remember who she is or even who you are right now.	COMMUNICATION: This father is confirming an important (though painful) reality for the child.
DYLAN: Mommy tried to hurt my neck.	
DAD: That was so scary. Your own mommy, who you love, tried to hurt you when her mind was so sick and mixed-up.	COMPASSION: Here he offers the child empathy.
DYLAN: Why did Mommy hurt me?	
DAD: She didn't mean to, honey. When Mommy gets sick, it's like a bad nightmare inside mommy's head. She doesn't realize that she's your mommy and you're her Dylan. She can't think or understand or take care of you. That's when she needs to go to the hospital to calm down and get better.	COMMUNICATION and COMPREHENSION: Now this father tries to offer his son a broader understanding of the situation.

NARRATIVE	REPARATIVE ELEMENTS
DYLAN: Will Mommy get better?	
DAD: We don't know. The doctors are trying to help her with some new medicine, so her sickness will go away.	More COMMUNICATION More COMPREHENSION
DYLAN: Will she come home?	
DAD: I hope she will come home soon, but if she does, I'm never going to let you stay alone with Mommy again. There'll always be someone to help Mommy and there'll always be someone to help you. That way you don't have to be afraid that Mommy will get sick or hurt you again.	COMPETENCE: In this last explanation, the father tries to offer his son a more hopeful resolution for the future.

A Death in the Family

Death is inevitable. Nothing we can say or do can subvert its claim on our lives. We can only comfort the mourning child or adult by offering our compassion for their grief—and our presence to help fill the void. And death is irrevocable. When there is a death in the family, a chapter in the family's story is abruptly terminated. We can no longer collaborate together to produce new material in the family narrative; we can no longer say, "This story is to be continued."

The loss of a child literally breaks parents' hearts. But no matter how heartbroken, adults have greater resources with which to deal with their grief. They have more experience in dealing with loss in general. Children are more vulnerable. When a child's parent dies, all of the child's energies must be given over to sustaining herself in the face of this unexpected devastation. This loss opens up a psychic rupture in the child's inner world. Children who have suffered a death in the family will naturally show a wide array of profound reactions to this traumatic event. These reactions may include significant disturbances in sleeping and eating, an inability to concentrate or attend, regressive infantile behavior, depressive feelings and thoughts, mood swings, aggressive outbursts, and withdrawal or retreat into fantasy.

There are four factors which determine the developmental outcome for a child who has lost a parent:

- The *psychological health* and resiliency of the child before the death of the parent.
- The *nature of the relationship* to the deceased parent.
- The *emotional availability* of the remaining parent to the child.
- The immediate opportunities for the child's *return to the ordinary rhythms* of her life.

Although children under six years old may not be able to understand the permanence of death, they can express sadness and grief, even though their feelings may not be able to be sustained. If children lose someone they love, they may become particularly worried about other losses in their lives. They may begin to ask you how old you are or get worried that you will become ill. They may become clingy and afraid to be alone. They may continue to ask about the person who has died or to wait for him to come back, resisting all your attempts to teach them about the finality of death. Even after your explanation, they may say, "When can I see Grandpa? Will he come to my birthday party?" As a protective parent, you must be both patient and consistent as you remind your child that this loss is permanent.

Children older than seven are capable of more sustained grief, but they may also have more specific fears about the rites and rituals of death and more terror about its consequences in their lives. They may want to know what happens once the dead person is buried or whether there's life after death. They may become worried about the family's finances or about any realistic changes that the death entails: "Will we have to move away to take care of Grandma, now?" They may express concern for others who are bereaved—"Will Aunt Marion live alone, now?"—or fears about whether you or they will die.—"Can children die?"

No matter what your child's age, try to include her in the funeral arrangements, so that she can participate in the mourning process. Children need to know that it's all right to feel sad and cry when someone dies; they need to realize that we comfort one another when we lose someone we love; they need to use the rituals of death to help them say good-bye. No matter how old your child is, make sure she understands these three concepts about death:

- Dying is *not* the same as sleeping. When we sleep, we're alive and our body is just resting.
- When a person dies, their body stops working and they don't feel anything anymore.
- Once a person dies, their body can never live again; they can never come back or be with us.

Be sure to listen for the five basic fears hidden beneath your child's questions about death:

- "Where will I go when I die?" *(fear of the unknown)*
- "Is Grandma lonely under the ground?" *(fear of being alone)*
- "Will it hurt when Uncle John gets burned?" *(fears about the body)*
- "Will God kill me if I'm bad?" *(fear of the voice of conscience)*
- "Will I still be me when I'm dead?" *(fears about the self)*

Here's how to construct a reparative narrative that addresses nine-year-old David's normal fears about his parent's death, after experiencing the recent death of his grandmother.

DAVID: Will you die, Mommy?

NARRATIVE	REPARATIVE ELEMENTS
MOTHER: Everyone dies sometime, just like we're all born. But people don't die unless they're very, very sick, very, very old, or they've been in a terrible accident. I'm not going to die for a long, long time.	COMMUNICATION: This mother is offering information and confirming reality for her child.
DAVID: I'll be lonesome if you die and I can't see you anymore like I can't see Grandma Bessie anymore.	
MOTHER: Grandma was very, very old when she died. She lived a long, long life and she got to be a mommy and grandma and even a great-grandma. She was eighty-two years old. I'm still a young mommy. I'll always be here when you need me. By the time I have to die, you will be all grown-up. You'll be an old man with your own family. You might even be a grandpa, and a great-grandpa, too.	COMPASSION, COMPREHENSION, COMPETENCE: This mother opens with an empathic statement and then tries to help her child understand the situation better. At the same time, she describes an outcome for him that offers hope for the future.

Sudden Death

Of course, none of us can ever be prepared for sudden death—the massive stroke, the devastating car accident, anaphylactic shock, a fatal heart attack. In these cases, the remaining parent or family and friends must bear the psychological consequences of the event. It is they who must convey the shocking news to the children, creating a narrative that can be absorbed and used. Here's a grandmother talking to her two grandchildren, Sophie, ten years old, and Ben, five, about their mother who lies in a coma after being hit by a car:

GRANDMOTHER: Mommy is very, very sick. When the car hit her, her head was so hurt that the doctors don't know if she'll ever wake up. Your Daddy is staying with Mommy in the hospital now, and I'm going to stay here and take care of you.

SOPHIE *(crying):* Will Mommy die?

GRANDMOTHER: I don't know, Sophie. I'm hoping and hoping she'll live, but the doctors don't think she will.

BEN *(crying):* Wake her up! Wake her up! I want to see her.

SOPHIE: Stop it, Ben, you're making Grandma cry.

GRANDMOTHER: We all want Mommy to wake up, and we all want to see her. We're going to the hospital today, but it's going to be very hard because Mommy can't see you or talk to you—she's not conscious. She would wake up if she could, but she can't.

THE SPECIAL CASE OF SUICIDE

Suicide is the most shocking death of all for us to accept. Most of us hold onto life so dearly that it's hard for us to face the idea that someone would want to die. Yet as your child grows, she is bound to hear (or overhear) about someone who has killed himself—a neighbor's son, a teacher who was depressed, a well-known movie star. Because suicide is a willful death, it raises unique feelings and fears in all of us. This is because suicide is the ultimate act of hostility and abandonment toward those who are left behind, and the anger and guilt toward the person who committed suicide are bound to be particularly intense.

A parent's suicide is the worst death of all for a child to bear. While an adult can intellectually understand that a suicidal person is mentally ill and not really responsible for his actions, this is very difficult for a child. The child of a parent who committed suicide feels she just wasn't good enough or important enough to keep her parent alive. In order to help a child face the devastation of suicide, you need to emphasize that a person's mind can get sick just as a person's body can get sick. The child of a parent that has killed himself can be told:

> "Daddy's mind was so sick that he wasn't able to think about things clearly. He got very confused and thought the only way to solve his problems was to kill himself because he felt so bad."

Children trying to cope with a suicidal death may feel particularly enraged at the dead parent ("How could Daddy leave me like this if he loved me? I hate him!") or even responsible for the death ("If I had been home with Daddy when he got so confused, I could have helped him and he wouldn't have killed himself. It's my fault.") These are perfectly normal feelings, and an empathic understanding of the child's emotional plight goes a long way to helping a child cope. "Of course you're angry. I am, too," you might say, or "When someone we loves dies, we often think we could have saved them, but it just isn't true."

Here's a reparative narrative that tries to help an eleven-year-old child understand and cope with a teenage brother's suicide.

Lucy: Why did Andy kill himself?

NARRATIVE	REPARATIVE ELEMENTS
FATHER: He'd been very, very unhappy for a long time, and no matter how much we tried, we couldn't seem to help him.	COMMUNICATION: This is a confirmation of the reality for the child.
Lucy: But why would he leave us? Didn't he love us?	
FATHER: That's the saddest part. We can't understand how he could do this terrible thing to himself and to us.	COMPASSION: Here, the parent shares his own feelings empathically with his child.

NARRATIVE	REPARATIVE ELEMENTS
But the doctor tried to explain to us. He said that Andy was very, very depressed, and that depressed people's minds get sick and confused. Maybe he just wanted to sleep his problems away and didn't realize he had taken so many pills.	COMPREHENSION: Now, the parent tries to enlarge his child's understanding of the situation.
LUCY: He was really stupid. I'll never forgive him.	
FATHER: We're all very angry with him for dying. We wish he had never done this horrible thing.	More COMPREHENSION More COMPASSION
LUCY (crying): I really miss him, and I'll never see him again.	
FATHER (crying): This is so, so sad for all of us. We all miss Andy so much. We have to help each other now.	COMPETENCE: This parent isn't afraid to share his grief with his child, helping her to find her way to a healing resolution.

It's hard to speak to our children about death. Sometimes we don't want to talk about it because we're afraid to say the wrong thing and sometimes we don't say anything because we want to protect our kids from this most painful reality. But death is a part of life. The earlier you help your children to cope with "little deaths"—the pigeon on the street, the goldfish that went belly-up, the bad accident on the corner—the better prepared they will be for the more significant losses they will need to face later on. But we've been learning that before you can help your kids, you have to know yourself. This is true about disease and death, too.

What Should I Ask Myself?

The way we feel about our bodies is formed early in our lives and transformed through our bodily experiences as we grow and develop. Were you a healthy, sturdy, baby, or were you described as sickly? Did you struggle with any chronic illnesses as a child? Did you have any operations? or any long recuperations? How did your parents handle your health? Did they fuss and worry? Were they casual and laid-back? Do you feel they taught you to feel confident or fearful about your health? Was any member of your immediate family chronically or gravely ill when you were a child? Did any family members or friends die when you were growing up? Did you go to the funeral?

How would you describe the way you feel about your body now? Do you think of yourself as strong? weak? vulnerable? invulnerable? Are you hypochondriacal, always worried about every ache and pain? or do you ignore and obliterate your symptoms? Have you learned to live with your own physical limitations? or do you get cranky and depressed every time you get a cold? When you're sick do you like everyone to give you a lot of attention? or do you just like to be left alone?

Don was much better at taking care of his six-year-old son, Jake, who was home in bed with the flu, than Jake's mom, who fussed and fretted, increasing Jake's discomfort and irritability. "Jake is just like I am," Don told his wife. "When either of us gets sick, we like to crawl into our caves like animals and lick our wounds. Just leave him alone to sleep it off—don't keep trying to amuse him."

And what about you as a parent? Are you relaxed about your child's body, or fearful? Do you panic every time your child tumbles from a swing or climbs a tree? Do you show it? Do you worry that she could die every time your child gets sick? Sally was concerned about her eight-year-old daughter, Melanie, who'd recently been diagnosed with a heart murmur. The minute she heard the doctor's pronouncement, she became convinced that Melanie was going to die, even though she'd been told that Melanie's heart murmur wasn't serious and wouldn't interfere with Melanie's leading a completely normal life. Sally's dread made no sense in the present. It wasn't until she remembered that she'd had a best friend in third grade who had died of a heart defect when she was the same age as Melanie that she realized her irrational fears for Melanie originated in her own past.

As protective parents we want to help our children to manage the realities of life. Illness and death are two of those realities. Even though they fill all of us with frightening images of the unknown, of loneliness, of bodily damage, of dreadful punishment, and of the final obliteration of the self, we must deal with them. We can help our children to gain strength and resilience by exposing them to the right information at the right developmental time and by creating reparative narratives to help them deal with the losses we will all inevitably face throughout our lives.

6

Dark Passages:
Helping Kids Deal with Anger,
Envy, and Hatred

Violence in Your Child

All of us are born with the capacity to hate as well as to love. Aggression is not abnormal, it is all too normal—normal to our species, normal to our human condition. The infant that screams in rage when she's put in her crib, the toddler who bites his playmate in the park, the school girl who taunts her best friend, the adolescent boy who fights for his gang are all expressing their aggression—a potential for anger, hatred, and violence that lies within each of us, hidden in our deepest and darkest core. It is parents who must teach their children to become civilized. This means helping kids to modulate and transform their aggressive impulses into more useful and acceptable forms—into assertion, competition, activity, force-fulness.

One bewildered mother and father brought me their aggressive, unmanageable eight-year-old son for treatment. "We can't understand what's gone wrong," they exclaimed. "We've never expressed any aggression toward Brandon. We've always tried to let him develop freely, without any restrictions. We've never even let him play with toy guns in our home. How did he end up so angry?"

Sometimes our best intentions backfire in surprising ways.

Brandon's parents hoped to convey their personal values to their only child through a policy of parental noninterference, but they were unaware of the principles of protective parenting. Without his parents' help, Brandon had been unable to "modulate or transform his normal aggressive impulses into more useful and acceptable forms." Instead of a calm, peaceful child, Brandon's parents had produced a child whose aggression had run wild, beyond his own or his parents' control.

In order to achieve our civilizing goals, we must strike a balance. We want to raise a child with enough control to channel his aggression into effective action in his world, but not so much control that his energy and spirit are suppressed or his ability to act is paralyzed. In order to reach this healthy balance, we must start at the beginning of our child's life, setting appropriate restraints on aggression as it appears at each point in development. As protective parents, we must shield our children from the damaging effects of their impulses as well as from the dangers of the world. We start this process in infancy, as we help our baby learn that he will not be able to have everything he wants exactly when he wants it. In the beginning, we talk gently to the baby as we welcome him and help him to settle into the rhythms of our life. But soon we begin to talk more firmly to the baby, helping him to begin to understand both his own boundaries and ours. This process is called *setting limits*, and most parents have a lot of problems deciding what limits to set for their kids and when to set them.

It's important to understand that limit-setting is your first opportunity to help your child to begin to control his aggression. At first, your child needs you to tell him how to behave— "Don't touch!" "Don't grab!" "No biting!" "Big boys don't kick!" "Stop screaming!" But by the time your child is three years old, he will begin to internalize your expectations. Now, your child can begin to determine for himself what's right and what's wrong, what's good and what's bad, what's safe and what's dangerous. We call this internalizing process the development of the "voice of the conscience." When your child's conscience has crystallized, he will no longer need you to be there to set limits for him—he will be able to do it for himself.

When a child accomplishes this developmental task, we say he has self-control: now he is able to master his aggressive impulses. But if a child is unable to achieve this mastery over aggression, we say he is out of control. A child who is out of control will have great difficulties living in the real world. He can't adjust his impulses or modify his needs to take into account the impulses or needs of others; he can't master his thoughts, his feelings, or his actions; he can't calm himself down; and he has no brakes on his behavior. An uncontrolled child acts and feels like a monster. He can't calm himself and often no one else can calm him either! This is pretty frightening in a three-year-old, but it's even more frightening to imagine these feelings and this sort of behavior in a thirteen-year-old—or in a thirty-year-old. The older the child, the graver the consequences of a lack of aggressive control are likely to be. An out-of-control three-year-old can only throw tantrums, but an eight-year-old can get into fights. And an out-of-control teenager can become a juvenile delinquent.

Mastery of the violence within us is extremely difficult. Evidence of our continuous struggle with aggression is everywhere around us. We see domestic violence, violence in the schools, violent crimes by youths, racial and ethnic violence. Wars between parents occupy our courts, wars between gangs disrupt our streets, wars between nations disturb our lives. If we want to help our children survive, we need to help them to master their own aggression: In a broader sense, we need to help them master aggression if we want to help our world survive, too!

What Should I Ask Myself?

Before you can teach your child to be appropriately assertive but not inappropriately aggressive, to be a good loser as well as a good winner, to be cooperative as well as competitive, you have to know how you really feel about aggression—in your child and in yourself.

Think back to your own childhood. How was competition handled in your family? Did your parents value good sportsmanship? or were they only interested in whether or not you won the game? When you came home with a 97 percent on a test, did your father ask you what happened to the other three points? Was your mother a "killer" competitor, always invested in winning, even when she played Monopoly with you? Were you always compared to your siblings? Was the comparison favorable? or unfavorable? Were both of your parents high achievers? One of them?

Ray, who grew up with a brilliant older brother, Tim, who seemed to do everything well (and to whom he was always unfavorably compared), is now the father of two sons. He finds himself continually sympathizing with his younger son and relentlessly critical of his older son. It wasn't until his wife said to him "Boy, you must never have forgiven Tim" that he realized that he had identified with his younger son, who reminded him of himself as a child, and was reliving his childhood anger about his brother with his older son.

What about assertion and aggression? Did members of your family scream and yell at each other in arguments? or were voices always kept hushed? Were you permitted to talk up or talk back to your parents, or were you punished for bold or brazen behavior? Did your parent(s) hit you as a child to punish you? Did they hit each other? Did they humiliate you in front of others? Were your parents sarcastic or contemptuous of you? or of each other? Were you and your siblings permitted to "fight it out" with each other, or did adults intervene?

Tanya never felt accepted by kids her age when she was growing up. A shy, timid child, she was always particularly worried about being hurt by more aggressive children. Her daughter, Michelle, has been disciplined several times in school for disruptive behavior and aggression toward other youngsters. Tanya is bewildered by her daughter's aggression, but proudly declares, "At least she's no pushover like I was." Without realizing it, Tanya is subtly encouraging her daughter's aggression in order to ensure that Michelle has the power over others that Tanya never had as a child.

What family values about aggression were passed down to you? Do you feel that "nice guys finish last?" Do you think that we live in a "dog-eat-dog world"? Do you believe in the "survival of the fittest"? Do you think that it's "every man for himself"? Or do you believe in brotherhood or sisterhood? Do you feel virtues like kindness and sensitivity are valuable? or foolish?

And what are your feelings about aggression now? Do you or your spouse fight a lot? Do you ever "lose it" or become violent? The single most important influence on the development of aggression in children is exposure to aggression in the adults they live with. Marital strife produces sibling strife. Spousal abuse produces child abuse. Do you have a bad temper? Does your child?

Do you believe that if someone hits your kid, he should hit back? Try to reason with his attacker? Get an adult to mediate? Do you believe it's important to be tough in today's world? Do you rate the kids your child hangs out with as "winners" or "losers"? This can be important. Todd, who felt he was a "loser" as a child, wants his daughter Jessica to only hang out with the right crowd so she'll be one of the "winners." He's forever quizzing her on her friends and rating them from one to ten. But Jessica doesn't feel her dad should have anything to say about who her friends are. Finally she said to him, "If you think these kids are so great, *you* play with them!"

Most of us feel ambivalent about the role of aggression in our own lives and confused about what role we want it to play in our children's lives. You need to be clear about your own priorities before you can help your child to set his.

Discipline Versus Punishment

We've all seen spoiled, obnoxious children—children whose bewildered parents seem unable to soothe or satisfy them, no matter what they do. How do they get that way? Too much love? No! Too little *discipline*. A protective parent knows that discipline is an important part of his civilizing job. Parental discipline is your child's first "brush with the law"—family law. Discipline means setting standards for your kids and having clear expectations about their behavior; it also means encouraging your children to meet the standards that you set. It is a way to tame aggression. It's a way to help your child achieve self-control. But discipline is not the same as punishment—there's an important difference. Discipline means "laying down the law"; punishment is the price one is asked to pay when the law is broken. Parents often resort to punishment when discipline has failed.

Here's an example of a parent who is unable to discipline her two-and-a-half-year-old and is already beginning to spoil him, losing an opportunity to teach him self-control:

DALE: I want an ice cream cone.

MOTHER: It's too close to dinner time.

DALE *(kicking and screaming):* I want it, I want it now!

MOTHER: Stop making a fuss. Everyone's looking. All right! I'll get you a cone if you stop screaming.

Here's another example. This parent is also unable to discipline his young five-year-old daughter, Abigail, and instead resorts to punishment, losing a chance for learning self-control and demonstrating lack of self-control himself!

ABIGAIL: I want an ice cream cone.

FATHER: It's too close to dinner time.

ABIGAIL *(kicking and screaming):* I want it, I want it now!"

FATHER *(smacking the child):* Don't you scream at me. If you don't stop right now, you'll be sorry. You'll get a real spanking right here in front of everyone!

Remember, children pay attention to what we *do*, not only what we *say*. Parents lose a lot of credibility with their kids if, while disciplining them, they display the very behavior they are prohibiting in the child ("How many times have I told you not to hit your sister? Now you're going to get a real spanking!").

Here's an example of a protective parent using discipline to help her four-year-old son, Chris, learn about limits—his limits and the limits of others.

CHRIS: I want an ice cream cone.

MOTHER: It's too close to dinner time.

CHRIS *(kicking and screaming):* I want it. I want it now!

MOTHER *(restraining child's tantrum by holding child's arms, etc.):* I can see you're very angry with me because you really, really want an ice cream. But unless you stop kicking and screaming *right now*, we're leaving this store. I won't even talk to you about ice cream, and you certainly won't get any.

CHRIS *(stops kicking, now just crying):* I want an ice cream cone.

MOTHER *(looking in child's eyes with hands on child's shoulders):* I know you want ice cream. You can't have it now no matter how much you scream because we're going to have dinner soon. But if you show me you can calm down, I'll get an ice cream that we can put in the freezer and you can have it *after* your dinner. You can pick your favorite flavor if you stop crying.

CHRIS *(stops sobbing):* Can I have chocolate?

What has this protective parent conveyed to her four-year-old?

- We can't always have what we want when we want it.
- Crying, kicking, and screaming aren't effective ways to get what you need.
- You can get more of what you need through reasoning and talking.
- Self-control brings rewards.

This protective parent has disciplined her child and helped him to learn how to modulate his own aggression. She's helped him to keep his loving connection to her while still obtaining what he wants for himself. She hasn't let his aggression overwhelm him or her. As a result, her little son has managed to negotiate an important developmental path successfully. He's controlled himself, maintained his good relationship to his mom—and he's gotten his ice cream.

Many parents are reluctant to discipline their children because they feel that in doing so, they are hurting, restricting, or criticizing their kids, but discipline is an important part of protective parenting. It helps your child learn self-control early in his life; it addresses the social and legal expectations of the world at large (schools, laws, etc.); and it tells your child that you care about who he is and what he does.

I remember a period in my son's life when it seemed as if he and I were always at odds over his commitment to his school work. I began to feel that I was disciplining him endlessly, and that I was becoming a tedious nag. One evening I was talking to a friend who told me she *never* got involved in her son's work. She just told him, "I got through school once on my own, and I'm not going to do it all over again! If you want to work, fine, and if you don't, it's your life!" I was inspired by this eminently sensible conversation and decided to immediately try this approach on my son. He patiently heard me out and then replied, "Don't you care about me anymore?" Your child knows that you discipline him because you love him. Use this understanding to help him grow.

Here's an example of an ordinary family episode where aggressive feelings quickly escalate when the mother isn't able to bring her ten-year-old son's rebellious reactions under enough control.

Mom: I've told you to clean your room for three days. I'm tired of excuses. Do it right now!

Paul: You're such a nag. You're always on my back. It's my room.

Mom: You better listen to me.

PAUL: Why do I have to listen to you? You can't make me. I don't care what you do! *(slams door to his room)*

MOM: Your father will hear about this when he comes home.

This parent feels helpless to deal with her child's aggressive rebellion. She's unable to discipline him and abdicates, deferring handling the situation to his father. What has she taught her child?

- If kids are aggressive enough they can even intimidate their parents.
- My mom is not strong enough to manage me. I must be pretty powerful.
- Men have more clout than women.

If the previous parent threw in the towel too early, this parent is trying to bring her ten-year-old's aggressive reactions under too much control:

MOM: I've told you to clean up your room for three days. I'm tired of excuses. Do it now!

GREG: You're such a nag. You're always on my back. It's my room.

MOM: Don't you dare talk back to me, young man. You live in my house. I pay the bills and you do what I say, when I say it, or you'll be sorry. *(She smacks child across the face)* Now you march right into that room and start cleaning, or find someplace else to live.

This parent manages her son's rebellion, but only through resorting to physical punishment. She loses sight of the real issue: helping her son take responsibility for his room and for modulating his reactive anger. Instead, she escalates the event into a battle of wills and uses her hands instead of words to break down her son's resistance. She may have gotten him to clean up his room, but she's probably increased his underlying aggression rather than decreased it. What has she really taught him?

- The person who hits, wins.
- Kids have no right to talk up or talk back; adults have all the power.
- If you don't do what Mom says, you could get kicked out of your home.

Now let's look at the way a protective parent might try to construct a reparative narrative to help her twelve-year-old child respond and modulate his aggressive reactions in that same situation.

MOM: I've told you to clean up your room for three days, now, Richie. I'm tired of excuses. Do it now.

RICHIE: You're such a nag. You're always on my back. It's my room!

NARRATIVE	REPARATIVE ELEMENTS
MOM: You know, you're right. I am a nag. I've been hearing myself nag you and nag you, day after day.	COMPASSION: This mother uses an empathic statement to let the child know she understands how he feels.
But we have a problem here that isn't getting solved. I nag you and you ignore me, and both of us get very angry with each other. I'm very angry at you for not cleaning up your room like you promised, and you're very angry at me for being on your back all the time.	COMMUNICATION: Now, she's offering her child information and she's confirming the reality that has to be addressed. COMPREHENSION: This mother lets the child know she understands the situation.
We've got to find a way to solve this together. Do you have any good ideas?	COMPETENCE: Here, she's trying to help her child develop an outcome or come to a resolution.

NARRATIVE	REPARATIVE ELEMENTS
RICHIE: Let me keep my room the way I want!	
MOM *(laughing):* That would solve your problem, but not mine. Your room doesn't have to be perfect, but it has to be better than it is.	
RICHIE: I'm really tired tonight. Could I do half my room tomorrow and half on Friday, when I get out of school early?	CHILD'S COMPETENCE: The child comes up with his own resolution.
MOM: OK, that sounds reasonable. But how do I know your plan will work? I don't want to be nagging you all over again tomorrow and the next day. Then we'll be right back where we started.	More COMPREHENSION
RICHIE: If I don't do it this time, you can take away my allowance for two weeks.	More COMPETENCE

What has this child learned in this exchange?

- People are entitled to angry feelings, but they still need to meet their obligations.
- Promises should be kept.
- Words work: Reasoning and bargaining help to solve situations.
- Kids are powerful, too. They can speak up and negotiate on their own behalf.

Assertion Versus Aggression

We've been talking about the negative aggressive potential that lies within all of us, but aggression has positive uses as well. The positive aspect of aggressive energy is called *assertion*. With too much aggressive force, a child can become overbearing, spoiled, selfish, mean, domineering, and tyrannical. Without enough aggressive force, however, he would not be able to act with decisiveness, impact, and assurance in his life.

Some kids will need our help to be more assertive on their own behalf, while others may need to be constantly reminded to be less aggressive. Protective parents need to help their kids to know that there is a big difference between assertion and aggression as they go out into the world.

That's why protective parents have a tricky job. How can you ask a child to feel strong and powerful in the world while still encouraging him to restrain his power on behalf of others? How can you ask a child to actively pursue his own goals while still helping him learn how to accommodate? How can you ask a child to believe in himself while still urging him to respect the rights of those around him?

Protective parents help their kids to make choices between appropriate assertion and inappropriate aggression all the time. These choices will vary from family to family, with some parents tolerating a great deal of provocation, challenge, and rebellion, as other parents promote more restraint and require more respect from their kids.

But remember, it's important to keep that balance between too little and too much control in mind. At the same time we're limiting aggression we've got to know how to encourage healthy assertion. Children need to know how to speak up for themselves, how to challenge arbitrary authority, how to make choices, and how to take appropriate risks. And without healthy assertion none of these actions is possible.

Protective parents can help their children master aggression without suppressing assertion by setting developmentally appropriate expectations and limits as their children grow. In children under three years old, these limits have mainly to do with bodily controls—toilet-training and temper-training (no biting, no fighting). At this age, you need to encourage your child's increased language skills to help him control his impulses. When children are little, it is natural for them to discharge their aggressive feelings with their bodies—through movement and action. That's why so much early education is about getting kids to talk instead of hit. When we help our kids to modulate their aggressive impulses through language, we give them an enormously flexible, effective, and powerful tool for self-control and control over others. (That's why children who are late talkers are often frustrated and angry until they begin to speak.) Just teaching your child to use and respond to the word *no!* already safeguards him against many of the dangers he will confront at the beginning of his life (sharp knives, open windows, poisons, cleaning fluids, etc.), and will continue to confront as he gets older (drugs, sex, gangs, etc.).

As your child grows older, self-control over his aggressive impulses becomes more complicated. Now, he's going to need to control what he *says* as well as what he does; he's going to need to become aware of the needs and rights of others as well as himself; and he's going to need to learn to play by the rules and to become a good sport. How can you teach a child to compete without crushing his opponents? How can you teach a child to win, but to also play fair?

Competition Versus Cooperation

Many years ago, I consulted to a day care center in Manhattan that served some of the children of the Communist Chinese delegation to the United Nations. I was always impressed by how even the littlest Chinese children always saw to the needs of the other children before their own. When they brought in a special treat for their own lunch, they would always share it with all the children at their table; when a toy was in dispute, they would often insist that the other child take a turn first. I noted this behavior to one of the mothers.

"I know," she replied. "We teach our children to be cooperative because it is one of the principles of the Communist revolution."

"In the United States," I replied, "we try to teach our children to share and cooperate with each other, too. It's one of the principles of a democracy."

"Yes," she stated, "but your government doesn't enforce it!"

Perhaps she was right. As citizens, we elect officials to govern on our behalf, but our society is very ambivalent about the uses and abuses of aggression. On the one hand, we try to teach our kids to cooperate with each other; on the other, we encourage competition. On the one hand, we profess to be against violence; on the other, we have the highest incidence of murder among the civilized countries of the western world. On the one hand, we tell our kids "to play by the rules"; on the other, we often admire people who do anything to win. On one hand we say, "It's how you play the game that counts"; on the other, we say, "Winning isn't everything; it's the *only* thing!" No wonder we can't decide as parents whether we want to raise assertive, self-centered achievers, or cooperative, selfless, good samaritans! We all want our children to be successful, yet the qualities emphasized in the climb to the top may be qualities we don't like to live with—particularly in our own families.

This is where the voice of conscience, with its accompanying fourth basic fear (guilt), becomes extremely important in your child's development. Your child's conscience (the internalization of parental standards and expectations), and the guilt that he needs to feel when he fails to meet these standards, can now help him to begin to regulate his behavior. Conscience can tell your child when he's stepped over the line, when he's hurt someone else, when he's betrayed or violated the principles you value. A child without a conscience is tragic, but an adult without a conscience is terrifying. Helping your child develop "good character" is one of your most important jobs as a protective parent. And there is no such thing as "good character" without conscience.

But don't go overboard! Be careful, too, to keep your expectations of your children balanced and appropriate. Too many harsh expectations and perfectionistic standards can crush your child's character, just as too few expectations and low standards of behavior, can leave him with "bad" character, one that's selfish, aggressive, and out of control. Sometimes parents consciously convey one set of values, while unconsciously conveying another. They may, for example, tell a child not to hit other kids, while secretly admiring and even encouraging their child's aggressive power ("He's a real little fighter, isn't he!"). Remember that children are very adept at picking up hidden messages. If you consciously profess nonviolence, but unconsciously admire aggression, your children will learn to be aggressive!

Empathy and Compassion: The Civilizing Emotions

Helping your child to develop an internalized voice of conscience is one of the ways to control the aggression that lies within him, but is not the only way. In addition to absorbing your standards and values, and differentiating between right and wrong, your child also needs to know what impact his words and actions will have on others. This knowledge is embedded in that characteristic we've called empathy or compassion. Protective parents can start to teach their kids how to empathize with the feelings of others as soon as the child is old enough to understand the effects he may have on those around him, usually between two and three years old. Empathy and compassion also help your child to begin to modify and constrain his own anger and aggression: "You can't hit Tony; that hurts him." "How would you like it if he hit you?" "If someone hit you, would you want to play with him?" We point out the impact our child's aggression will have on others and try to get him to think about the consequences. We also try to get our child to put himself in the other person's place—to imagine what it is like to be them, or to feel like them. Teaching our children to feel empathy and compassion is not only meaningful for their own lives; it has profound consequences for society. It is one of the emotions that enables us to stop our own hostility short of hurting another person. If every parent was able to teach this to every child, our world would be a far better place for us to inhabit. No wonder we call empathy and compassion the civilizing emotions.

Envy: Another Aspect of Aggression

It is hard for all of us to be content with our lot in life. There is always something more for us to want—more money, more success, more power, more love, more attention, more recognition, more excitement, more glory. Children, too, are envious. They want to have long blond hair, or be the best on the team, or be the teacher's pet, or be chosen for the lead in the school play. When they see that they don't have things that other children have, they feel angry and frustrated. They cry, "It isn't fair!" And indeed, it isn't.

One of the most painful aspects of being a parent is explaining the inequity of life to our children. We all aren't born with the same potential. Life will not offer us all the same opportunities. And each of us will be marked by destiny in unique ways. It's natural for children to envy those they feel have it easier or better than they do. But envy is not a pleasant emotion: It undermines character, erodes our good will, and heightens the fifth basic fear (fear about the self). Envy is also an aggressive emotion. We feel hostile toward the person who possesses what we want. Envy of others can quickly consume all the energies we need in order to pursue the goals we want to achieve. A little envy, in that moment when you wish the good news had happened to you, is normal. But too much envy can leave you with a bitter legacy. Here's a protective parent who's trying to help his ten-year-old daughter cope with the consequences of losing, and the aftermath of envy.

RACHEL: Charlotte's going to be the princess in the school play, and I only get to be the sister. It's not fair! Just because she's pretty and has long blond hair, she thinks she can get everything she wants!

NARRATIVE	REPARATIVE ELEMENTS
DAD: I'm sorry you didn't get the part of the princess, honey. I know how disappointed you must feel. You know, when actors try out for parts in plays, sometimes they're "typecast." That means that they get the part just because they look like the part. But other times, just looking pretty has nothing to do with who gets the part. It has more to do with who's the best actor.	COMPASSION: This father gives his daughter empathy. He also begins to open COMMUNICATION with her, offering her information, and confirming her reality. And lastly, he's showing through COMPREHENSION his understanding of the situation.
RACHEL: I wish I looked like Charlotte does. Then I'd get to be the star.	
DAD: I know you do. It's hard not to be envious of how Charlotte looks, but she's who she is and you're you.	More COMPASSION
RACHEL: But she's so pretty and I'm not.	
DAD: Yes, Charlotte is pretty. And sometimes she's going to get things that you want because of her looks, but sometimes you're going to get things that she wants, too. She doesn't have your sparkling blue eyes, and she doesn't sing as well as you do. The more you waste your time envying her, the less energy you'll have for being yourself.	More COMPASSION More COMPREHENSION More COMMUNICATION and COMPETENCE: Now, he offers his child a resolution that offers hope for the future.

NARRATIVE	REPARATIVE ELEMENTS
Up until now, you and Charlotte were friends. If you keep hating her just because she got the part of the princess and you didn't, you're going to lose a friend, too. Think about it.	

Here's a reparative narrative constructed by the parent on the other side. Her child is the object of envy and needs help to cope with the consequences of winning.

MOM: What's the matter, honey? I thought you'd be really happy today. You got to be the princess in the play. That's the biggest part. You're the star!

CHARLOTTE: I know, but Rachel was really mean to me today, and I thought we were friends. She told me I thought I was such a big deal, and I didn't, Mommy. I didn't do anything to her.

NARRATIVE	REPARATIVE ELEMENTS
MOM: Well, now I see what the problem is. Something did happen that made Rachel upset with you. *You* got the part of the princess and *she* didn't. Sometimes when you get something that your friends want, too, they feel envious or jealous of you, and that makes them angry and frustrated for a while.	COMPASSION: By using empathy, this mother lets her daughter know she feels for her plight. COMPREHENSION: She also tries to help her understand the situation, by naming the emotions involved.
CHARLOTTE: But I still want Rachel to be my friend. I don't want her to hate me.	

NARRATIVE	REPARATIVE ELEMENTS
MOM: Give Rachel a little time to get over being hurt that you got the part and she didn't. Try not to mention being the princess when she's around, and let's see if she's able to get over her envy of you. If she doesn't, then we'll figure out a way to talk to her about what happened, so she knows you wanted to be princess but you didn't want to hurt her.	COMPETENCE: Finally, she helps her daughter see a possible resolution or outcome that offers hope for the future.

As they learn to be civilized, children have to learn to moderate their expressions of pride in self in order not to make others feel bad. Here's a reparative narrative a protective parent might use to help a boastful child to win without wounding others.

SCOTT: I got the highest mark in my class on my math test! But Mark only got 79 percent. Boy, is he stupid!

NARRATIVE	REPARATIVE ELEMENTS
DAD: I can see that you're really proud of yourself! It feels good to be the best. Mark didn't do so well, and I bet he doesn't feel good about it, just like you didn't feel so good when Mark won the spelling bee and you didn't. Sometimes it's not enough when we *win*, we also want our friends to *lose*. That's called "gloating"—when you feel good *because* your friends feel bad. Think about it.	COMPASSION: This parent shares an empathic statement with the child. COMMUNICATION: He also expands the child's information. COMPREHENSION: Now, he broadens the child's understanding of the situation.

NARRATIVE	REPARATIVE ELEMENTS
Would you like it if Mark gloated when you lost at spelling? You can still feel big without making Mark feel small.	COMPETENCE: Finally, he offers a better outcome or resolution to the situation than boasting.

Protective parents also need to provide a cushion of safety for their children when they lose. They need to help their kids to accept their losses gracefully, to gather their energies to try again. You don't want your child to be a "sore loser." Here's the other side of the coin—a reparative narrative that helps your child deal with losing without lessening his sense of self.

HANK: I really screwed up today. I was supposed to spell *mortgage* in assembly and I forgot how. I couldn't figure out if it had a *t* or not. Finally, Ms. McCarthy said, "Henry, are you still with us?" Everyone laughed at me and I felt like a jerk! I'm such a loser. Jethro won. He's really smart.

NARRATIVE	REPARATIVE ELEMENTS
MOM: It's really hard when you screw up. You must have felt awful, particularly when everyone laughed. But I think kids laugh when things like that happen because they're all remembering times when they screwed up, too. I remember when I was in the fourth grade, I was in the school chorus and we were all supposed to stop singing quickly together at the end, but I forgot and I just kept on singing! I thought I would die, I was so embarrassed. You just felt like a jerk at	COMPASSION: This parent begins with an empathic statement. COMMUNICATION: Next, she offers the child more information. COMPREHENSION: Then she enlarges her child's understanding of the situation by sharing her own experiences as a child.

NARRATIVE	REPARATIVE ELEMENTS
the moment. It happens to everyone, sometimes. It feels bad today, but you'll have other chances to win. There'll be other spelling bees.	COMPETENCE: Last, she suggests another outcome, one that contains more hope for the future.

BOYS VERSUS GIRLS

What are little boys made of?
Snips and snails and puppy dogs tails!
What are little girls made of?
Sugar and spice and everything nice!

It may be true that many boys are "naturally" more aggressive than girls throughout the entire course of life, but even this biological predisposition can be modulated by protective parents who are mindful of their children's development. The problem for parents is not who starts out with more innate aggression; the problem is how we can help both our boys and our girls to modulate and channel their normal aggression in healthy and productive ways. Some boys may need to learn how to face verbal challenges as well as physical ones, and some girls may particularly need how to learn to face physical challenges as well as verbal ones (just as boys seem to rely more on aggressive action, girls show a propensity for reliance on their verbal skills).

Some children who have trouble standing up for themselves (boys or girls) may need your help to strengthen their resolve, while other children (boys or girls) who are "too pushy" may need your help to modulate their forcefulness. Parents need to be watchful about gender bias. Often we encourage or suppress aggression along gender lines. Before you can help your children grow without gender bias, you have to make sure you're not biased.

Do you think that it's all right for boys to fight it out, but that girls should never get physical? Do you roughhouse with your boys but treat your girls gently? Do you buy cars and trucks for your boys and dolls for your girls? In all of these subtle ways we cue our children to so-called masculine and feminine behavior. In all of these ways, we're teaching boys that being assertive and forceful is OK, but we're teaching girls that being assertive and forceful is *not* OK. Even if boy children start out with more innate aggressive potential, the strong social cues we give them from the time they are born often continue to emphasize this aspect of their development, while the social cues we give to girls de-emphasize it.

But even when we are able to permit girls more assertion and aggression—"tomboys" are admired in childhood as long as they don't carry it too far into adolescence—we still leave very little room for boys to repudiate or relinquish aggressive behavior. We don't even have an equivalent positive term—"janegirls?" A boy who shows gentle tendencies may wind up being called a "sissy," or at best, "sensitive." Protective parents try to help their children reach their true potential *without gender constraints*. It's important for us to realize that both boys and girls need to use action and language to communicate; both boys and girls need to learn how to be bold as well as tender; both boys and girls need to know how to be good nurturing parents; both boys and girls need adventures; both boys and girls need emotional as well as intellectual and physical strength.

Once you've helped your child to channel his own aggression into constructive action, to know the difference between assertion and aggression, to respond to the voice of his conscience, to develop "good" character, and to play by the rules, your child is well prepared for his encounters with our world. Now, what can you do as a protective parent to help your child to face the aggression, hostility, and violence around him?

Violence in Your Child's World

Verbal Violence: Dealing with Bigotry

One of the unfortunate ways human beings try to build themselves up is to put other people down. To do this, we often choose to ridicule characteristics the other person has, such as how they look, how they talk, what they like, what they do. But one of the most painful ways we put someone else down draws on who they *are*—either their religious or their ethnic origins. To be subject to such slurs triggers the fifth basic fear, fears about the self. Obviously, this kind of aggression has to be learned by the child—children are not born with racial or ethnic prejudice. That's why it's extremely important that you understand your own bias and prejudice, now, when you're a parent—because your children are likely to carry your feelings into a new generation.

What Should I Ask Myself?

What are your feelings about people who are different than you? Are you secretly prejudiced? Did you grow up in an ethnic neighborhood where virtually everyone you knew shared your ethnic heritage? Or did you grow up in a mixed neighborhood with children from many different backgrounds? Were your parents tolerant and open-minded in their views about other people? Or were your parents narrow-minded or even bigoted in their views about the world? Was it common to hear racial and ethnic slurs in your household? Did your parents refer to "wops," "kikes," "chinks," "niggers," "micks," "pollacks," "spics," "spades," "honkies"? Or was this kind of name-calling unthinkable in your family? This kind of thinking about groups is based on prejudice and bigotry. It doesn't look at the individual with all his capabilities and vulnerabilities, it just looks at his ethnic classification. Do you want your kids to grow up thinking this way? Do you want others to think this way about your kids?

Here's a reparative narrative that can help your child cope with the painful hostility that's directed toward him in an ethnic slur:

CARLOS: Daddy, what's a "spic"?

DAD: Where'd you hear that word?

CARLOS: I wanted to play baseball in the park with Kevin, but his friend said, "We don't let spics on this team," so I walked away.

NARRATIVE

REPARATIVE ELEMENTS

DAD: A spic is an ugly name that ugly people call Hispanics. You did the right thing, walking away from that kid. He doesn't even know you and he's calling you names. It means he's just prejudiced against Spanish people.

COMMUNICATION: This father is giving his child information and confirmation of the reality he's facing.

COMPASSION: He's also offering his child empathy about the situation.

CARLOS: Next time, I'll punch him in the nose, if he calls me that—and I'm going to punch Kevin, too.

DAD: I can understand why you want to punch him out, but that kid isn't worth getting into a fight about. We don't know who he is or who his friends are. But Kevin is different. You're right. He's supposed to be your friend. I don't blame you for being angry with him. But maybe you and Kevin need to talk this through some more, before you do any punching.

COMPREHENSION: He's also letting his son know he understands the whole event and all its implications.

CARLOS: I'm going to tell him he's not my friend anymore if he hangs around with jerks. I wouldn't let anyone call *him* names.

CHILD'S COMPETENCE: By dad's having empathized with his son and heard him out, his son comes up with his own resolution.

DAD: You feel you'd stick up for Kevin, and you're upset he didn't stick up for you. You need to talk to Kevin and find out why.

The father also offers another possibility that may produce another outcome with hope for the future.

But what if your child isn't the victim of a racial slur? What if your child is (unwittingly) the *aggressor*? Many young children overhear words and phrases that they imitate—often without realizing that their language is offensive. Here's how one mother handled a situation like this with her eight-year-old son:

MOM: Who do you want to come to your birthday party this year?

OLIVER: Ned and Julian, and Mario and Brett. I don't want any girls, and I can't have Lloyd and Andrew come because they're niggers.

NARRATIVE	REPARATIVE ELEMENTS
MOM: Oliver, where did you hear that awful word?	COMMUNICATION: Here this mother is trying to get information
OLIVER: Ned told me his father doesn't like him playing with niggers.	
MOM: So you've decided not to invite Lloyd and Andrew, even though you like them, because you're worried that Ned won't come.	COMPREHENSION: Now she's trying to understand his plight.
OLIVER: It wouldn't be a good party without Ned.	
MOM: You have a real problem here, but there's something even more important for us to discuss. "Nigger" is a terrible word—I never, ever want you to use it again. It's a word to hurt someone who's black or Afro-American. I know you don't realize how ugly it is or you wouldn't have said it. People like Ned's father are prejudiced. They may hate all	COMPASSION and COMPREHENSION: The mother remains empathic but tries to help her child to understand this complex situation.

NARRATIVE	REPARATIVE ELEMENTS
black people without knowing them, or all Jewish people like your teacher, Mrs. Rosenberg, or Italian people like your friend, Mario. Ned's father has a hating problem.	
OLIVER *(cries):* I wanted to ask Lloyd and Andrew. I really did.	
MOM: I know you did and we *are* going to ask them. You can tell Ned that you're asking *all* the kids you like to your party. You can tell him you hope he comes because he's your best friend.	COMPETENCE: Now this mom helps her child to come to a resolution of this problem that represents the family's values.
OLIVER: What if his father doesn't let him come?	
MOM: If Ned can't come then, we'll ask him over by himself for a birthday sleepover later on. I don't want Ned to be punished because of his father's problem. Maybe we can talk to Ned about all of this and find out how he feels.	COMPETENCE: She also offers her son hope for the future without compromising her family's values or permitting her son's life to be contaminated by another parent's bigotry.

Physical Violence: Dealing with Physical Threats

As the breakdown of the American family continues, as poverty, homelessness, and joblessness increase, as racial and ethnic crimes rise, as drug abuse proliferates, all of us are drawn into a web of increasing violence. Even the nature of the crimes committed by youngsters has shifted. Most juvenile delinquents used to commit crimes against property like car theft, arson, and larceny, but now most of these youngsters commit crimes against people, like rape, assault, and murder.

The mean streets of our cities are getting meaner, and violent crime by young people has increased by 25 percent in only the last ten years. It is important for all of us to note that this increase is not only among poor, urban youths in urban areas, but among people of all races, social classes, and life styles. In fact, crime is even increasing at a faster rate in our suburbs and rural areas than in our cities. This means that how we raise our kids is more important than ever, and how we prepare them to protect themselves is crucial.

Once your child begins to go to school, he will have to learn to deal with the violence and aggression he meets in the playground and on the streets. Even when children are still quite young, they are already bewildered and frightened by the aggression around them: "Mommy, why does Shawn grab things? He hurts me when he pushes." Some children are ready and waiting to mobilize their own energies to fight back: "Daddy, Steven took Patricia's pail and shovel, so I just took them right back. I'm not scared of Steven." Other children are already in retreat from the hostile confrontations: "Mommy, I don't want to go to the park. Shawn will be there." "Steven can have my pail and shovel, I don't care."

Protective parents need to be alert to the role their child seems to choose in his dealings with other children. Does your child always seem to get manipulated by other kids? Is it hard for him to speak up or speak out? Does he have trouble defending himself? If this is the case, he may be taking on the role of "the victim." A child in this dilemma has usually suppressed aggression and assertion out of his own fears and anxiety. He may permit himself to be "scapegoated" in order to gain the pity of other children, or to punish himself for imagined wrongdoings. Children struggling with this issue need to be supported to stand up for themselves even when they're little. You need to help them to rehearse assertion. You can say, "Now, if Margie takes your apple at lunch, remember to tell her, 'No, that's mine!' in a loud voice," or "When Jeremy tries to be first in line again, be sure to say, 'It's my turn.'"

But what if your child takes on the role of the aggressor in his dealings with others? What if he's the class bully? Kids who boss and bully other kids are struggling with fears and anxieties, too. They don't operate out of personal strength, but rather out of personal weakness. They need to have power over others in order to begin to feel good about themselves. They are not able to stop their aggression, even at the thought of another person's pain. This means that if your child is a bully, not only is he acting big because he feels small, but his empathic capacities are insufficiently developed, as well. You'll need to help your child to increase his compassion and gain a more secure sense of himself—a self that doesn't have to be bolstered by bullying others. Here's the way a parent might talk to her nine-year-old son, Peter, who's acting like a bully:

NARRATIVE	REPARATIVE ELEMENTS
Mom: We spoke to your teacher last night, and she told us that you're having a lot of trouble with the other kids in your class.	COMMUNICATION: This parent is informing her child, and confirming an important reality.
Peter: I don't have any trouble with anyone. I can take care of myself!	
Mom: That's just it. You seem to be taking care of yourself without thinking about anybody else. Your teacher was afraid that you're turning into a bully—bossing other kids around who aren't as strong as you are.	More COMMUNICATION: Here, she's offering more information about the event.
Peter: They're just wimps. The minute anyone comes near them they run to the teacher. They're babies.	

NARRATIVE	REPARATIVE ELEMENTS
Mom: If kids are weaker and more babyish than you are, then you need to be particularly careful not to hurt them. We need to find out why it's so important for you to frighten other kids. You must be angry or unhappy about something. Boys who are really strong don't become bullies. Boys who are really strong become leaders, and leaders take care of all the kids they play with; leaders are fair. When you boss around another kid you may get him to listen to you, and maybe even to be afraid of you, but you'll never get him to like you.	COMPASSION: Letting her child know she feels empathic will help him face his problem. COMPREHENSION: Here, this mom offers her child understanding of the situation. She tries to expand his understanding.
Peter: I have lots of friends.	
Mom: I know that you *want* to have lots of friends, but you're not going about it the right way. We need to help you figure out how to get friends that *really* like you, not friends who are only afraid of you. We've got to help you to stop being a bully.	COMPETENCE: Now she offers her child hope for the future including a possible resolution.

What do you do if your child hasn't asked for coaching in dealing with aggressors, or if the coaching hasn't worked. Here's a reparative narrative that can help your child deal with the experience of being bullied:

NARRATIVE	REPARATIVE ELEMENTS
DAD: How come you don't like to play in the park anymore?	COMMUNICATION: This question confirms a reality the parent has observed.
CRAIG: I'd rather stay home.	
DAD: I've noticed that, but something must have happened that made you feel upset. Can you tell me about it?	More COMMUNICATION: Now the parent asks for more information about the reality.
CRAIG: There's this kid there that always tries to pick on me.	
DAD: What does he do? Does he tease you or hit you?	COMPREHENSION: Here, the parent is trying to understand the situation and to absolve his child of responsibility.
CRAIG: Sometimes he just calls me names, but when I try to ignore him, or get away from him, he pushes me. And once he twisted my arm behind my back.	
DAD: Is he your age, or bigger than you?	More COMPREHENSION: The parent asks more questions to enlarge his and his child's understanding of the situation.
CRAIG: He's bigger than me and he's stronger.	
DAD: No wonder you don't want to go to the park alone anymore. He sounds like a bad bully.	COMPASSION: Empathy lets your child know you know how he feels.

NARRATIVE	REPARATIVE ELEMENTS
You can't win over a bully alone. You need some help. Maybe I need to go with you next time.	COMPETENCE: After hearing about the situation, the parent offers a possible resolution that might produce a different outcome.
CRAIG: Then he'll just call me more names. He'll say I'm a baby.	
DAD: I see. OK. Do you have any other ideas?	
CRAIG: Maybe I could go to the park with some of the kids on the block. Maybe I could get the bigger kids to come with me.	CHILD'S COMPETENCE: The discussion has encouraged a competent resolution by the child.
DAD: That's a great idea! Maybe we could talk to John and Mickey. They're twelve years old, and we could ask them to help you get rid of this bully. When he sees you with *them*, maybe he won't pick on you anymore. That's worth a try.	More COMPETENCE: The parent confirms that the resolution/ outcome proposed by the child is effective, and offers hope for the future.

In helping your child to deal with aggression in his world, remember the third basic fear: fears about the body. Your child's natural fears about his body play a strong role in keeping him worried. He's trying to do everything he can to keep himself safe. But he can't feel strong or brave if he avoids all confrontation. If he feels weak and humiliated he will experience fear about the self. This fear needs to be addressed if you're going to help your child feel more self-esteem. Sometimes a protective parent will need to help a child keep his body safe at the expense of his self-esteem: "Even though you may want to punch him in the nose, he's much bigger than you are, so it's smart to walk away." And sometimes, a protective parent will need to help a child to maintain his self-esteem, even at some risk to his body: "I know Jimmy's always teasing you because you can't climb that tree and he can. Even though it's scary, if we practice together, you'll be able to do it, and then he'll have to shut up!"

As protective parents we hope to keep our kids safe, but we all know that our kids can be unexpectedly exposed to aggression and violence that is beyond our control. Whether on city streets, in suburban malls, or on country roads, kids can be mugged or assaulted by other kids, or molested and robbed by unscrupulous adults. Up until now, we've been helping you to help your kids to prepare themselves against aggression, but what can you tell your kids if they've already suffered through violence?

Here's a protective parent talking to a ten-year-old child who has been surrounded by a group of teenagers who threatened him, pushed him off his bike, and stole it. He has just come home, bruised and crying, from the park. He is still overwhelmed by the event and trying to cope with many emotions at the same time. He's frightened and hurt and will need to be comforted and attended to. He's sad and upset about the loss of his bike and will need to be consoled. He's angry and enraged by the event and will need to be calmed down, and he's feeling humiliated and powerless and will need to have his self-esteem restored. It's useful to address as many of these different emotions as you can. The following reparative narrative tries to do just that:

EDDIE *(running in the house):* Daddy, Daddy. *(crying)* They stole my bike.

NARRATIVE	REPARATIVE ELEMENTS
FATHER *(hugging child):* Oh, no. What an awful, awful thing! Are you hurt?	COMPASSION: First the parent offers the child immediate empathy for all his feelings and fears.

NARRATIVE	REPARATIVE ELEMENTS

EDDIE *(crying):* They pushed me and hit me.

FATHER: What happened?

COMMUNICATION: He tries to obtain more information about the event.

EDDIE: I was just riding up the hill when they came out on the road. A lot of them.

FATHER: You must have been so upset and mad. Your new bike! Were they kids your age or big kids?

More COMPASSION: This parent is still taking care of the child and offering more empathy.

EDDIE: They were big and they had baseball bats, too. They said they'd hit me if I didn't give them my bike.

FATHER: That sounds so scary. We're so lucky that they didn't hit you and really hurt you. It's a good thing you gave them your bike immediately.

COMPASSION, COMMUNICATION, COMPETENCE: Here, the parent confirms the child's resolution of the situation, and accepts the outcome.

EDDIE: I didn't. I just fell off because they pushed me. I should have done something. I shouldn't have let them take my new bike.

FATHER: You did exactly the right thing. Remember how we've always told you never, ever to fight back when someone mugs you or robs you. You're much more important to us than any bike.

More COMPETENCE: This father tries to absolve his child of blame and to confirm the outcome again.

EDDIE: But it was brand-new.

NARRATIVE	REPARATIVE ELEMENTS
FATHER: I know it was your birthday bike, but the important thing is you're not hurt! We can always get another bike!	More COMPREHENSION: Finally, he helps the child to understand the situation and offers hope for the future.

Note that this parent doesn't judge, criticize, moralize, or lecture to his child in these typical ways:

"How many times have I told you not to ride your bike in the park?"

"What were you doing playing when you had homework to do?"

"It serves you right! It's your own fault!"

"Why didn't you yell for help? There must have been people around."

"Maybe those boys were poor and needed your bike more than you did!

"Why didn't you ride away from them?"

"If you can't take care of your bike, you don't deserve to have one!"

This protective parent's reactions are geared to protect and comfort his child against the violence of the event (addressing fears about the body) and to confirm and support the child's behavior (easing the child's fears about the self).

Today's children need to know how to handle themselves on the street, how to protect themselves against danger, and how to avoid experiences which might prove to be violent or aggressive. Here's a list of some cautions that protective parents can share with their kids as they grow older and are exposed to more of the dark side of life:

- "Don't walk down dark streets; always take the best lit way, even if it's longer."

- "Pay attention to other people when you're outside. If someone seems to be angry, or scary, or if you see a group of teenagers being rowdy, walk away from them."

- "If you get scared when you're out alone, find someplace with people (like a store or a restaurant or a gas station) and go inside."

- "If you're carrying money with you, put most of it in your shoe, and only keep a few dollars in your pocket." [City kids call this money "street rent."]

- "If you're threatened or mugged, give up your money, your clothes, or your possessions immediately. Never, ever protest or fight back, no matter how upset you feel. Never say anything to make the kid who's stealing from you angry. Keep quiet!"

- "If someone tries to grab you or push you into a doorway or a car, try to run away and scream or yell as loud as you can to attract attention."

But don't overdo caution. Remember that your goal is to protect your child without alarming him. So don't tell him all these things at once! Build them gradually into his awareness as he grows up, particularly during the years between seven and twelve. And don't keep repeating your warnings every time he goes outside. Most kids don't need to be reminded about these dangers—they've heard about them, read about them, and seen them on television and in the movies. Instead, focus on helping your kids to feel that you trust their judgment, that you think they will make good choices, and that you feel that they're competent to deal with themselves and their world!

7

Separation, Divorce, and Abandonment: Telling the Kind of Truth Kids Need to Hear

We Didn't Live Happily Ever After

Unfortunately, there are many times in the life of every family when the needs of the parents will necessarily conflict with the needs of their children. The decision to separate or divorce is one of the most serious of those times. While moving out and moving on may provide the solution to conflicts between a man and woman, it is usually perceived by children as a problem—and it's quite a pervasive problem. In fact, divorce has almost become an ordinary event in the lives of American parents and their children. The fairy-tale ending, "... and they got married and lived happily ever after," seems either nostalgic or ironic to today's youngsters. The persistent battle between the sexes is also producing a great many casualties. The more we know and understand about the developmental impact of divorce, the more we realize that these civil and un-civil wars produce profound consequences for our children—consequences which reverberate all our lives.

All marriages are structures. They may be in need of a paint job, or a new roof, the foundation may be shaky, the whole building may even be in need of major reconstruction—but whether good, bad, or mediocre, as long as you're married, the building remains standing. Divorce, on the other hand, hits

a family like an earthquake; the family's structure is shattered. As in an earthquake, too, there is both the initial damage and the aftershock to be dealt with. Children need to be
protected before, during, and after a divorce, no matter how
amiable or adversarial the divorce may be. If both parents are
fighting over them, they need to understand that, despite this
present bitter custody battle, *both* parents still love them and
want to spend time with them. They also need to understand
that one parent's gaining custody of them does not mean that
they will not be able to see the other parent.

Some parents, faced with increasing tension and turmoil in
their marital lives, become unable to attend to their responsibilities as parents. This means that the children will begin to
feel the emotional loss of *both* parents long before the actual
physical separation is accomplished. These children have been
living in the eye of the storm for a long time; they've seen it
coming. Other parents are able to preserve their relationship
to their kids even though their relationship to each other is
pulling apart at the seams. On the plus side, they've been able
to protect their children; on the minus side, divorce may come
as a surprise to these children, since the rents in the fabric of
family life were not so visible. When separation or divorce is
contemplated, parents will need to know what to tell the kids.
They will also have questions about when the kids should be
told about their decision to separate.

As a protective parent, you can help your kids to absorb
even events as disruptive as the dissolution of the family if
you:

- Tell as much of the truth as you can.
- Tell it in the form of a story, a reparative narrative with
  a beginning, a middle, and an ending.
- Tell the story in language that your kid can understand.
- Don't include more detail than is necessary.
- Don't speculate about what you don't know.

Remember, the younger the child, the more concrete her
comprehension of events will be and the less understanding
she will have about the nature of cause and effect. A very

young child is apt to connect events that happened together. For example, if a parent walks into the kid's messy room one day and says, "I can't stand this mess anymore. I can't bear to look at your room one more day!" and then, the very next day, the messy child is informed that her father is moving out, she may conclude that he's leaving because she kept such a messy room.

Remember, too, that children between the ages of two and five (during oedipal development) often love the parent of the opposite sex in a special way and wish that the parent of the same sex, whom they often perceive as a rival, would go away. If, in fact, this happens, as a result of a separation, an abandonment, or a divorce, the child may believe that her angry or competitive wishes drove the parent away. The child may then react with sharply felt guilt, sadness, and subsequent depression.

Finally, remember that both you and your child are likely to react with many different emotions at many different times during the disassembling of your family. At first, the child may be quite calm, or even appear indifferent, only later to dissolve in grief, erupt in rage, or feel overwhelmed by anxiety and rising panic. Similarly, you as an adult may be angry, then relieved, and finally, saddened.

Since so much of a child's world is defined by her parents, the way the child receives the news about the impending disruption of family life largely depends on how the parents themselves have come to understand the separation. If it is friendly, a mutually agreed-upon separation (and these are rare indeed), the impact of the event may be softened by the absence of bitterness, rage, or grief. If the custodial parent has left an abusive partner, the kids may even feel relief at escaping this atmosphere. If one parent has largely been responsible for the care of the kids, and that parent remains the caregiver, then the longing for the absent parent may be minimized. But even in these optimal conditions, the event will evoke strong feelings in all concerned.

What Should I Ask Myself?

Before you can help your child to cope with the effects of a separation, abandonment, or divorce from your partner, you need to understand how you really feel about these events.

First, search your own memory. Were you yourself from a divorced family? If so, how old were you when your parents parted? Thinking about how you felt then (and what you would have wished that your parents had told you or done for you) will help you now to decide what you should tell your kids.

Do you believe that every kid needs to feel good about his mom and his dad? Or do you feel so angry at your partner that you feel that your children are better off without him or her in their lives? Are your feelings based upon what your ex did to you or to your kids? Do you feel your ex is dangerous to you or your kids? Is he or she violent and abusive, mean and cold, or irrational or abandoning? Are you afraid of him or her? Are your kids? Do you feel that your ex is likely to be a better parent once the two of you are separated? A worse parent? Do you like him or her? Are your kids close to your ex even though you're not?

Helene couldn't get over her bitterness toward her ex, who had left her for his travel agent, Maria, with whom he had been engaged in a long-term affair. Her twin six-year-old daughters adored their father and found Helene's open antagonism toward him troubling and confusing. Because Helene was so hurt, she frequently would tell her girls, "Your father left us for Maria. That's how much he cares about our family," without realizing that the twins needed to feel that their father still loved them, even though he no longer loved their mother.

What kind of relationship would you like your kids to have with your ex? What kind of relationship did they have before the separation took place? Is there any room for improvement? On your part? On his or hers?

Truth and Consequences

When a marriage dissolves, there are many consequences for kids. Even very young children should be told about some of these consequences right away in order to help them know the basics of their new lives. Remember the first basic fear, fear of the unknown. It's reassuring to children to be able to know what to expect when their parents are parting.

The first thing that kids need to know is that, while their parents are no longer able to love each other in the way a husband and a wife should, they both still love their children very, very much. Remember, when you get divorced, your kids get several messages loud and clear: Love doesn't always last. Things are often not what they appear. And life can change in profound and unpredictable ways. These are harsh messages; even adults have trouble understanding them. But for kids, they are particularly painful. After all, if you could "fall out of love" with your mate, couldn't you also "fall out of love" with your kids? If you wish to live alone, without a partner, couldn't you also wish to live alone, without your children?

If you and your partner are involved in a particularly adversarial divorce, it's also very important to let your kids know that Mommy and Daddy are very angry and upset with each other right now, and family life may be difficult and disturbing for a while until things get settled. If custody is a major issue, and the children will be part of a psychological examination or be required to appear in court (always painful for kids and something to be avoided, if possible), explain to them that *both* Daddy and Mommy want to live with them most of the time, and the judge needs to know as much as possible about everyone's feelings, particularly their feelings, in order to make the right decision for them. Make it clear that they should speak to the judge or the person conducting the psychological evaluation as honestly as they can, to help make this decision, but be sure to emphasize that the decision is not up to them! This is vitally important to your children's well-being. No child should ever have to face the long-term consequences of choosing between a mother and a father. Even in situations where the choice is clear, and the child has strongly expressed her feelings on the matter, she should be relieved of this burden. Be sure to assure her that the court takes into account all the factors, including her testimony, but that the judge is the one who makes the final decision.

The following are some of the things that will be part of your divorce agreement. Your kids need to be told about these arrangements:

- *Who has custody* of them and *what kind* of custody? What does it mean for the kids? For example, "You're going to live with Mommy, and I will decide most of the time about what you need. When it comes to big things, like where you go to school, or if you need braces, then Daddy and I will decide together."

- *When will your child get to see the noncustodial parent?* With older children, it makes a lot of sense for the child to be consulted about these arrangements before they become final. Children often have very definite and useful ideas to contribute to custody arrangements. (Although they are not automatically consulted, because of their legal status as minors, you must remember that your children's *emotional* status is central to all these issues!)

- *Who will support the family* and how will the custodial parent be helped (or not be helped) by the noncustodial parent? This should ease the constant bickering over money that plagues children of divorce, who are frequently asked to be a "financial runner," carrying economic messages back and forth from one parent to another: "Tell your father he's late again with the alimony check" or "Tell your mother I'm not going to pay for such an expensive camp this summer. I'm not made of money!"

- *How is their future secured?* Who will pay for medical, dental, and psychological treatment? Who will support the cost of primary schooling, and college and graduate school if needed?

Divorce and the Five Basic Fears

At the same time that a divorce changes the child's external world, her internal world is undergoing a similar change. When care and continuity are disrupted in a family, a child's trust and confidence in herself are also compromised. Children may now directly ask a parent, "Don't you love Daddy anymore?" or "Will you divorce me, Mommy, if you don't love me?" or "How could you stop loving Mommy?" For some of your child's questions, there may not be any easy answers, and for some there may not really be any answers at all. This is where a reparative narrative can help your child to bridge the frightening new gap that has opened in her life.

When you begin to talk to your kids about the impending separation of the family, keep in mind that your child will really be searching for reassurance about the five basic fears. Embedded in her expressed questions will be other unexpressed questions:

"What will happen to me now?" (fear of the unknown)
"Where will I live?" (fear of being left alone)
"Who will take care of me?" (fear of bodily harm)
"Was all this my fault?" (the voice of conscience)
"Why did Daddy leave me?" (fears about the self)

The five basic fears give you a map to your child's mind. They help you to know the direction your child's mind is turning. Understanding her fears will enable you to create a reparative narrative with your child that is appropriate for her age, answers her questions, and helps her to master her underlying anxieties.

Are You and Daddy Getting Divorced?

Children who overhear their parents arguing will often imagine the worst, especially since the parents of many of their friends may be divorced. If the argument simply represents the ordinary strains of intimacy, offer reassurance. It is easy to say, "Of course we're not getting divorced, honey. Daddy and Mommy are just having a disagreement about whether to spend Christmas at Grandma's. You know that sometimes we argue. That doesn't mean we don't always love each other and always want to be married to each other."

But suppose this argument, like the hundreds before it, is unable to be resolved, and suppose that each of you has begun to feel that life apart is beginning to look a whole lot more attractive than life together? Suppose the answer is "Yes, we *are* going to get a divorce." It is important to begin to help your child to understand that sometimes people *don't* live happily ever after with each other. Sometimes they need to make changes in themselves and in their lives in order to live happily at all. If this is the case, and your child has picked up on the tensions between you, then your child needs to be told.

Here's an example of how a mother might construct a reparative narrative to answer a seven-year-old's question.

CAROLINE: Are you and Daddy getting divorced, Mommy?

NARRATIVE	REPARATIVE ELEMENTS
MOM: I can understand why you're asking about divorce. Daddy and I have been arguing more and more, and we don't seem to be able to stop."	COMMUNICATION: This mom starts with a direct reference to the upsetting experience, which confirms the child's sense of reality.
CAROLINE *(crying):* Can't you be nice?	
MOM: We've tried but we can't. We're very unhappy over what's happening, and I can see that you are, too. It's really sad when parents fight and they can't stop.	COMPASSION: Now she makes an empathic reference to the emotional impact that the experience has for the child.
CAROLINE: I'll try to be good. I'll clean up my toys.	

NARRATIVE	REPARATIVE ELEMENTS
MOM: Our problems have to do with *us*, not with you. We both love you very much just the way you are.	COMPREHENSION: Here's a statement about the child's role in the upsetting experience and her lack of responsibility for the outcome.
CAROLINE: Please don't get divorced, Mommy.	
MOM: Daddy and I are going to see a marriage counselor to help us to see if we can be happier with each other and stop all this fighting. We hope it works so we can stay married.	COMPETENCE: A statement about what is done or might be done to resolve the upsetting experience comes next (outcome or resolution). This resolution offers hope for the child's future.

If the problems in the marriage have progressed beyond counseling, or if you've already made this effort and it's proved fruitless, or if you have no wish to even see a marriage counselor, then you might answer your child this way:

NARRATIVE	REPARATIVE ELEMENTS
DAD: Mommy and I have decided that we need to separate for a while and live in two different places.	COMMUNICATION: This father begins with a direct reference to the experience or event that offers the child information.
SAM: You're going to get a divorce, aren't you?	
DAD: We don't know, honey. We hope that when we have some time to think about things without arguing so much we might be able to work things out and be better friends.	COMPETENCE: Now, a statement about what is being or what might be done to resolve things and hope for the future is made.

NARRATIVE	REPARATIVE ELEMENTS
SAM: I don't want you to leave our house.	
DAD: This is going to be a big change for all of us. But both Mommy and I will see you and be with you, even though we may all be pretty upset for a while.	COMPASSION: An empathic reference to the emotional impact of the experience comes next.
SAM: Why are you leaving me?	
DAD: Sammy, Mommy and I are separating from each other, but not from you. This has nothing to do with you. It's *our* problem. Whatever happens between us, we'll always, always be your Mommy and Daddy.	COMPREHENSION: A statement that absolves the child of responsibility is made, and a possible outcome is suggested.

If there is no help and also no hope for the marital relationship, and things have gone beyond the point of no return, then the reparative narrative that you use to invite your child to talk about her thoughts and feelings might sound like this:

NARRATIVE	REPARATIVE ELEMENTS
MOM: Daddy and I have been fighting for a long, long, time. We've tried to work things out and be better friends, but it just doesn't seem possible, so we've decided we need to get divorced.	COMMUNICATION: This mother begins with a direct reference to the event and a confirmation of reality.
LESLIE: I knew this would happen.	

NARRATIVE	REPARATIVE ELEMENTS
MOM: You've been thinking about our troubles, too. You probably have a lot of feelings about what we're doing. I bet you're sad and mad at us because we couldn't keep things the way they were, but we still have to do this.	COMPASSION: She offers her child empathy.
LESLIE: Why can't you be friends? You always tell me to make up. I've been going to bed on time, and my room is cleaned up, too. Now, I'll have no family.	
MOM: You've been thinking that you can help us, but this has nothing to do with you. It's between Daddy and me. We need to get divorced from each other because our marriage isn't working out, but we will never, ever get divorced from you kids. Daddy is always your Daddy and I will always be your Mommy—your whole life.	COMPREHENSION: She emphasizes the child's lack of responsibility for the events to help her understand the situation. COMPETENCE: Finally, this mother offers her child a resolution that offers hope about the future.

Once you've gotten past the first big questions, your child may then ask the noncustodial parent, "Why did you leave us?" The following narrative, which is suitable for most children, contains all of the reparative elements that we have been discussing all along. It talks about reality; it is empathic to your feelings and the child's feelings; it relieves the child of responsibility for the outcome she faces; and it offers the child a resolution, however sad, of the marital difficulties.

NANCY: Why did you leave us?

NARRATIVE	REPARATIVE ELEMENTS
DAD: I know because I'm not living in the same apartment with you, it feels like I've left you. But I would never, ever leave you, sweetie.	COMPETENCE: This parent starts by reassuring his child about the future.
It makes me sad that I can't live with you and I know it makes you sad, too.	COMPASSION: He offers his child empathy.
But Mommy and I weren't happy living with each other. We tried but it just didn't work.	COMMUNICATION: Here, he confirms the reality of the situation.
We decided it would be better for us to live in two separate places. You're going to stay in your house with Mommy, so you don't have to move, and I'm going to get an apartment nearby, so I can see you a lot. You're going to have two houses, not just one. You'll be staying with Mommy sometimes and with me sometimes. One of us will always be with you, and you'll always be our child.	More COMMUNICATION More COMPETENCE MORE COMMUNICATION
Our divorce has nothing to do with you. Mommy and I need to live in two separate places so we can try to be happier. We'll never, ever leave you.	More COMPETENCE and COMPREHENSION: Now this dad emphasizes his child's lack of responsibility in the events and again offers the child a resolution.

So far, all the narratives have assumed a situation in which both parents cooperate with each other on behalf of their kids. What about a divorce in which the parting parents are bitter adversaries? Or a divorce caused by an extramarital affair? What can you tell a kid who says, "Daddy says you don't love us anymore. He says you're selfish, and you only love your boyfriend, Matthew. He says that *he* loves us better because he didn't want the family to get all broken up. He wants us all to stay together. The divorce is all your fault."

Many marriages end because of experiences that have nothing to do with kids, like sexual problems, or extramarital affairs. Protective parents should try to shield their children from knowledge of these intimate experiences. If all of the parties have been discreet this is possible, and children can be told that Mommy and Daddy had adult problems that made it hard for them to continue to love each other and live together. In many cases, however, the warring partners have been indiscreet. Loud accusations may have surfaced during heated arguments ("You slut, you've been running around behind my back!" or "I should have known better than to trust you and your secretary and all those late nights at the office!") Children may have seen or discovered you with a lover, or they may have overheard others talking about an affair. Once a child has picked up clues about the problems in the marriage, it's best to offer her a chance to ask her questions and to construct a narrative that helps her to understand what has happened. Once a child has developed her own perceptions about the event, you cannot deny them or pretend that they're not there.

Here's an example of how to take up the issue of a protested or unilateral decision to separate, with an older (nine- to twelve-year-old) child.

NARRATIVE	REPARATIVE ELEMENTS
MOM: I know that you can see how much I like Matthew and how we want to be together. That's the way it was with Daddy and me when we were first married and in love. But it hasn't been that way between us for a long time.	COMMUNICATION: This mother tries to confirm the reality for her child, while offering important information about the event.

NARRATIVE	REPARATIVE ELEMENTS
Our marriage had problems way before I even knew Matthew. I've been thinking about getting divorced for a long time now."	
BETH: But Daddy said you don't love us anymore!	
MOM: I guess Daddy's right when he says I don't love *him* anymore, but he's wrong when he says I don't love *you*. I love you more than anything in the world. And I know how hard this is for you; I wish it had worked out for your Dad and me. But it didn't. I want to live with someone I love, and who loves me.	COMPASSION: She offers her child empathy for her feelings about this complicated change.
BETH: Daddy said you ruined our lives.	
MOM: This is really awful for you because Daddy wants you to be as angry with me as he is. But you don't have to choose sides. You're probably angry with both of us.	COMPREHENSION: She's also absolving her child of responsibility for the upsetting events and tries to expand her understanding of the entire situation.
BETH: You're both stupid! I don't want to hear you talk about each other.	
MOM: I'm going to tell your dad not to put you in the middle, but you know that he may not listen to me because he's so angry with me. That means that *you* may have to tell him to leave you out of it. If he	

NARRATIVE	REPARATIVE ELEMENTS
doesn't listen to you, either, just walk out of the room or let me know and we'll get someone to talk to Daddy that he'll listen to.	COMPETENCE: Last, she suggests a possible outcome or resolution that offers hope for the future.

When a Parent Is Abusive or Mentally Ill

What if one parent is violent, abusive, or unable to properly assume his parental responsibilities? Even though the child has a clear sense of the parent's limitations and may verbalize fear, anger, or even hatred of this parent, it is still important to create a narrative for the child that absolves the child of responsibility and guilt. Here's a mother creating a reparative narrative for an older child (nine to twelve) with an abusive parent:

LUKE: I don't want to see Daddy. He always yells at me and scares me, and he hit me all the time with his belt. Do I have to see him after the divorce?

NARRATIVE	REPARATIVE ELEMENTS
MOM: I've gone to court to ask Judge Hillman to give me sole custody of you once your dad and I get our divorce. I've asked the judge not to let Dad see you until he deals with his temper. People who get as angry as your father gets are sick and they need help. Meanwhile, I've asked Judge Hillman for an "order of protection." That means that your father can't come near us or hurt us in any way, or he'll to to jail. I don't want him to go to jail. But more than that, I don't want us to	COMMUNICATION: Here, the mother offers information that confirms the reality for her child.

NARRATIVE	REPARATIVE ELEMENTS
get hurt, and I don't want you to see your dad until he can control his temper.	
LUKE: I hate him; I never want to see him, and he'll never control his temper.	
MOM: I know there are times when you feel very angry with your father and even hate him. You may be pretty angry with me, too, for getting you into this mess by marrying him.	COMPASSION: She also makes an empathic statement.
LUKE: It's not your fault. He and I just push each other's buttons.	
MOM: That may be true, but remember, no matter what you think you may have done to make him angry, a good father is still not supposed to hurt his son. We can't trust your dad to control himself, and we're not going to take any chances. Your father's temper is his problem. He has to stop it.	COMPREHENSION: Absolving the child of responsibility is an important priority here, along with enlarging the child's understanding of the situation.
LUKE: Do you think he'll ever change?	
MOM: I don't know, but meanwhile, you could write to your dad if you want, and he can write to you. But he can't see you or me until we know for sure that he won't lose his temper. That's going to take a long time. Meanwhile, we're safe, so don't worry.	COMPETENCE: The resolution or outcome she offers holds out some hope for the future, but ensures her child's safety.

Similarly, if a parent falls physically or mentally ill, and the child must be separated from this parent for a substantial amount of time, it is important to define what is happening for the child, so that the event can be understood. When a mother must be hospitalized for depression, for example, or a father must go into a drug rehabilitation hospital, the child should be told as much truth as possible. A reparative narrative for a four-year-old child whose father is an alcoholic might sound like this:

CLAIRE: Why is Daddy going away?

NARRATIVE	REPARATIVE ELEMENT
MOM: For a long time, Daddy has been drinking a lot, and when he drinks he gets angry with everyone and can't work and can't be a good daddy and can't be a good husband in our family. Daddy and I have talked about this again and again. You've heard us fighting about how much he drinks.	COMMUNICATION: Here the mother confirms her child's reality.
CLAIRE: Why doesn't Daddy stop?	
MOM: Daddy has decided that he can't stop drinking without help, and he can't get help unless he goes to a special hospital where they help people to stop drinking.	More COMMUNICATION and COMPETENCE: Some resolution is offered for the problem and more information is offered to the child.
CLAIRE (crying): I don't want Daddy to go. I'll miss him.	
MOM: It's going to be hard for us because he'll be away for two months, and we'll miss him and he'll miss us, but unless	COMPASSION: Here, this mom offers empathy to her child and helps her understand that her feelings are shared by the family.

NARRATIVE	REPARATIVE ELEMENTS
Daddy can stop drinking, we won't be able to live with him anymore.	
CLAIRE: Will they help Daddy? Will he get better?	
MOM: Daddy's drinking is Daddy's problem. He used to get drunk way before you were born. He has to stop. We can't help him.	COMPREHENSION: Now, this mother tries to help her daughter understand the situation, while absolving her of responsibility in it.

Don't be afraid to tell your child that you don't know how bad things like this happen. "Sometimes things happen in life that we didn't expect" is a useful thing to say to a bewildered child. Real life is filled with inexplicable events.

Divorce When a Parent Is Gay or Lesbian

It's hard enough trying to explain how a man and a woman can fall in love and out of love, or to explain an affair that breaks up a marriage, or a parent who skips town, but what can you say to a kid when your marriage is breaking up because one partner has discovered or has always known that he is homosexual? What does it mean to a child when a mother walks out on a father because she cannot love or live with a man (or vice versa)?

And what about the heterosexual parent? Left for a homosexual lover, the parent may feel particularly deceived, betrayed, or embittered. It is tempting to give way to your rage and sadness by telling your child the truth—but in such a way that the child feels as awful as the abandoned parent does. This kind of truth-telling sacrifices the child's ability to heal their complicated wounds. Parental hatred infects the situation and permits the wound to fester.

Here's a mother trying to explain her husband's "coming out" to her child:

"Sometimes, a man finds out that he can't love his wife or live with her. He feels better if he lives with someone who is a man like he is. And that's happened to Daddy. He's going to be living with his friend, Jack, and Daddy and I are going to get a divorce so we can both live the way we like."

This explanation can address the needs of a young child (ages three to seven). But as the child gets older (ages eight to twelve), more of the meaning of homosexuality and its place in our society will need to be discussed, and more room will have to be given in the conversation for the child's own questions and concerns.

LAURA: Tommy said my Daddy's a fag, and that's why you're getting a divorce.

NARRATIVE	REPARATIVE ELEMENTS
MOM: When Daddy and I were first married, we thought that we could love each other and we both wanted a family, so for a while things were okay. But as we got older, things started to go wrong, and one of the things that went wrong is that Daddy realized that he couldn't really live with or love a woman. He felt he really could only be happy living with his friend, Gene. When two men love each other we say they're "homosexual," or "gay." They're also called names that are not so nice like "fags" and "queers," so you may hear people call Daddy one of those words, like Tommy did.	COMMUNICATION and COMPREHENSION: Here, the mother informs her child and confirms reality, absolving the child of responsibility for these events.

NARRATIVE	REPARATIVE ELEMENTS
LAURA: I don't like all of this. I don't want Daddy to live with Gene.	
MOM: This is going to make us all pretty upset for a while, but Daddy and I are going to feel better when we can live away from each other and both get on with the kinds of lives we really want to live. I know it's hard to understand what happened to Daddy, and you'll have lots of questions that I'll try to answer. You can also talk to Daddy about all of this.	COMPASSION: She makes sure to empathize with what her child must be experiencing.

This is a beginning reparative narrative to create for your older child. It will permit her to think about things in a new way, and it leaves room for all kinds of questions that she might have. Her questions will then form the basis for a continuation of this narrative. Remember, though, even when you've been thoughtful and honest with your children and helped them to heal their hard times, you can't control your child's experiences with other people who may make matters worse.

Here's a mother who's trying to help her eleven-year-old son deal with his grandfather's angry reaction to his son's homosexuality:

JOEY: Grandpa Harold said that Daddy is committing a sin. He said that homosexuality goes against the teachings of the Bible.

NARRATIVE	REPARATIVE ELEMENTS
MOM: Grandpa is an old-fashioned man, and he takes the Bible very seriously—almost like a law. He thinks a lot of things are sins.	COMMUNICATION: This mother is trying to help her son confirm an important reality.
JOEY: Is Daddy a sinner, Mommy?	
MOM: Some religious people like Grandpa believe that homosexuality is wrong, but many people believe that it's not—it's just a different way of life and love. Some people even believe you're born gay or not.	COMPREHENSION: Now, she's trying to help him better understand the whole situation.
JOEY: He sounded pretty angry with Daddy.	
MOM: He's upset, just like we're all upset. I think he's angry because he's shocked. He doesn't understand what Daddy did, and Daddy's his own son. He's also upset because he loves us, and when Daddy left us, it broke up our family.	COMPASSION: Now, she's enlarging her son's capacity for empathy.
JOEY: If Daddy's a sinner, am I a sinner, too?	
MOM: Absolutely not! As far as I am concerned, Daddy's not a sinner, and this has nothing to do with you.	COMPREHENSION and COMPETENCE: Here, she's absolving her son of responsibility and also trying to offer him a resolution of his concerns.

Here's a narrative constructed by a gay mother to explain her separation from her husband to her eight-year-old daughter and her seven-year-old son. She is involved with a lesbian lover but has not yet made the decision to move in with her.

NARRATIVE	REPARATIVE ELEMENTS
MOM: I know it's hard for all of us right now because Daddy and I have decided to get divorced. I know Daddy told you that it's because of my friend Mary Margaret, and that's true in a way, because I learned that I really can't love Daddy or any man the way a wife should. Some women love men and some women find they can only love women. I found out that I really love Mary Margaret.	COMMUNICATION: This mother is trying to communicate information to her children in language they can understand.
WARREN: But mommies can't get married to each other.	
MOM: Yes, that's right. But women who love each other can live with each other and be a family, too.	COMPREHENSION: Here she's trying to help her children understand the situation.
EMILY: I don't want two mommies. I want a daddy and a mommy.	
MOM: Mary Margaret isn't your mommy, honey. I'm your mommy forever and ever and Daddy's your daddy. Mary Margaret is someone I love. We don't know yet whether she'll live with us or not, but I hope she will.	COMMUNICATION: Again, this mother conveys important information to her children.
EMILY *(angry):* I hope she won't!	

NARRATIVE	REPARATIVE ELEMENTS
WARREN *(cries):* Me, too.	
MOM: I can see all this is making you very mad and sad now. But we've got lots of time to talk about this. Mary Margaret will stay in her apartment, and we'll be right here in our own house for a long time before anything changes. By then, you'll have a chance to know her better and you'll also see that Daddy and I are always here.	COMPASSION and COMPETENCE: This mother remains empathic to her children's feelings even though they differ from her own. COMPETENCE: Here she offers her children a possible resolution and some hope for the future.

About Separation

Although divorce disrupts a child's ongoing development, at least it's a decisive event in a child's life, with a beginning, a middle, and a discernible end. But some parents are unable to decide if they can continue to live together. They may opt to live apart for a time, so that they can evaluate their situation. A trial separation, while holding out hope for kids that their parents may be able to return to each other, also puts a great strain on all the members of the family because everyone has to live with uncertainty. Children, in particular, have difficulty when things are uncertain. Uncertainty can cause your children to act up. They can express their conflicts and concerns over what is happening in the family through behavioral problems—sassiness at school, an inability to concentrate, delinquency, or physical symptoms, such as headaches or stomachaches. If you're contemplating a trial separation, you need to explain clearly what this means to your kids. They need to be told that you are trying to make things better, but that you don't know yet whether it will work.

Young children can be told that "Daddy is going to sleep at

his office for a while, so that we don't fight so much at home. We're going to talk to a marriage counselor who can help us understand each other better. We hope we'll be able to live together again, but we'll have to see what happens." If older children ask about divorce, they can be told, "We hope this will work. If it doesn't, then we may need to get a divorce." Both younger and older children need to know that there is nothing that they can do to help in the meantime; it's not their problem. They need to be told that they will be able to see both parents even though they are separating and reassured about schedules and routines (a calendar that lists "daddy days" or "mommy days" is useful).

About Abandonment

What if a child must face an abandonment by a parent? In this case, the care-giving parent will be hard-pressed to offer the child any comfort (or to find any comfort herself or himself). The psychological loss of a parent is, after all, the most significant loss a child can experience. In a way, it's even more bitter than the death of a parent, because a child can understand (on some level) that a parent is not responsible for his own death. But a parent *is* responsible for abandonment. How can we explain abandonment to a child so that we help the child resolve her sense of herself? How can we keep the damage to a minimum?

Where Is My Daddy? How Come I Never See Him?

Separation and divorce are difficult enough for kids to understand, but hardest of all is *abandonment*. An abandoning parent has demonstrated through his or her reactions that the child is not important. It is hard to feel that you're lovable when you feel that your very own parent doesn't love you enough to stay with you.

It is also hard to know what to say to a child in this situation. Faced with this dilemma, some parents are so angry at being abandoned that they try to "kill off" the absent parent and tell the child that the parent is dead. Other parents, hoping to cushion the blow, sometimes try to create a mythical father or mother who can never come to visit the child because he or she is too busy with work in a foreign country.

A parent can say, "Your father was a no-good alcoholic bum who couldn't hold down a job and beat me up when he drank," but this exposes her child to harsh reality without offering him any emotional protection against the impact of the abandonment. This mother is forgetting that every child identifies with both of his parents, even one who abandons her. She is not building any emotional cushion of safety into her explanation to help reassure her child about himself. How can a kid hear that Dad was a no-good alcoholic bum and still feel good about himself? This mother doesn't realize that the child of a despised parent will be haunted by that fact for the rest of his life.

Another parent might tell his child, "Your mother was a wonderful woman, but she really liked to have fun and to go to parties, so she moved to New York." This father has told his child a story that he hopes will protect his kid so she will not be damaged by her mother's abandonment. But unfortunately this story is not *reparative*, because it doesn't address the mother's emotional and physical abandonment of the child. It leaves the child feeling she wasn't important enough to keep her mother's attention. It doesn't locate the problem with the *mother*. This kind of incomplete story may cause more problems for the child to manage later in life than it solves. For example, the party-loving mother in New York can be idealized by the child, who may yearn throughout her life to be a part of her mother's good time. She may feel that her mom left because neither she nor her dad was exciting enough. As she grows to be a woman, she may seek out excitement as the only worthwhile goal of adult life. Similarly, a child who has been told that her father is dead, and learns otherwise later in life, may never forgive her mother for the deception. And the child who's been told that his mother is "too busy" with work is still left with the knowledge that "work" is more valuable to his mother than he is. Children are practical creatures. You cannot tell a child that Daddy loves her, but has no time for her.

There is another reason to tell your child the right kind of story. Mothers (who are more often the abandoned marital partner) are seen as all-powerful by their kids. If anything goes wrong in the child's world, she is likely to blame her mother. Stories that overexpose the child to too much rage may backfire as the child struggles to protect the father from her mother's aggression. Stories that overprotect the child from the father's faults may also backfire, as the child blames her mother for her father's disappearance. For many mothers, the whole experience of separation becomes a no-win situation. Not only did she lose out in the marriage, but now their kid seems to hold *her* responsible for loss of the father!

This is where the reparative narrative can be particularly useful to parents. It can help the child come to terms with an unpleasant reality without absorbing blame or laying blame. It can help the mother and the child begin an important dialogue about the disappointments of love. Let's take a look at a situation where a mother is trying to explain an abandoning father to her five-year-old daughter and see whether we can construct a narrative that includes all of the reparative elements we've been emphasizing:

MAGGIE: How come I never see my daddy?

NARRATIVE	REPARATIVE ELEMENTS
MOM: When I married your dad, I was very young, and I didn't know what to look for in a husband and father. He was handsome, and he was a good dancer, so I liked him. I realized that your dad wanted to go to parties a lot and drink beer and stay out late. He was a good date but not a good husband. I wanted a	COMMUNICATION: This mother opens with information about the reality of the upsetting event.

NARRATIVE	REPARATIVE ELEMENTS
baby and I wanted us to be a family. After you were born I realized he wasn't going to be a good father. I couldn't count on him. I guess he didn't really want to be a husband or a dad; he just wanted to keep being a kid himself. One day, when I came home from work he wasn't there. He'd just left.	
MAGGIE: He was mean to you, Mommy. Did you cry?	
MOM: At first, I felt awful and alone. I was really sad and mad that he'd left, probably like you feel sometimes when you wonder about him.	COMPASSION: Now, she shares an empathic response with her child.
But then I realized that it really had nothing to do with me and nothing to do with you—because you were just a baby. He never even really knew you. It had to do with *him*. He wasn't ready to love someone and take care of them.	COMPREHENSION: Here, she's absolving the child of responsibility while expanding her understanding of the situation.
MAGGIE: Can you get a better daddy for me?	
MOM: I really made a mistake marrying him, so that's why I'm very careful now about dating. This time I want to choose someone who knows about love.	COMPETENCE: This possible resolution or outcome offers her child hope for the future.

Any divorce or abandonment raises anxieties in your child. You can use reparative narratives to try to address the five basic fears for your kids. Fears of the unknown are put to rest by outlining what will happen to the child. Fears about being alone and fears about the body are addressed by the emphasis on continued parental caregiving. Fear of the voice of conscience and fears about the self are assuaged by relieving the child of any guilt or responsibility for the breakup of the marriage.

Family Breakups and Your Kids

We've been focusing here on what to say to your children, but remember to *listen* to your children, too, when you speak to them. Some children want to know a great deal, but many children want to know as little as possible, and some children may openly tell you, "I don't want to know *anything* about your divorce or any reasons. I just want to know who I'm going to live with and when I'll see each of you."

Also, be prepared to accept your child's initial angry and unforgiving feelings toward you. Many children will continue to harbor wishes and fantasies about their parents' reunion even years after a divorce; hard as it is to accept, the fact is that many children feel they will never, ever forgive their parents for getting divorced in the first place. These feelings can be hard to bear—for you as well as for your child. But they are often an inevitable consequence of the rupture in the life of the family. Sometimes, no matter how well you address the issues, or how many reparative narratives you construct to help your child and you to understand the events, only time will ease the pain that your child feels.

The breakup of a family is not a single event. First, there are all the bad experiences leading up to the dissolution. Then there is the breakup itself, with its attendant legal negotiations, financial adjustments, and reversals of fortune. Finally, there is the aftermath, with its delayed reactions, its bitterness, its sadness, its relief, and ultimately, its resolution. Every broken relationship then is the midpoint in a series of events that had a beginning in the decision to become a family and will have an ending that extends far into the future for all of you.

Talking to your child about how a separation or a divorce or an abandonment happened may also help *you* to cope with your own disappointment and despair. The very act of trying to make sense of the breakup of the family for a child may help you to recognize and realize where and when things started to go wrong.

Don't be afraid to let your child glimpse your own pain and bewilderment about a separation or a divorce or an abandonment. These events *should* make us unhappy. A child can survive these events with the idea that people can make mistakes, that you can't count on happy endings all the time, that parents aren't perfect, and that things are not always what they seem. Although these are not cheerful messages, they are real responses to real events in the real world. This may be the most important legacy that you can give to your kids: that pain is a necessary part of life, but important lessons can be learned from painful experiences. The next generation of children may indeed be sadder—but also wiser about love than we have been.

8

Single Parents, Double Efforts

The Facts of Real Life

The image of an "intact" family has a powerful hold on us. We picture a calm, cookie-baking mom, a dad who goes fishing, and a big rambling house full of mischief-making kids; there are white cotton sheets on the bed and meatloaf and mashed potatoes on the table. But is this reality? I vividly remember how troubled I felt in the early years of my marriage, when my husband was working long hours to launch his career, and I was studying for my doctorate in psychology and raising our sons, with the help of caretakers, in a small city apartment. Our situation presented quite a contrast to my own childhood, which featured a full-time, stay-at-home mom, a large suburban home, kids to play with on my own block, lots of space for roaming around, and a father who was always home for dinner by 6 P.M.!

We've been trying, as protective parents, to learn how to help our kids deal with real problems in the real world. In today's times, we can no longer expect our kids to understand family life by talking to them about the traditional family with its full-time housewife, hard-working dad, and their 2.3 kids. This is only one of the many kinds of families that we see around us.

In only one generation, the structure and life of the American family has changed significantly—who's in it, where we live, how we work, what we want, and even what we eat. As we saw in the last chapter, with one out of two marriages ending in divorce (and with many of these divorces occurring earlier in the course of the marriage than ever before), it's doubtful that even half of our country's children are currently being raised in traditional families. Single-parent families are no longer the exception to the rule, they nearly constitute the rule itself. "Father Knows Best" is fast giving way to "Murphy Brown."

We also need to recognize that American families are in a process of metamorphosis. Many of our children will actually live in several different kinds of families throughout their childhood and adolescence. They may start out living in a traditional "mom and pop" family, and then, five years later, Mom and Pop may decide to get divorced. They may begin life with an unmarried mother in a single-parent home, and then Mom may fall in love and marry a man who already has his own children, creating a new "blended" family of step-parents and step-siblings. Kids can be raised by their father, who subsequently marries a woman who then gets pregnant and has a child. Or either Mom or Pop can leave married life in order to live with a homosexual lover, who then becomes part of the child's family.

A child can now also be adopted into many different kinds of single-parent homes. He could have been adopted by a couple (either heterosexual or homosexual) who were together, and then split up, leaving him in the care of one of them. Some children may be adopted by a relative, or raised for many years by a grandmother, or aunt and then returned to a single mother's or father's care later in his life.

All of this demonstrates the reality that, today, the children we see around us may be raised in all kinds of families, by all kinds of parents, for all kinds of reasons. Neither parents with partners or parents without partners have a monopoly on the "right" reasons to raise a child. A married woman can choose to have a child because she is lonely, because she feels it would be the culmination of her love for her mate, as an affirmation of life, because she feels she has a talent for motherhood, because she feels she has a moral commitment to the next generation, because she wants company in her old age, or because she wants control over someone's life—and so can a single woman. A married woman can get pregnant by accident or by plan, on a whim or with serious intent, with a man she knows and loves or by alternative insemination—and so can a single woman.

Neither those with partners nor those without have a monopoly on the mental health and emotional well-being of their children, either. Normality and abnormality are not narrowly defined areas of human behavior. Rather, they are points located on either end of a continuum, with many possible variations in between. Parents with and without partners can be represented at any point on this continuum, as can children of parents with or without partners. Children who come from "intact" families can be strong or vulnerable, happy or depressed, anxious or calm, competent or overwhelmed—and so can the children of single parents.

No matter how much we all cherish the notion of family values and believe in the sanctity of marriage, no matter how seriously we personally take our wedding vows, we must also understand that many people—especially women—are not given the opportunity to sustain these choices. They have either been widowed or abandoned or separated or divorced from their partner in child-rearing. These are the hard facts of life.

The good news is that children seem to be able to flourish in all kinds of families, from the most conventional to the most unconventional—as long as they have people who love them and are capable of caring for them. The bad news is that children need a tremendous amount of time, energy, effort, devotion, and commitment. In short, they need a lot of hands-on care in order to grow and develop. The more hands, therefore, the easier this task becomes; the fewer hands, the more difficult this task becomes. That's why I've called this chapter "Single Parents, Double Efforts."

Single Parents, Plural Meanings

Before we can begin to help single parents we need to know who they are. Some of them are unwed teenage mothers; a few of them are men who are raising a child or have adopted a child; a growing group are unmarried heterosexual or homosexual women who have elected to have a child or adopt a child; others are women with children whose husbands have died.

But the overwhelming majority of single parents are divorced women who entered into marriages that they fully expected to last. Not only did they start out believing in traditional family life, most of them still do. If asked, they would tell you that they would much prefer to face the rest of their lives with a partner. Not surprisingly, many of them marry again, and some of them, again and again!

Obviously, the meaning of being a single parent will be vastly different for a mom whose husband has had a sudden heart attack and died, leaving her with two kids under five years old, than for a mom who is abandoned by the father of her child while she is still pregnant, for a mom whose husband has run away with his secretary, leaving her in charge of their seven-year-old twins, than for a divorced mom whose ex-husband is still her best friend and remains supportive of her motherhood in every sense of the word. The children, too, of all these single parents will feel differently about their families—depending on their age, their experience, and their relationship to their parents, both "before" and "after." Each single parent needs to consider the special meanings being single has for her, before she can help her kids understand the meaning of their experience.

What Should I Ask Myself?

So now that you're a single parent, how do you feel about it? Are you overwhelmed? anxious? resentful? saddened? bitter? angry? relieved? satisfied? excited? The way *you* feel about being or becoming a single parent has a great deal to do with how your children will feel about it, and how they will go on to develop as individuals and make their way in their world.

Do you want your child to have a close relationship with his father? a civil one? none at all? How has having (or adopting) a child changed your life? For the better? or are things worse? Not what you expected? Are your children a comfort to you? or a difficult burden? Is raising them on your own the best thing that ever happened to you?

Single parents need to take stock of all their resources, too. What about work? Are you financially self-sufficient? (Lucky you!) Do you have a good career? or are you still looking for a job, any job? Do you get alimony or child support from your ex? or do you have to drag him into family court for every penny? Does being single change where you and your children will live? Do you have to make a move to another house? another apartment? another city?

Has your relationship to your child changed since you've become single? Are your kids beginning to ask about their father, even though they've never known him? Do your kids have a good relationship with your ex? Do you? Is he a valued friend? a hated enemy? uninvolved? What is your kids' relationship to their dad? Are they hostile? loyal? indifferent? confused? What do you *want* their relationship to be?

Stephanie, who had separated from her husband, a perennially out-of-work actor, because she couldn't face the financial uncertainty or the ups or downs of his difficult career, was astonished to overhear the following conversation between her two children, Emma, age ten, and Jeffrey, age eight:

JEFFREY: What's Daddy going to get you for your birthday?

EMMA: I don't know. Mommy says he never has any money. He's such a bum.

Stephanie realized that her own often-expressed feelings about her husband's lack of financial resources were eroding her daughter's ability to feel good about her father. Once she recognized what was happening, she was able to help her daughter understand that even though her dad was struggling financially, he was still as responsible as he could be, that he was working as a waiter and was definitely not a bum.

While all parents can and do have problems raising their kids, if you're a single parent, you have four special problems that you need to be aware of:

- You are likely to have many *feelings and fantasies about the absent parent* (both open and underlying feelings) that can interfere with your child's ongoing development.

- You are likely to have *heightened anxieties and concerns* about raising a child alone.

- Single parents often find it particularly *difficult to set limits or keep boundaries* between them and their kids. Since your relationship to your child is not "diluted" by another parent or partner, it may be overly intense.

- Your *social and sexual needs as a single adult* will have to be integrated into your life as a single parent.

Here is an example of the first special problem I outlined—a single women who has let her underlying feelings about her ex-husband spill over into her relationship to her eleven-year-old son. When this happens, she overexposes him to her resentment, and is unable to keep boundaries between her son and his father, or between her past and her son's present. She cannot function as a protective parent.

MOM: Drew, where is my dress? I told you I needed it for tomorrow, and you were supposed to pick it up at the cleaners on your way home from school.

DREW: I meant to do it, but we went on a class trip today, and I wasn't walking home the way I usually do, so I didn't go past the cleaners.

MOM: You're always full of excuses, you're so irresponsible— just like your father. I could never count on him for anything, either. You're two of a kind. I guess if I want anything done around here, I have to do it myself.

This mom is understandably disappointed and angry, but instead of sticking to the situation at hand, she's drawing on her past memories of her life with her husband—all the broken promises, all the missed appointments, all the lies and betrayals. By comparing her son in the present to his father in the past, she's also not maintaining boundaries. She's hitting her son below the belt and interfering with his developing sense of self. Also, she's setting up the possibility of a self-fulfilling prophecy. Kids who are told over and over again that they're just like their fathers, when their fathers are "no good," have nowhere to go but down!

Mothers living on their own are often worried about their ability to keep their children safe. This can cause them to hold too tightly to their kids, a second problem single parents share. Here's an example of a mom who isn't aware of how her anxieties are crowding her nine-year-old daughter's development.

ALTHEA: Bye, Mom. I'm going outside to ride my bike now. I'll come back before it gets dark.

MOM: Honey, I don't want you going out on your own unless I know exactly where you're going and who you're going to be with. There's just the two of us, and I worry about you all the time. I couldn't take it if anything ever happened to you. You're all I've got!

This single mom is overprotective of her child. She's not able to keep her worries under wraps; they are spilling out and constraining her child's ordinary activities. She's also burdening her child with the intensity of their bond to each other, making her feel guilty about separating when her child needs to take important developmental steps toward freedom. This is the third special problem that many single parents share.

Sometimes, the circumstances of a separation or divorce can

leave one partner feeling responsible. Their guilt can cause them to see their children as the helpless victims of their actions. Remember, no matter what the circumstances, your kids need your *empathy* not your *sympathy* or *pity*. Empathy helps you to understand how your child feels and strengthens him; sympathy or pity can leave a child feeling vulnerable and powerless. Here's a dad who's feeling very guilty about his role in an extramarital affair that precipitated the breakup of his marriage. He's unwittingly placing his six-year-old son in the role of a helpless victim, rather than helping the boy (and himself) to face the facts of his situation with strength.

WILLIAM: Daddy, why are you living with Meredith instead of with Mommy and me?

DAD: Oh, God! I don't know how to explain it to you! You're too young to understand. I love Meredith, but I did a terrible, terrible thing to you and Mommy. I couldn't help myself. I'm so sorry. I hope one day, when you're older, you'll forgive me.

Here's the way a more protective parent could handle this same situation in order to leave the child with more comprehension of the situation and give the child more credit.

WILLIAM: Daddy, why did you leave Mommy and me? Why are you living with Meredith?

DAD: Mommy and I weren't happy living together, and we didn't love each other like a husband and wife should. I fell in love with Meredith, and Mommy was very hurt and angry with me, and she was right. Husbands and wives should love each other. But sometimes, even grownups do things that they can't help. I'm sorry Mommy is still so upset, but even if I hadn't fallen in love with Meredith we would still have gotten separated like we are now. I would never, ever leave you, and neither would Mommy. Just because I don't live in Mommy's house doesn't mean I've left you. As soon as Mommy and I are divorced, I'll be able to move to a bigger apartment and you'll have your own room in my house, too. Husbands and wives can get divorced, but parents would never, ever get separated from their kids.

Single parents who have once been married particularly need to guard their children against their own ongoing feelings of resentment. It's rare for a marriage to dissolve gently and gracefully, with both partners shouldering responsibility and neither of them attributing blame. Most separations are painful and acrimonious. But as a protective parent you need to try to keep your kids clear of these dark emotional tangles. Hate is a demeaning and difficult emotion to live with, and revenge between a mother and a father is seldom sweet. Besides, listing your ex's sins for his children and exposing them to how much you hate him can backfire, diminishing *you* in your kids' eyes, and possibly creating unwanted (and you would surely say unwarranted) sympathy for your partner. Trust your kids to know who's who and what's what—you don't have to spell it out for them.

And remember that once you become single, your needs as a *person* may be quite different from your needs as a parent. Many single parents take their time in rebuilding their social or sexual lives; others may immediately plunge back into the whirl as soon as possible to combat the loneliness they feel; and some (burned by their previous experiences) may even feel that they no longer wish to have a social or sexual life! Since your children will be affected by any decisions you make, they are bound to have strong feelings one way or another ("Mommy, please get married again," or "Daddy, you don't need a wife, I'll take care of you"). Try to keep your children in mind now, as you begin to integrate your new life as a single person with your life as a single parent.

Feeling at a Loss: Parents Single by Necessity

Parents who become single by virtue of an abandonment, death, separation, or divorce have become single parents by necessity and must come to terms with enormous and unexpected changes. It is completely understandable that there will be times when they or their children will feel "at a loss." Many of the losses that single parents feel are directly linked to the five basic fears we discused in chapter 2. Remember that these fears affect us as deeply and directly as they affect our kids.

The first loss for families is often a financial one. Many single parents find themselves in reduced financial circumstances after an abandonment, death, separation, or divorce because the family no longer has two incomes on which to draw, or because two households must now survive on one income. If a mother was a full-time housewife, she now must find work— any work—that will help her to support herself and her children. Choosing to work because it is a vital part of your sense of yourself, and being compelled to go to work, when you had envisioned that your job was going to be child care, are two very different circumstances. Many mothers feel hard hit and overwhelmed at this new responsibility.

Children, too, may feel at a loss. First, their original family has come to an end. Then they feel the loss of their father in their home. Next comes the loss of their father's income (which affects their lives). And finally they feel the new loss of their mother as she takes on part-time or full-time work to support the family. Children in this situation often feel like "emotional orphans," set adrift without either a father or a mother to anchor them to the new and unfamiliar world they occupy. We can easily realize that both parents and children of divorce are likely, at first, to experience fears of the unknown and fears of being alone, until the new single family gets its bearings.

Fears of one's body, too, may be particularly exaggerated in children living with only a female parent in the house. Most children are conservative creatures. They haven't caught up yet with feminism. They still see men as bigger, stronger, and more aggressive than women. Living without a man in the house can make both a mom and her children feel more vulnerable and less secure. This is particularly true in modern urban life, where we're all constantly exposed to the sights and sounds of the city—the homeless lying in the streets, fires in tenement buildings, pushers hustling dope, screaming ambulance sirens, double-locked apartment doors.

But children who live in the suburbs may also feel the absence of a father's presence in the home. In suburban communities, children may be exposed to additional feelings of humiliation when they attend the Little League games, church and synagogue functions, holiday parties, and school meetings where fathers are ordinarily participants. In this kind of community, the absence of a father may stand out more sharply, increasing the child's fears about the self ("Why me? Why don't I have a dad like the other kids do?").

And rural life has its own special problems, which can highlight the absence of a dad for a single mother and her child: It often requires physical strength and skills—chopping wood, driving in the snow, tending animals, planting crops, and so on. Here, too, a mother and her child may feel at a loss without a father in the house.

Single parents need to watch for fears about the self that may be revealed in their children's social experiences. Take some time to notice your children's reactions. How do they feel when Father's Day or Mother's Day comes around? Do they get nervous before family gatherings? Do they talk openly about their absent parent? Do they never mention him or her?

Another difficulty that contemporary single parents face is that the extended family that once might have been available to step in and help is no longer around. The maiden aunt who used to lend a hand with the babies is more likely to be a high-powered attorney today, and although Grandpa is retired, he doesn't have much time to go to ballgames with your daughter because he's working at the local hardware store to supplement his Social Security benefits. Sisters and brothers are at jobs or off at college or graduate school. Nobody's home anymore! No wonder single parents need to double their efforts. They have to make a special effort to provide their kids with that cushion of safety; they need to make a special effort to maintain the sanctuary of childhood for their kids; and they need to make a special effort to help their kids (and themselves) master the five basic fears.

As a protective parent, you need to recognize that your kids may have a very different "take" on their lives than you do. This means that you may have to let your children yearn for a daddy (even though you're relieved he's gone); it means letting your kids display anger at an abandonment (even though you may feel it was all for the best); it means letting your kids mourn for a loss that you may have precipitated; and it means helping your kids to bear the consequences of your decisions in their lives with as much strength and good will as they can muster.

"Who Needs a Father, Anyway?"

Why do we worry so much about the breakdown of the traditional family and the absence of the father in the lives of growing children? What's so important about fathers? When you come down to it, doesn't every society more or less leave the care of children to their mothers—at least until the child is five or six years old? And haven't women always carried the lion's share of child-care responsibilities?

Today's single-parent families, which are overwhelmingly headed by women, face a different and a more difficult life for several reasons. First, while fathers in many cultures may leave the psychological and physical upbringing of children to mothers, in the past, fathers were at least held to their financial responsibilities—Dad was the "breadwinner." Now, wholesale paternal abdication of financial responsibility has left many women and children severely deprived. All too often, these days, Dad just throws them a "few crumbs." With many families unable to make ends meet even with two incomes, and most women still paid at levels that are far below their male counterparts, this means that children raised by single mothers are likely to be poorer children.

Their lives may be poor in psychological, as well as material, ways. In the best of all possible worlds, fathers provide love and support for the mother of their child, better enabling the mother to make the sacrifices necessary to the care of a baby—the sleepless nights, the hourly feedings, the constant rocking and holding. A father's loving relationship to a mother forms the basis for their child's earliest experiences of *all* loving relationships and helps the child to have hope that he, too, can grow up and find a partner to love and support him in the world. Loving fathers also have a unique investment in their children and therefore can exert a considerable developmental influence over them. It's not just that "two heads are better than one," or that father offers another, much needed pair of hands: a father also offers the child a developmental way to move out of his mother's emotional orbit and into the world at large, going from mother to "other." (This "other," of course, does not have to be the child's actual father. It can be a lover, heterosexual or homosexual; it can also be a relative; it can even be a close friend.)

When fathers who have fully participated in making a baby do not as fully participate in raising that baby, we all suffer. Our society suffers since the economic plight of women raising their children alone has created what we now call "the feminization of poverty"; the mother suffers, since she must sacrifice so many of her own needs to fulfill her child's needs, without anyone to watch over her; and the child suffers, since two loving parents double the child's access to emotional, intellectual, social, physical, and financial resources.

Fathers (or "others") also offer the child another point of view, another place to turn to, when Mom is busy, or sick, or unavailable. And in the absence of a father (or "other"), there is no one around to dilute the strength of the mother-child bond—no one to help the child to separate from the mother *and* no one to help the mother to separate from the child. In the absence of a father (or "other"), mothers can come to depend too much on their children for the kind of emotional support that one would seek in a mate. This can produce what we call "parentified" children—children who subvert their own developmental needs in order to fulfill the needs of their parent. Single parents also can find themselves unable to restrain their children's desires because they're trying to make up for the loss of the absent parent. This can produce children who have difficulty accepting any limits, or who are unable to empathize with another's point of view. Finally, the ordinary diversity of opinion that occurs between two parents in the daily raising of a child is also absent in single-parent families, making it harder for the child to find "breathing space" in the family. All of these factors can make it harder for single parents to let their kids grow up and grow away from them.

While single parents may be more vulnerable to these difficulties, the fact is that all of these problems can occur in intact families. Nor is the mere physical presence of a partner any guarantee of his psychological presence in the life of a mother and a child. Nevertheless, most single mothers feel that raising a child on your own puts a special strain and a special responsibility on both mother and child, one that is different than the kind of strains children and parents experience within a traditional family.

Most single fathers feel this way, too! Although single fathers are a small segment of the single parent population, they are a fast-growing one. Many more fathers are now sharing child care in joint custody arrangements, and some fathers are willingly assuming sole custody of their children. Further, with women bearing children later in life, the death of a mother in her forties may leave children who are still young in the care of a widowed father. Many of these single fathers will remarry, creating second families for themselves and their children. But some will not, preferring to shoulder the responsibilities of raising their children alone. These men may have a particularly difficult time juggling the demands of their jobs with the more unfamiliar demands of caring for young children, but they may also find enormous satisfaction in the new connectedness they have to their children.

Parents Single by Choice

Up to this point, we've been discussing the mother or father who is compelled to raise a child alone because of separation, divorce, or a partner's death or abandonment, the parent single by necessity. But there is another kind of family, one that is formed by a parent who has *chosen* to raise a child alone. Some of these single parents are women who are unwilling to forgo the pleasures of child-rearing, despite the fact that they may not have been able to find a partner with whom they care to live. Some of them are single men or women who have chosen to adopt a child; some of them are women who, finding themselves pregnant, have no further interest in the father of their child but a great deal of interest in having a baby. As little girls they may have jumped rope to the old rhyme, "First comes love, then comes marriage, then comes a mommy with a baby carriage," but as women they do not subscribe to this sentiment.

The problems of a parent single by choice are bound to be quite different from those parents who unwillingly find themselves raising a child alone. Some of the issues we've been discussing may be less of a problem, but new problems also emerge. For example, parents who are single by choice have usually thought ahead and planned for the day when they could become parents, so they do not have to figure disappointment, disillusionment, depression, or despair about the breakup of a relationship into their family calculations. Whatever difficulties they face, at least they are chosen difficulties, and that fact alone sometimes makes hard times easier to bear.

Another factor that can ease the burden for parents single by choice is that many of them are older. They have waited a long time to be able to raise a child, and in that time, they have usually gathered together their emotional as well as their social and financial resources. Third, parents single by choice do not have to juggle the requirements of being a wife (or husband) along with those of being a parent. This can simplify their lives, leaving most of their emotional energy for child care.

On the other hand, they must face some bewildering questions from their kids. Most children have some knowledge of their father, even if he is absent. This knowledge can range from the bare minimum (a photo of a dad who has died, for instance), to a good relationship with a father who spends more time with them now than he did when he was married to their mother. But a single mother who chose to be alternatively inseminated, or who may have arranged a pregnancy "with the help of a friend," or who has had intercourse with several men so that neither she nor her child knows who the father is, must face some complicated concerns when the children begin to ask the ordinary questions kids inevitably will: "Where is my daddy?" "Why don't I see him?" "Doesn't he like me?" "Will you get me a daddy?" "Can I ever see him?" Here's where reparative narratives can help. What kind of narratives can single parents create to help their kids understand their choices? How can a single mother whose child has never seen his father still enable him to feel wanted and worthwhile? How can a lesbian mother explain her special choices in ways her kids can comprehend and respect?

Here's a narrative created by an older heterosexual woman who chose to conceive a baby through alternative insemination and raise the baby herself. Her daughter is now five years old and beginning to ask some important questions.

VALERIE: How come I don't have a daddy?

NARRATIVE	REPARATIVE ELEMENTS
MOM: Everyone has a daddy, because it takes a man and a woman to make a baby. But we don't know who your daddy is, because I got pregnant a special way. I went to a special doctor who helps the mommy to get sperm to meet her egg, so she can have a baby.	COMMUNICATION: This mom offers her child confirmation of the special realities of her life and gives her appropriate information.

VALERIE: But I want a daddy.

NARRATIVE	REPARATIVE ELEMENTS
MOM: I know you must wish that you had a daddy, that you could see him and know him. Sometimes I wish I could have a husband, too. I had wanted to have a baby for a long, long time, but I never met anyone who I wanted to live with me and be my husband. Getting pregnant with you was the best decision I ever made. I was so happy when you were born, and so were Grandma and Grandpa, and Uncle Woody, Aunt Janet, and all our friends, and your godfather, Justin, too.	COMPASSION: This empathic statement lets the child know that her mother understands how she feels. COMPREHENSION: By telling this story, this mother is helping her child to understand the entire situation.
VALERIE: Madeline has a daddy.	
MOM: Yes, she does. But all families are different. Leah's mom adopted her and brought her over to live here from Vietnam; and Calvin's parents are divorced, and he spends half his week with his mommy and half his week with his daddy; and Pamela has two mommies and no daddy, so lots of kids have lots of different families. You and I are a family, too."	COMPETENCE: In this statement, this single mother offers a resolution and an order to the story of her child's life. She also tries to "normalize" her child's special situation.

Here's a narrative created by a single unwed mother who has decided to keep her baby and raise him herself. She knew the baby's father, but he has no ongoing involvement in the child's life and has been unwilling to assume any responsibilities for his child. Her little boy, James, is seven years old.

JAMES: Why doesn't Daddy live with us? Where is he?

NARRATIVE	REPARATIVE ELEMENTS
MOM: I don't know where he lives now. When I first met your daddy, I was only a teenager. When I found I was pregnant with you I decided that I really wanted you to be born and to be my baby.	COMMUNICATION: Here, the mother is informing the child and confirming his reality.
JAMES: Did he live with me when I was a baby?	
MOM: He was still too young to be a good daddy for you or a good husband for me, so I didn't want to get married to him, and he didn't live with us.	
We lived with Granny May when you were born, and she helped me to take care of you. I am so happy that I decided to have you because otherwise I would never have known you!	COMPREHENSION: Here, she's trying to let her child know the story of his birth so he can understand the situation.
JAMES: But will I ever see my real daddy?	
MOM: I know you really wish you could see him, and it's sad that we can't now.	COMPASSION: This empathic statement lets her child know that his mother understands how he feels.
If you still want to try to see your daddy when you get older, I can try to help you find out where he is.	COMPETENCE: This mother is suggesting a possible resolution to her child's questions—a possible outcome.

NARRATIVE	REPARATIVE ELEMENTS
Meanwhile, Uncle Stuart loves you and you have Grandpa Arnold to love you, too. And I will always love you, forever and ever.	

The mother in the following narrative has been abandoned by the father of her child. She has begun to date and hopes to remarry. She has constructed this reparative narrative for her nine-year-old daughter:

ELISE: Why can't I see my daddy?

NARRATIVE	REPARATIVE ELEMENTS
MOM: I wish that you did have a daddy that you could know and see.	COMPASSION: This is an empathic statement that offers the child comfort.
When I got married to your daddy, and we decided to have you, I hoped that he would become a good father, but that never happened. Instead, he just left one day, without even telling me. You were three years old. Do you remember any of this? You were very little when he went away, and it had nothing to do with you. He left because he didn't want to be a husband.	COMMUNICATION: This gives the child information and confirms the reality of her life.

COMPREHENSION: Here, the mother is trying to help her child understand the situation. She's also absolving the child of responsibility. |
| ELISE: I remember Daddy was tall and he had fuzzy hair on his arms. | |

NARRATIVE	REPARATIVE ELEMENTS
MOM: Yes, he did, but he wasn't able to be very loving or responsible. He liked to party and hang out with his friends. We need someone who can stay with us and love us. I'm looking for a really good father for you and a really good husband for me. I hope that I can find someone who will love us and take care of us. What do you think about my friend Jay? I've been liking him more and more.	COMPETENCE: This story helps the child to know about the outcome in the past, and to look ahead with hope for the future.

Often when kids fight with each other, they reach for ammunition in each others' families, saying things like, "Your mother is fat," "Your father has an ugly car," "Your parents adopted you—they're not your real parents." Here's a mother trying to comfort her ten-year-old child after one of these "below the belt" punches about his family.

NARRATIVE	REPARATIVE ELEMENTS
MOM: What's the matter, honey?	COMMUNICATION: Here this mom tries to elicit information from her son.
GEORGE: I hate Bradley. I hate him. He's so mean.	
MOM: It sounds like you two had a pretty serious fight, and you feel pretty bad about it.	COMPASSION: She offers him empathy for his situation.
GEORGE: I'm never, ever going to talk to him again.	
MOM: I hear you loud and clear. What about talking to *me* about what's upset you so much?	COMMUNICATION: Now she tries to encourage her child to speak up.

NARRATIVE	REPARATIVE ELEMENTS
GEORGE: We were fighting about who was winning at Monopoly, and he said I cheated and I said I didn't, and he told me I didn't know anything because I didn't even have a father and he was probably a cheater, too. He said maybe he was in jail.	
MOM: Boy, that must have hurt your feelings. What a dumb thing for Bradley to say. It sounds like he was looking for a way to make you mad and he'd use anything—even stuff he knows nothing about.	COMPASSION and COMPREHENSION: Again, this mom empathizes with her son and also tries to enlarge his understanding of the incident.
GEORGE: But he's right. Why don't I have a father like everyone else does? I don't even know if he's in jail.	
MOM: No, honey. Your dad isn't missing because he's in jail. He just didn't stay around to be a husband or a father. He left when you were only nine months old.	COMMUNICATION: Here she confirms an important reality for her child.
But you're right, it's mean of Bradley to throw your dad up at you in a fight. What do you think you should do? Never talking to him won't let him know how you feel. Maybe you could think of something to say to him.	COMPETENCE: Now this mom, after empathizing, tries to help her child come up with a solution.
GEORGE: I'm going to tell him I'd rather have no father than a bald, ugly father like he has!	

NARRATIVE	REPARATIVE ELEMENTS
MOM: You want to get back at him the same way, but you like Mr. O'Conner. Do you really want to say that?	COMPREHENSION: She tries to help her son understand more about the implications of his actions.
GEORGE: I'll tell him he wouldn't like it if I said bad things about his father, and he doesn't fight fair.	
MOM: Those are two important ideas. I bet Bradley will feel differently about what he did when you tell him that.	COMPETENCE: Finally, she offers her child hope for the future.

Since many children of single parents are worried about what would become of them if something happened to their single parent, a reparative narrative that lists all the people who love and care for your children is also important in helping them feel more secure. Here's one sort of narrative that a parent could construct to reassure a school-age child who's worried about who would take care of her should something happen to her mother:

MILLIE: Who will take care of me if you die?

NARRATIVE	REPARATIVE ELEMENTS
MOM: I know that when parents get divorced, sometimes kids get worried about who'll be there to take care of them.	COMPASSION: This empathic statement lets the child know her mother understands her worries.
Even though Daddy* doesn't live in our house anymore, he would always come to take	COMMUNICATION: Here, the mother offers information and confirms the child's reality in a consoling and supportive way.

*If a father is not available or has never been available to you or your child, this reparative narrative would simply omit his name as one of the persons to whom your child can turn.

NARRATIVE	REPARATIVE ELEMENTS
care of you if we needed him. And if Daddy couldn't, then Grandma and Grandpa would come to stay with you; and if they couldn't come, Aunt Sylvia and Uncle Ethan would come here, or you could go visit them in Florida. And don't forget your babysitter, Zoe. There are so many people who love you and care about you, you never have to worry.	COMPETENCE: This mother ties up the narrative with a reassuring resolution for her child.

Remember, knowing who you can count on in an emergency is not only important for your child, it's also an important consideration for you. Whether you are single by choice or single by necessity, you need to build up all of the "people resources" you can. All single parents must remain alert to the following developmental pitfalls:

- *Don't ask your child to "fill in" for the absent parent.* Single parents often feel lonely, and they can keep their kids too close to them, way past the time when children need this kind of attachment. Try to keep appropriate emotional and physical boundaries between you and your children, particularly at night. Don't make a habit of taking them to sleep with you.

- *Don't overburden your child with too much responsibility.* In the absence of a partner, single parents can ask children to assume tasks that are beyond their capacity. (Remember the little girl who was caring for her sick father and all her siblings?) And don't constantly ask one child to be responsible for another. This creates unhealthy tensions and rivalries among kids in the same family.

- *Don't make your child your confidant.* This both exposes children to matters beyond their understanding and burdens them with worries that should be shouldered by parents. This applies equally to talking about your sex life (past and present), money worries, job concerns, or health problems. Find adults to talk to—friends, family members, or counselors.

- *Take care of yourself as well as your child.* Single parents particularly may find that it's very hard to get their own needs attended to, since there's so much to do and so little time to do it! But sacrificing too much for children can backfire, causing them to grow up self-centered or even selfish, just as not sacrificing enough can cause them to feel deprived or neglected. A proper balance leaves children room to give *and* take.

- *Let your child leave you in developmentally appropriate ways.* Remember, children need to grow up and grow away from you. (This is sometimes hardest for single mothers of single children.) Don't make children feel guilty for moving on or leaving you. Be alert to the development of this situation and be prepared to cope with it.

SPECIAL QUESTIONS FROM SINGLE PARENTS

Following are some of the most common questions single parents have asked me:

- Will my son grow up to be homosexual if he doesn't have a good relationship (or any relationship) with his father?

    Many single mothers of male children have concerns about the absence of a father in their families. They hear a lot in the media about the importance of "good male role models" in development and wonder if this means that their son won't be able to become a man without a man around. They worry that the absence of a close relationship to a father will predispose their child toward homosexuality.

    In fact, consolidation of both heterosexual and homosexual

identities are very complex developmental outcomes and don't simply depend on the absence or presence of a loving father. (If that were the case, every son whose father died in a war would grow up gay!) On the contrary, most gay men seem to grow up in *intact,* rather traditional families.

To help your son (and daughter—both boys and girls benefit from loving male attention!), call upon male members of your family and friends to "fill in" for your child's absent or inattentive father.

- How will my choice to live alone affect my children? Will they make the same choice later on in their lives?

Children learn all sorts of complex lessons in life, including lessons about love. If you have chosen to live alone, your children may come to admire and respect your choice. They may resent and regret it; they may understand that it makes sense for you but not for them. A lot depends on what overt and covert messages you give to your kids: Do you enjoy being alone, or are you despairing? Do you feel marriage is a great deal or a thoroughly unsatisfactory one?

My mother, the shy eldest daughter of a family of six, didn't marry my father until she was almost thirty years old (in her generation, a spinster!). All our lives, my sisters and I heard the story of "her last chance at love," and how happy she was to have met my father at the "last minute." No wonder we were all married by the time we were twenty-one years old!

- Are my children adversely affected by the fact that I've had to change care givers several times?

All parents who must leave their children in the care of another feel worried about the outcome. And most children do not respond well to abrupt or frequent changes in their routines, so try to choose carefully the first time around. Interview, check references, and spend time with your care giver and your child together before you leave your child alone with her or him.

But the best-laid plans go awry—a care giver can get married or get ill, requiring you to find someone new; a mother can change her job or her city, requiring her to hire a different care giver. In these unpredictable instances, if you let your child know what's going on and use your knowledge of the five basic fears and the four C's to construct a narrative for your child that explains the events, you will create the cushion of safety that helps him cope with these changes.

- Will my child love his care givers better than he loves me?

  Children have very special feelings for their mothers (and fathers), feelings that are sustained despite the inevitable absences that today's times require. Try to spend as much time as you can with your kids, and remain emotionally available to them when you are with them.

- Do children absolutely *need* to be raised by two parents?

  There are no absolutes about family life. While it's true that a man and a woman are necessary to make a baby, children can be raised by grandparents, uncles, aunts, sisters, brothers, cousins, strangers, and even other children. If a child has two people who have the intellectual, emotional, and financial resources to take care of him, he is very lucky. But if he has one person willing to love and cherish him, he is still pretty lucky.

The Dating Game: Some Rules for Single Parents

For most single parents engaging in active social and sexual lives, the dating game is difficult and confusing. In chapter 7, we have already discussed the kinds of narratives you can construct to help your children understand and accommodate your separation or divorce. But now, you also need to develop some ways of talking to your kids about your new role as a single parent. If and when you find yourself ready to date again, you need to prepare your kids to understand this next phase of your life. Since children understand things best in terms of their own lives, the first step is to link your new wish to meet and date people with your child's understanding of his own need for friends. Here's how you could talk to a very young child (three to five years old) about dating:

"You know how you have friends over to play sometimes, or I bring you to their house for a playdate? Well, now that Daddy doesn't live with me anymore, I need to have some time to find new friends—friends that I can talk to and play with, just like you do. Children see their friends during the day, but grown-ups work during the day, and they need to see their friends at night. Sometimes, I'll be going out to meet my friends at night after you're in bed, and Nanna will stay with you until I come home. Sometimes I'll be having dinner with my friends, or going out to a movie, and I'll need to leave before you go to sleep. Then, the babysitter will put you to sleep. But I'll always be here when you wake up."

As much as you may feel that it's *your* time to have the life you want to lead, try to keep your children in mind, too. Remember, you're a single *parent*, not just single, and this means that, once again, it's going to be a balancing act between your needs and your children's needs. Your new social life may be good for you, but it imposes some new deprivations on your children. Previously, you may have been able to be home to put them to bed (their most vulnerable time); now you may be out several nights a week, leaving this task to others. Children begin to act up if they begin to feel abandoned. Make sure that you're home at least every other night to put your children to bed or you'll find that they begin to show the wear and tear of your lack of attention and wind up displaying behavioral disruptions that only make your life more difficult in the long run. (With very young children—under three years old—you may not be able to leave them at night more than once or twice a week, unless they are staying with people that they love and trust.) Once you begin dating, make sure you take stock of the "people resources" that you have around you—babysitters, friends, relatives, and so on—and alert them to this new phase of your life, so that they'll be ready to help you.

What about sex? Most single parents are hoping there's still sex after separation. What should you tell your kids if you start to become sexually active? *Should* you tell them? Don't be surprised if your older child takes you aside with his worries about whether or not you're practicing safe sex and using condoms! But even if your kids sound cool and sophisticated about your becoming sexually active, it's never easy for a child to imagine their mom or dad in the arms of a lover. Single parents need to keep their sexual lives private as long as they can to protect their children from sexual overexposure and overstimulation. (This is true for all parents!) This means trying to conduct your sexual life away from home when your kids are there, until it's someone you'd want to bring home!

Children who are overexposed to a single parent's active sexual life may be burdened with all kinds of upsetting thoughts. They may be angry at you for betraying the missing parent (remember Hamlet?); they may be distressed because they still hold out hope that you and their father may be reunited; they may be jealous and protective of you and hostile toward your lover; they may be envious of you and compete for your lover's attention; they may feel disgusted or embarrassed by a parent openly engaging in sexuality (this may be particularly true of older children). They may be saddened by their exclusion from this new phase in your life and feel isolated from you; they may feel you've betrayed them by being capable of loving someone else; they may be frightened and anxious that you will abandon them for your new life.

Do yourself and your kids a favor: Leave them out of the dating game—unless or until you find someone you're serious about. It's very wearing for children to meet each new guy that Mom dates or each new girlfriend that Dad takes to dinner. Keep your social life private until it becomes a *love* life. Once you've reached the point where you're serious about someone and you want to see as much of them as possible during your days, it may become difficult (and feel artificial) to avoid sharing your nights, too. At this point, you need to make sure your kids get to know and feel comfortable with your partner. Now's the time to make an effort to do things "as a family." But try to let your children find their own way to friendship with your new beau—don't push it. Wait for your child to shape and define the relationship he wants with your new partner.

If you've found someone you love, who's willing to love you and to love your child, then your family is about to change and you're no longer going to be a single parent. It's time to turn to the next chapter in this book, chapter 9, "Second Families, Second Chances."

9

Second Families, Second Chances

When parents remarry, they imagine beginning their new life with a new family that will heal all the wounds they suffered in their old marriage. They are resolved that they will never make the same mistakes they made the first time round; they are sure that their children will warmly welcome their new spouse; they dream that their stepchildren and their own children will blend together lovingly—just like "The Brady Bunch." But this is seldom the case. Being a good parent is a difficult job, but being a good stepparent can feel impossible!

Yet, with one out of two marriages ending in divorce, bereaved parents left without partners, and many single parents choosing to remarry within three years, there are bound to be more and more stepfamilies. In fact, there are more than thirty million mothers and fathers struggling to be stepparents in this country right now.

Any marriage gives us a developmental opportunity to work through some of the problems we experienced in our original family. We can choose a partner who is supportive of us to contravene a mother's criticism, or a partner who respects us to mitigate against a father's contempt. But if we are unable to transform our early experiences, we can wind up repeating the pain of our past in the present. When this happens, we wind up choosing a partner who always erodes our self-confidence, like our carping mother, or who demeans and destroys our self-respect, like our haughty father. Often, when a marriage falls apart, it is because these old painful patterns from our past continue to show up in our present lives. A second marriage raises our hopes for a second chance to heal our wounds—a second chance to repair the damage of our childhood, a second chance at growth, and a second chance at getting the love we need. But with a second marriage, the developmental opportunity is encumbered. Not only does the spouse carry his childhood baggage into the new union, each also carries the baggage from the first marriage, as well.

And although you may have learned a lot about yourself through your marriage and your separation, divorce, or widowhood, now the scene has shifted, and you have to master a whole new role—stepparent. Suddenly you're being asked to be a new partner and a new parent at exactly the same time. This is a formidable expectation, with the potential for double trouble. Settling into a new marriage and a new family always produces unpredictable conflicts and entangled loyalties.

Stepmothers, since they are traditionally perceived as wicked and heartless, often feel used and abused in their new families. Stepfathers, often portrayed in life and literature as cold and cruel, feel rejected and exploited. When we get a second chance at family life, hopes run high, but, sadly, they are often dashed by the real problems all the members of second families face. How can you love someone else's children? What if you don't even like them? How can a second wife accommodate to the constant shadow cast by the first wife's presence? How can a second husband earn the affection of a child who sees him as an intruder? How can a parent treat her own child and someone else's child equally? Can she? How can a child accept a stepparent into her life when her own parent is alive and well? What if a child feels the breakup of her parents' marriage was the stepparent's fault? What can a stepparent do to help this important transition from one life to another go smoothly?

No matter how much thought you gave to becoming a stepparent, no matter how much you tried to anticipate all the problems, the reality will always be unpredictable and complicated. This is because there are four hard facts that all step-parents must face:

- Your spouse has loved and lived with another person, who may always have some sort of prior emotional claim on him.

- Your spouse's children are a constant living reminder of this prior relationship.

- The children you live with (or some of the children you live with) are not yours, and they never can be yours.

- These children are bound to have hostile (or at best, mixed) feelings toward you and to see you as a powerful rival for their parent's love and attention.

One stepparent captured her plight in the following statement: "The painful part about being in a second marriage is that, on some fundamental level, you feel you can never come first."

Step by Step

Even though your child may have known and liked your new partner over months and even years of courtship, it's a whole new ballgame once you decide to get married. Now you're asking your child to accept him as a member of the family. Now your child knows that it's serious; now there's no going back. A child whose mother or father is about to re-marry is going to have mixed feelings about the event, no matter how comfortable or prepared she is.

First, the announcement of your remarriage ends, once and for all, your child's fantasies that her mother and father will be reunited and she will be able to have her family together again. This reunion fantasy can persist for years in children of all ages, despite all evidence to the contrary, and it is painful for kids to relinquish.

Second, even though your child has already mourned the

original breakup of her family, she may experience a resurgence of grief when you tell her of your plans to marry again. A child's unexpected grief at the very time when a parent has found happiness can be hard to take—for both of you. This is true whether you have been widowed or divorced.

Third, when children are informed about a parent's remarriage, they often become deeply concerned about the well-being and happiness of the parent *without* a partner. Their sympathies may be stirred up in his behalf. "Who will take care of Daddy?" "Will he be more lonesome now?" or "Why can't you love Mommy anymore?" are questions your child may ask. And they may feel compelled to come to this parent's rescue, particularly if the parent is indeed unhappy or even depressed by the ex's remarriage, and shares this with his child. A child who is placed in the real (or imagined) position of comforting a vulnerable parent may also feel upset with the remarried parent, whom they perceive as heartless and hostile, or toward the stepparent, whom they see as the villain of the piece. (It's a whole lot easier for kids to be angry at a stranger than it is to be angry with you.) When you've been widowed and plan to remarry, your kids may accuse you of forgetting your first partner.

Last, your child's feelings don't necessarily match yours. She still loves the parent you divorced. She is still having a hard time figuring out how you could "fall out of love" with her daddy. Your ability to remarry raises troubling questions for her about the nature of love. Similarly, your child may see your decision to remarry as proof that you are being disloyal to his dead mother's memory.

Here's a mother who isn't alert to her child's inner experiences, and so she can't understand or manage her seven-year-old daughter's reactions to her remarriage very well:

MOTHER: I wanted you to be the first to know that Stan and I are getting married. Isn't that wonderful news?

CAROL: But what about Daddy?

MOTHER: What do you mean, what about Daddy? Daddy and I were divorced three years ago. Now I've found someone I love, and we're going to all live together and have a new family. It'll be great. You'll have a new daddy.

CAROL: I don't want a new daddy.

MOTHER: What's the matter with you? You like Stan; we have good times together. Why are you being so negative?

In her happiness over her remarriage, this mother has forgotten that the meanings of this event are bound to be complicated for her young daughter. Then, to make matters worse, not only does she miss addressing her daughter's worries about her father, but she also suggests that her new husband will be her daughter's "new daddy," further saddening, angering, and alienating her child from her.

This is a tricky emotional time for all of you. You want to feel happy and hopeful as you open a door to a new life, while your child may feel angry and bereft as the door is slammed shut on her old life. The more aware you are of all the psychological meanings of the events, the more you can help your children to become aware of their hidden feelings.

Here's a protective parent facing the same situation. She is armed with her knowledge of the four C's so she can build a reparative narrative:

NARRATIVE	REPARATIVE ELEMENTS
MOTHER: I wanted you to be the first to know that Charles and I are getting married. I know this is big news, and you probably have a lot of different feelings about it.	COMPASSION: This mother begins the conversation in the same way, but follows-up with an empathic statement about her child's feelings.
TED: But what about Daddy? He'll be all alone now.	
MOTHER: I can see you're worried about Daddy. But we've been divorced for three years now, and meanwhile,	More COMPASSION, COMMUNICATION, COMPREHENSION, and COMPETENCE: Now, this

NARRATIVE	REPARATIVE ELEMENTS
we've both been dating. I found Charles and fell in love first. I hope Daddy will find someone to love, too.	mother lets her child know she can see how he's feeling. She gives him information and tries to expand his understanding. She also offers a possible outcome for the child's father that holds out hope for the future for him.
TED: Charles is not my daddy, though.	
MOTHER: Of course not. You only have one real daddy. Charles will be your stepdaddy.	More COMPETENCE: This mother offers a possible resolution of the child's conflict of loyalties.

Of course not all parents remarry as a consequence of divorce. For some, death has prematurely claimed a partner, leaving the family bereft. This may present the child and the parent with quite a different set of difficulties. Here's a father trying to help his nine-year-old daughter come to terms with his decision to remarry three years after her mother's death:

NARRATIVE	REPARATIVE ELEMENTS
DAD: Helen, I want to tell you something important. You know that I've been seeing a lot of Allison this past year. Well, we've decided to get married this spring.	COMMUNICATION: Here this father offers important information and confirms an important reality for his daughter.
HELEN: How could you get married again? How could you forget about Mommy?	

NARRATIVE	REPARATIVE ELEMENTS
DAD: I can see you're upset with me, and I understand why. You think marrying Allison means I'm forgetting Mommy, but it doesn't. We both loved Mommy so much.	COMPASSION: He tries to let his daughter know he can empathize with her feelings.
HELEN: You didn't love Mommy! If you loved her, you couldn't marry Allison!	
DAD: No, sweetie, you're wrong. I loved Mommy and I'll always love Mommy, but she's been gone for three years now, and we can never have her back.	More COMPASSION and COMPREHENSION: Offering more empathy, he tries to expand his daughter's understanding of the situation.
HELEN (*cries*): You can get another wife, but I can never have another mommy.	
DAD: You're right. Allison likes you very much, but she can never replace Mommy. She can never replace Mommy for me, either, but I don't want to live alone the rest of my life.	More COMMUNICATION: Here he again tries to share his experience with his daughter and explore a mutual understanding of the situation.
HELEN: I'll take care of you, Daddy.	
DAD: No, Helen, I don't want you to have to take care of me. I need someone like Allison now, and you need to grow up and find someone to love as much as I loved Mommy. Someday I hope you'll have your own husband and family.	COMPETENCE: Now this father relieves his daughter of responsibility for him and offers her hope for her future.

What Should a Stepparent Do?

When we first get married, we often take time to be alone with each other and get to know each other before we have children. But when we marry again, and our spouse has children, there is often no time for this beginning adjustment as a couple. The children (and the children's parents) are a part of marital life right away. Some stepparents have a lot of trouble with this fact. "Can't we ever be just a couple?" they say, or "What do you mean, you have to help your ex-wife paint the house?" But even when stepparents have been looking forward to taking on family responsibilities, even when they want the children to feel welcome, there are questions. How much of a parent should a stepparent try to be? To decide about the limits of your role, you need to know the answers to four important questions:

- How much of a parent does your stepchild *want* you to be, or let you be?

- What kind of relationship does your stepchild have with the custodial parent?

- What kind of relationship does your stepchild have with the noncustodial parent?

- What kind of a child is your stepchild?

You'll need to do a lot of psychological fact-finding about your new family, and you'll need to take time to get to know your stepchild in order to be informed. It's not a matter of "love me; love my child." You've fallen in love with your spouse, but you have to *learn* to love your stepchild. The more information you gather, the more you will be able to decide what steps will be safe to take.

Generally, the younger the child, the greater opportunity you will have to build an ongoing relationship. Children under five years old often are not engaged by the complex loyalties, jealousies, and competitiveness that can make a stepparent's life so miserable. They are primarily concerned with affection, care, and security. As long as you offer friendship, don't stand between the child and your spouse, and don't try to compete with or criticize the natural parent, you'll probably find things settling down well. But older children are much more likely to experience all these conflicts of loyalty and to feel challenged and threatened by a stepparent's entry into the family. Further, they are much more likely to have known about the tensions and troubles of their parent's marriage, to be privy to the details of the divorce, and even to have taken sides. Your spouse could be on the child's wrong side, making life difficult for both of you. Then adjusting to your role as a stepparent will have to be laid aside until your spouse and the child work out *their* conflicts.

If your stepchild has a very good relationship with your spouse, and your spouse is loving toward both of you and supportive of your relationship toward each other, the child is more likely to let you into her life in a meaningful way. But even this ideal situation can be constrained if your stepchild feels compelled to protect her natural parent or feels that her affection for you is a betrayal of her parent. Stepparents need to know when to *step in* and when to *step back* from situations with their stepchildren that could be potentially destructive.

Here's a protective stepparent trying to handle a prickly situation with her stepson, who is ten years old and very close to his mom. By *stepping back*, she's avoided a conflict of loyalties.

NARRATIVE	REPARATIVE ELEMENTS
STEPMOM: I was thinking that it would be fun to buy you a new baseball jacket for your birthday. Your old one is getting pretty shabby.	
DOUGLAS: There's nothing wrong with my jacket! I like it, and besides my mom always gets me a new jacket on my birthday!	COMMUNICATION: Here her stepson conveys important information to his stepmom.

NARRATIVE	REPARATIVE ELEMENTS
STEPMOM: Oh boy! I was pretty dumb to just barge in like that. No wonder you're annoyed with me. I didn't realize your mom gets you these great jackets every year. Of course it's getting a little worn—she'll be getting you a new one next week.	COMPREHENSION and COMPASSION: This stepmom lets her stepson know she understands that she's put her foot in her mouth, and knows how he feels about it (empathy).
DOUGLAS: Well, I guess I never told you that.	More COMMUNICATION: Both stepmom and stepson exchange information.
STEPMOM: I'd still like to get you a birthday gift from me. Is there something you'd really like that no one else is getting you?	
DOUGLAS: I need a new basketball. Maybe we could buy that.	COMPETENCE: Here her stepson comes up with a resolution.

Here's another situation in which a stepfather *steps in* successfully to help his eight-year-old stepchild and his mother solve a family problem:

NARRATIVE	REPARATIVE ELEMENTS
MOTHER: If I hear one more time about how all the kids go to the park after dinner, I'll scream. You're not old enough to go alone, and that's that!	
NEIL: But everyone hangs out in the park. All the kids in my class play ball on Fridays. Besides, I promise I'll come home before it gets dark.	COMMUNICATION: This child tries to inform his mom about his wishes.

NARRATIVE	**REPARATIVE ELEMENTS**
STEPDAD: I can understand that your mom is worried that the park might not be safe in the evenings. What about this? I'd be willing to walk you over to play ball while I take my run and then pick you up on my way back home, if it's OK with your mom. That way, she wouldn't worry so much, and you can still get a chance to play ball.	COMPREHENSION and COMPETENCE: By understanding this situation and offering a resolution that addresses both the mom's needs and her son's, this father has stepped in successfully and gained his stepson's affection.
MOTHER: That'd be all right with me.	
NEIL: That'd be great! Thanks, Dad.	

Stepparents need to build their relationship to their own spouse first, their stepchild next, and their relationship to their stepchild's parent—if at all possible—last. That's because you will need your spouse to support the steps you take; otherwise it's easy for your stepchildren to "divide and conquer" both of you. Remember, parents share an emotional "bank account" with their children from the time they're born. While anger, and disappointment, and frustration may temporarily diminish the balance in this account, deposits are made daily, so there are such plentiful resources to draw upon and neither parent nor child feels totally depleted. But stepparents do not share such an account with their stepchildren. That's why the very first step a protective stepparent takes is to build up such an emotional bank account. This is the best investment a stepparent can make in the new family's future. How can you build this emotional bank account?

- Try to understand that *your gain may be your step-child's loss.* Many single parents invest a lot of their emotional energy in their kids. Now that energy is invested in you. Try to balance the books by offering your stepchild your support.

- *Don't take a stepchild's hostility personally.* Recognize and acknowledge the complex mixed feelings your stepchild is likely to have toward you, no matter how nice you are.

- *Don't push it!* Only offer what you and your stepchild can manage. Offering too much, too soon—whether it's discipline or affection, gifts or advice—will usually backfire. Many stepparents overextend themselves for a stepchild (who does not appear grateful) and then they are resentful and angry that their efforts weren't appreciated.

Here's a stepfather who's "pushing it" and offering more discipline than he and his ten-year-old stepson can manage:

DAD: Are you still watching TV, young man? You're never going to amount to anything if you don't spend more time on your school work and less time goofing off.

LEE: Just cause you're married to my mom doesn't mean you're my father! I don't have to listen to you.

DAD: Don't get fresh with me!

Here's a stepfather who is careful not to offer too much discipline too soon:

DAD: Are you still watching TV, Lee? It's getting late, and I was wondering if you have enough time left to finish up your homework. I know your mom worries about your math. Do you need any help?

LEE: I'm almost finished, I just want to watch the end of this show. There're only two more long division examples. I hate long division!

DAD: I know what you mean!

WHAT'S IN A NAME?

We've already talked about the importance of naming in our lives. In addition to the names we give to each other and to the things in our world, there are special names we give to people to define their function in our lives: doctor, wife, professor, husband, officer, teacher, and so forth. Mother (Mom, Momma, Mommy, etc.) and Father (Dad, Daddy, Poppa, etc.) are the first and most important names we ever say. Parents, anxious to help a child to bridge the gap between one family and another, sometimes ask a child to call her new stepmother "Mom" or her new stepfather "Dad." A mother may say, eagerly, "Carl is going to be your new 'dad.'" Some children, who are aware of the symbolic importance of this title, but are anxious to please, will make a personal differentiation that preserves the distinctions between the original parent and this new version—"I'd like to call you Poppa; I call my real father Dad."—while others will immediately bristle at any suggestion that the stepparent is trying to take over any of the functions of a natural parent. These kids might say, "Carl isn't my father and he never will be. He's just Carl."

Protective stepparents will realize that it's best to take it slow and easy as you build a new family. Children need to spend time with a stepmother or stepfather before they can feel comfortable even referring to them as their "stepmom" or "stepdad." If you compel a child to call you Mom or Dad, you may get sullen compliance, but you'll never get the acceptance or affirmation you want. Letting children choose what they want to call you, while letting them know you'd like them to *feel* like calling you Mom (or Dad) someday, leaves your new relationship room to grow.

What Should I Ask Myself?

Stepparents have a hard job sorting out their conflicted feelings about their new families. Here are some questions that may help you to focus on the source of the problem.

Do you find yourself constantly comparing yourself to your spouse's ex? Do you feel superior? inferior? Are you often angry and resentful at the amount of time your ex spends with his "old" family? Do you feel it's at your expense or the expense of your children?

Angela and her husband have a two-year-old son, Randy. But her husband also has children by a previous marriage—a twelve-year-old boy, Connor, and two girls, Penny and Johanna, ages ten and six. Her husband still feels guilty about leaving his first family and tries to "make it up" to his kids by spending as much time as he can with them on weekends and holidays. Angela likes the fact that her son has stepsiblings, but she resents never having time alone with just her husband and her son, without her husband's other kids, who tend to focus on their time with their dad and ignore her.

Once she realized that she was becoming tense and irritable every time a weekend approached, Angela was able to sit down with her husband and work out some time for the three of them to be alone together as a family without his children.

Do you feel your spouse never takes your side in disputes you have with your spouse's children? Do you get into disputes with them often? Do you feel your spouse indulges or favors his or her children at the expense of yours? Do you feel your spouse resents your children and makes them feel unwelcome?

Cliff's parents divorced when he was eight years old and his father remarried a woman that Cliff felt was cold and hostile toward him. Now he's divorced and remarried, too. Whenever his twin boys visit his home, he becomes very tense, and afterward he often accuses his new wife of not being nice enough or welcoming enough to the twins. It wasn't until his wife sobbed, "No matter how nice I am to the boys, you always make me feel mean," that Cliff realized that the memories of his stepmother's hostility toward him were coloring his vision of his wife's behavior toward his children, which was actually quite affectionate.

Do you feel your spouse takes parenting responsibilities more seriously than marital responsibilities? Do you feel your spouse's children come between you?

Were your parents divorced when you were a child? Did either of them remarry? Did you like or dislike your stepparent? Do you have any stepsiblings? Are you close to them?

Stepparents need to be especially mindful of the way their own past can exert a powerful hold on their present relationships. It's so easy to feel excluded when you're "the newcomer" joining "the old family club," and it's even easier if you actually were excluded at some important point in your own past life.

Stepsibling Rivalry

When children grow up together in the same family, they normally jostle one another for a place in their parents' affections and attentions. It's perfectly ordinary and inevitable that siblings will feel competitive toward each other over some of their differences: Who's taller? thinner? smarter? Who's more musical? better at math? Protective parents need to work hard to create an open family atmosphere in which individual differences are accepted, unique characteristics are respected, and no child is made to feel inferior or superior to any other. This is no easy task, since children's personalities and abilities vary widely, as do our reactions to our kids' personalities and abilities.

Even normal sibling rivalry can be hard for families to tolerate, but heightened sibling rivalry can feel like bitter warfare, with no holds barred. Each child can plot and plan to defeat the other. Persistent hostilities over everything and nothing can take a daily toll on everyone's well-being; verbal sparring can quickly deteriorate into physical fights; and intimidation, hatred, and revenge can come to define the relationship between sisters and brothers. This kind of heightened sibling rivalry is often a fight to the finish, with the siblings unable to control their rivalry, and their parents unable to control them.

Heightened sibling rivalry is usually linked to four family problems: inadequate parental controls over aggression among family members; heightened marital strife between parents; observable discrepancies in health, looks, skills or competencies among children of the same family; and distinct parental preferences for one child over another. Protective stepparents try hard not to participate in these distortions, but it's hard work. In an old family, members share an ongoing history. This history enables family members to build up emotional reserves with each other, to cushion hard times with good times, and to balance competition and rivalry with cooperation and empathy. New stepparent families have not yet had time to build emotional reserves.

Further, in a second marriage, a mother and a father have chosen each other, but their combined children have had no choice at all in the matter. Sometimes the two sets of children are so far apart in age or temperament that rivalry is not an issue. When rivalry does emerge among stepsiblings it's particularly complicated for the following reasons:

- Stepsiblings have no shared history to fall back on to counterbalance their antagonism.
- Children may displace their anger and hostility toward their parents (for their divorce and remarriage) onto their stepsiblings.
- In moderating stepsibling rivalries, each stepparent may feel compelled to come to the defense of his or her own child.

Yours, Mine, or Ours?

We all have positive and negative feelings toward each other and toward our kids, and they have positive and negative feelings toward each other and toward us. But overall, we know we always can count on each other because "we're family"—we've grown up together. The stepfamily needs time to grow up together, too.

Yours: A Stepmother's Story

In this scenario for a second marriage, a woman without children marries a man who has children by another woman. If the children's mother is very much in the picture, she is probably the custodial parent, and you are probably seeing your husband's children every other weekend and during the vacations. Since your job as stepmom is only *part-time*, take advantage of it! Try to enjoy your visiting stepchildren without feeling too resentful of the responsibilities. You'll have the lion's share of your husband's love and attention; you just need to make room for the cubs to come and play every so often.

Remember, stepmothers get their bad press from their tendency to resent their stepchildren. But the man you married is always going to be a parent. Even when his children are grown and on their own, they will always have a prior claim on him. If you can't accept this proposition, you're in for a lot of misery.

Here are some useful tips for protective stepmothers:

- Don't criticize the way your husband raised his children.
- Don't compete with the child's natural mother.
- Don't try too hard and resent it afterwards.
- Don't expect gratitude and recognition for your efforts.
- Don't take anything personally.

And if you're the dad in this situation, you need to think about how to help your new wife accept and enjoy your kids— and how to help your kids to accept and enjoy your new wife. Without you running interference, sometimes it's hard for things even to get underway.

Here are some guidelines for protective fathers who have remarried:

- Leave time in your life to see your kids alone and your wife alone. Don't always throw them together.

- Don't expect your kids or your wife to love each other (or even like each other) right from the start.

- Don't take sides with your children against your wife or with your wife against your children.

- Permit everyone the free expression of *feelings* but insist on appropriate restraints on *behavior*. Your wife can tell *you* your kids are a royal pain in the neck, but not *them*.

- Make sure your wife and your kids feel you have enough love and attention for both of them.

Mine: A Stepfather's Story

In this scenario, you're already a mother and marry a man without children. He becomes your children's *full-time* stepdad. Unless you're a widow, you've divorced your husband, and this means you probably have some negative feelings toward him. Here your job as a protective parent is to remember that while you've chosen a new husband, your children still cherish their old father. A stepfather's role is difficult because he's assuming responsibility for someone else's children, and because many mothers become apprehensive about letting their spouses play an active role in raising their children. It's difficult to live with children full-time, yet feel limited or constrained about participating in the daily decisions of their lives.

As a mother, you're going to need to help your children to accept this new man in their lives without feeling that they're losing you (or their biological father!). Here are some suggestions to help smooth the way:

- Give your children time to learn to live with your new husband and your husband time to live with your children. Don't rush it!

- Expect resentment and antagonism and anxiety from both your kids and your husband. Try not to be upset by negative feelings—they're natural.

- Remember that your husband has never had children, much less any that are not his. Leave room for mistakes.

- Don't make your children choose between their biological father and their stepfather. Let them know they can keep a connection to both of them.

Protective stepfathers need to remember some helpful hints, too:

- Don't try to outdo the children's father.
- Don't discipline the children without their mother's consent and cooperation.
- Don't take charge or take over the children.
- Don't disagree with your wife about her children in front of them.
- Don't take anything personally.

Ours: The Blended Family

When two people with children marry, the complexities are multiplied. Now, not only do you need to learn to live with each other, you've simultaneously got to get *your* children to learn to live with each other. The potential for problems in such situations is greater. For instance, if you're a mom and your children live with you, and his children live with his ex-wife (their mom), your children are likely to see more of your husband than his own children are. This fact alone can cause his kids to feel considerable resentment toward your kids!

A second problem stepfamilies face is that parents often feel more protective of their own children and, in a dispute, may spring to their child's defense. Protective stepparents need to guard against this tendency to play favorites. Children who have lost a parent may face a particularly poignant dilemma if their surviving parent remarries. Sometimes they are able to lay aside their conflicted loyalties and welcome and embrace their new stepparent, but often they hold onto the memory of the dead parent and resent this new version of the mother or father they have lost. The situation can become particularly problematic if the child must not only accept a stepparent but a stepparent with his or her own children. Then the sadness and anger about the child's own parental loss may be displaced onto the stepsiblings.

Problems may start when you both begin to see each other and your children are first thrown together. Sometimes parents forget that, while they have selected one another, their kids have not. If the children are of many varying ages and sexes, the "blend" may turn out to be very complicated indeed. Your new family may now include children ranging in age from two to twenty-two—all with different personalities, interests, and needs. Coping with the dynamics won't be easy. But if your children are few and close in age to each other—a ten-year-old and an eleven-year-old, for instance, or two six-year-olds and an eight-year-old—blending them together can be even harder. Unless your kids take to each other, they may immediately become rivalrous and resentful in the face of their unsought and unwanted instant familial relationships.

Wise parents anticipate difficulties and try to take actions to resolve them as they arise. Here's a new blended family holding a family council to discuss the difficulties they've encountered in melding their families together. The parents are setting down guidelines for co-existence at the same time that they are trying to help each other. The mother has two children—Robin, a six-year-old girl, and Martin, an eight-year-old boy. Her husband, a widower, also has two children—Max, a nine-year-old boy, and another son, Buddy, who is eleven. They have all moved into the wife's home.

NARRATIVE	REPARATIVE ELEMENTS
Mom: We're holding this family council because none of us are happy with the way the family is living together. We have to find a better way.	communication: Here this mother offers important information to her family.
Buddy: You said it! I can't do my homework at night. Martin and Max are always fighting.	
Max: It's not my fault. Martin is such a baby.	

NARRATIVE	REPARATIVE ELEMENTS
MARTIN: I am not!	
ROBIN: He is not!	
MAX: You are too!	
BUDDY: Shut up!	
DAD: See, this is what we mean. We can't even begin a conversation in this family without it turning into a fight. This has got to change. We're going to go around the table and ask everyone what they think the problem is and what they think would help. Buddy, why don't you start?	More COMMUNICATION: Now the father again confirms an important reality. COMPREHENSION: He tries to expand the family's understanding of the situation.
BUDDY: It's Martin and Max. They always get on each other's nerves, and they ruin everything. Max is bossy and Martin doesn't defend himself. He always runs to his mom to protect him.	
MOM: You have some good ideas about what the trouble is. Do you have any good ideas about how to help?	COMPETENCE: Here this mother tries to encourage her stepson to offer a solution.
BUDDY: Max should keep his mouth shut, and Martin shouldn't be such a crybaby.	
MARTIN: I'm not a crybaby. Before Max came, I never cried. I had my own room and things were good.	

NARRATIVE	REPARATIVE ELEMENTS
MOM: It's been the hardest for you because Robin has her own room, and Buddy is older and sleeps in our guest room, but you have to share your room with Max.	COMPASSION: Now this mom offers empathy for her son's feelings.
MARTIN: It's not fair.	
DAD: But your mother and I hoped you and Max would become good friends.	
MAX: I can't be friends with a crybaby.	
ROBIN: He only cries because you pick on him.	
MOM: You and Martin stick together and protect each other. Maybe it's been hard on Max, too, coming into our family. He doesn't really know us well.	MORE COMPASSION: Here the mom offers empathy for her children *and* her stepson.
MAX: When I lived with my mom, she always believed me.	
DAD: So it's been really hard since Mom died. You must feel no one is on your side.	
MAX (*cries*): I want to live in our old house.	
BUDDY: Max, we can't do that. I miss Mom, too, but we live with Dad and Nora now. (*hugs him*) Don't cry.	

NARRATIVE	REPARATIVE ELEMENTS
DAD: It sounds to me like maybe you feel really angry with Martin because he has his mom to protect him. No wonder that makes you sad and mad.	COMPREHENSION and more COMPASSION: Now this dad offers empathy for the real underlying tension in the family. Max's resentment of Martin's relationship with his own mom and sadness about his mother's death, which has him feeling deprived and excluded in his new blended family.
MOM: You know, Max, now that I've had a chance to hear what's been bothering you, I think your dad and I can both help. I know I'm not your mom but I'll try to be fair and listen to you both when you and Martin get into fights.	COMPETENCE: Now, having understood the situation better, this stepmom can reach out to her stepson and offer him a possible resolution with more hope for the future.
DAD: And, maybe you two boys also need some space of your own. I'm going to build a partition in your room, Martin, so you and Max can each have some privacy. But Max, you're going to have to talk to us about your feelings instead of taking them out on Martin.	COMPETENCE: This dad, after comprehending his stepson's resentments and his son's sadness and anger, can offer a possible solution that may offer more hope for the future.

If, down the line, the parents in a second family decide to have children together, it can be a bitter pill for all of the children to swallow. Both sets of children may join forces now and resent these new intruders. It's hard for you, too, not to show more love for the children you have together than for the children each of you had with someone else. After all, the children you share together represent all the hopes and dreams of your new union—without the sadness and despair of old, failed, or fractured liaisons. Remember to spend some special time reassuring each of your children that the birth of a new baby won't ever change your love for them. Remind them that love is *not* like a pie, with a limited number of slices, but that love expands to include everyone in the family.

When I was a little girl, I used to ask my grandmother, who had had six children, to tell me which she loved best—hoping, of course, that she would pick my mother! She would reply by holding up six fingers and saying, "Do you think I love any one of these fingers better than the others? I love them all equally, and if I had four more, I'd love them, too."

No matter what the specific circumstances, if you and your spouse have the strength to pull together and become protective stepparents, your second family can give *you* a second chance at romance and *your child* a chance at living in a family that *works*.

10

Tobacco, Drugs, and Alcohol: Straight Talk About Use and Abuse

Pharmaceutical Living: The American Way

You have a splitting headache, so you take two aspirin; your son takes cough medicine for his scratchy throat; your daughter has hay fever, so you give her an antihistamine; your teenage niece is taking Tetracycline to clear up her acne; your aunt is on hormone replacement therapy for her menopausal symptoms; your husband's treating his athlete's foot with a fungicide; and the doctor just gave you a cortisone shot for your bursitis.

You're afraid to fly, so your best friend gives you a Valium; your stepson studies for his college exams with the help of some "bennies"; a chunky cousin is trying to lose weight with appetite depressants; your mother relaxes when she comes home from work with the help of a vodka and tonic; your father's a heavy smoker; and you and your husband just celebrated your anniversary with a good bottle of champagne.

We all take drugs. We take them throughout our lives, and we take them for all sorts of reasons. We use them to ease our physical pain; we use them to ease our emotional pain. We take drugs when we feel ill, when we feel good, when we're tense, when we're relaxed, when we're sad, and when we're happy. Some of these drugs are prescribed for us by our doctors. But many more of the drugs we take are not prescribed—they're just part of our ordinary repertoire of home remedies. A well-stocked medicine cabinet, like a well-stocked refrigerator, has become part of our way of life. Some of the drugs we take have become so much a part of our lives that we may not even think of them as drugs anymore: the caffeine boost in that cup of morning coffee, the nicotine in your daily cigarettes, the alcohol in your six-pack.

As parents, we may not even be aware of our own kids' substance abuse. We overlook the clues, or, if confronted, deny the evidence, or excuse the behavior. I remember a mother and father who came to consult with me about their twelve-year-old son's behavior. They were concerned that most of his friends were older than he was, and they were beginning to get worried that he was running around with the wrong crowd. They described him as moody and irritable, reported that he seemed to have lost his appetite, and noted that he appeared excitable one moment and exhausted the next. Additionally, these troubled parents reported that "peculiar" things were happening in the house. Some jewelry and their radio had disappeared. Money was missing, and their son had asked for a mirror in his room, but he never hung it up and they kept finding it on the floor! Despite all of these signs clearly pointing to cocaine abuse, these parents were shocked and even angry with me when I suggested it as a real possibility. ("He's only twelve," they insisted. "He's a good boy.") When I confronted this youngster, he confirmed my suspicions and was actually relieved to have someone discover what was going on.

Drugs can save our kids' lives, and drugs can destroy them. It's up to us, as protective parents, to make sure our kids use drugs properly—when they're good medicine. It's also up to us to make sure our kids don't use drugs to short-circuit their own development, as a way to feel strong or cool or bold or smart. Every time you or your child relies on a drug to feel good, you undercut your reliance on yourself. Every time the drug is powerful, you or your child loses power.

Sometimes we forget how pervasive the use of drugs is in our culture. Unless we realize how much we all *use* drugs in our daily lives, we can't begin to understand how easy it is to *abuse* them. Just one more beer ... one more Valium ... who's counting? It's the American way. But this use (and abuse) is not confined only to our country, nor even to modern times. Drug use has a long history in human affairs.

All over the world, in every era, people have cultivated and used drugs—to heighten feelings, to alter consciousness, to celebrate events. Working people have turned to drugs so they could work beyond their endurance. People of all classes have used drugs to deaden their pain. Thousands of soldiers became drug addicts during the Vietnam War, and in the last century, women drank teas and tonics laced with opium derivatives.

Drug use is not confined to the adults of a society, either. In many cultures, drugs mark the adolescent rite of passage. The thirteen-year-old in New Zealand who drinks a fermented beverage to enhance his experience of becoming a man shares this ceremonial use of alcohol with the college freshman who chug-a-lugs beer at his fraternity initiation. Today's teenager who's snorting coke to feel high, or swallowing LSD to "expand his mind," or smoking pot to feel cool, is only a more recent example of a long and extensive human history of drug use and drug abuse.

If this is the case, if drugs are so much a part of our history and our lives, why should parents be so alarmed? What's the difference between this long history and the drug abuse we see around us now?

First, drug use in modern cultures is not confined to shared cultural or religious ceremonies. Modern drug use is not even able to be controlled by the laws of our society, let alone the customs. This means that when it comes to drugs, every kid is on his own. He must decide whether and what, when and where he uses drugs. No adults are around to help him. Second, no culture has ever had the ability to produce the range and complexity of drugs—both legal and illegal—that we have, with so many dangerous effects on the body and on the mind. The array of American drugs is literally mind-boggling.

Third, the effects of many of these drugs are unpredictable and idiosyncratic. This means that, when it comes to drugs, simple curiosity (which is normal for children) can kill. Our kids can experiment with drugs and die! Fourth, much of the drug use parents fear is illegal drug use, and therefore its distribution is directly tied into violence and crime. This means that your kids are at risk by just purchasing illegal drugs—even before using them. And last, but perhaps most important, drugs interfere with psychological development. At the very time in their lives when your kids need to be relying on themselves (their minds and their bodies) to grow and develop, they may be relying on drugs instead. This is what we mean when we say that drugs can be psychologically addictive.

But wait a minute, you may say. If drug use is so common and so widespread, won't all youngsters inevitably experiment, at least with cigarettes or marijuana or alcohol? Does this mean that *all* our kids are doomed to drug abuse and addiction? Isn't there something we can do?

That's what this chapter is all about: to help you help your child make responsible choices about all drugs. The use of drugs may be an integral part of our culture; but the abuse of drugs need not be.

Parents often feel powerless when they begin to think about drugs. But that's because they're trying to think about it on the broad societal level. Parents are aware that they don't have the resources to stem the tide of drugs, or to hold back the hand of organized crime, or to eliminate pushers and drug peddlers. But parents do have enormous power with their own kids, who are the potential customers of the drug trade. Just as you don't have to cure the social problem of rape to ensure that your son doesn't become a rapist, or address the issue of white-collar crime in this country to ensure that your daughter doesn't forge your name to a check, you don't have to cure the problem of drug distribution in this country to prevent your kids from using drugs.

What Should I Ask Myself?

How can we start becoming protective parents about drug abuse? First, we can start where we've always started—at home, with our own attitudes toward drugs. Do you think, for example, that drugs are all right for adults but not adolescents? Do you think *legal* drugs are OK but *illegal* ones are not? Do you think it's fine to use illegal drugs that have so-called "mild" effects on the body—marijuana, for instance—but not "harder" drugs, like heroin? Do you think occasional drug use is all right, but habitual use is bad? Do you think all drug use is dangerous?

Today's youngsters, more than any other generation, are bombarded with media messages that drugs are good, thera-peutic, and necessary to our lives—that they provide a "fast, fast, incredibly fast" solution to all our problems. That means that it's up to us to make sure our kids are prepared to make responsible choices as they grow up and become adults. But before we can begin to talk about drugs with our kids, we have to take a hard look at our own use and abuse of drugs. You can't ask your kids to live by a set of standards that you flout. One of the things we've been emphasizing all along is that children do what we do, not what we say. If you smoke a joint to relax, or take a drink when you're tense, or pop Valium when you're feeling strung out, your kids, no matter how small, are already getting the message that drugs are the way to ease your day and get you through the night.

Since kids learn what they live, long before they become teenagers, your young children already understand that you don't want to feel certain feelings because they're too fright-ening or upsetting. The mom that gives her four-year-old daughter half a sleeping pill so she'll go to sleep without fuss-ing, and the dad who lets his eight-year-old share his beer to calm him down before the Little League game are already teaching their kids to rely on drugs to short-circuit distressing thoughts and feelings.

Children quickly absorb this message. After all, from the time they're toddlers part of their job is to learn the values and standards of your family. They see what you embrace and what you reject, they hear when you say no and when you say yes, and they learn to model their behavior after yours—whether you want them to or not. That's why now is the time to evaluate your own use (or abuse) of tobacco, alcohol, pre-scription medicines and over-the-counter drugs, as well as ille-gal drugs like coke, pot, hash, speed, and the like. If you have no trouble with your children using or abusing any illegal drugs, then you don't have to read any further in this chapter, but if you're concerned, then it's time to take stock of where you stand.

Parents' choices often predict their kids' choices. We now know that a parent's heavy use of tobacco or alcohol vastly increases his or her children's chances of growing up and using them. Further, alcohol addiction tends to run in families, and there may be a physiological vulnerability to its effect that is passed down from one generation to another. This means you have to be particularly alert if you're a problem drinker, because your children are probably already "at risk" for addiction.

Being a Protective Parent

If you use marijuana or cocaine recreationally and think your kids won't know or don't know about it—think again! Very young children see and hear and understand much more than we realize, and older children are alert to any changes in their parent's behavior. Children frequently report all kinds of memories of the drug and alcohol use of their parents. They remember "when Mommy's eyes were bright and she talked fast," "when Daddy couldn't walk up the stairs," "when the bedroom smelled funny," and so on.

Keep in mind, too, that drug and alcohol abuse unpredictably alter a person's personality. This is particularly frightening for children, since this makes it hard for them to trust or depend on the parent, and adds to their anxiety about the safety of their world.

This entire book is about helping you to become a protective parent—a parent who is willing to recognize real problems in the real world, who finds ways to enable your kids to recognize these problems, and who strengthens your children *early* in their lives to develop the resources to manage later on. This means practicing prevention—building understanding and mastery into your child's life all along the way, as your child grows. Protective parents help shield their kids from danger right from the beginning. And drugs are dangerous.

What you say now and what you do now, when your children are still young, will largely determine how they cope with drugs as they become older. As protective parents, you can start off by making three crucial distinctions for your young children:

- You can help them understand the difference between medicine and drugs.
- You can tell them what's legal and what's illegal.
- You can explain what's appropriate for adults and what's appropriate for children.

Now that you're a parent, it's time for you to take a hard look at kicking your own habits. Let your children know that you regret your addiction. Warn them about your own experiences and demonstrate some effort to change. Here's a typical exchange a smoking parent might have with any child who's curious and concerned.

MARSHA: Why do you smoke, Daddy?

FATHER: Smoking is a really bad habit, but once you begin it's very hard to stop. I started when I was a teenager, and back then I didn't realize how bad smoking was. I've been trying to cut down my cigarette smoking, and I don't smoke in the house around you because I don't want you to breathe smoke. I hope I'll be able to stop soon. But it's not easy to give up a habit when you're used to it. That's why the best way to stop smoking is never to start. I hope you'll never, never be as foolish as I was, now that we know how bad smoking really is for your body.

Cigarettes, Marijuana, and Alcohol: The "Gateway Drugs"

If you only have trouble with your children using "hard" drugs, but don't mind them smoking cigarettes, having a few beers, or passing a joint, then you should know that drug experts don't share your point of view. The pre-teenage and teenage use of alcohol, nicotine, and marijuana are seen as dangerous precursors to more serious abuse. These three drugs in particular are often described as "gateway drugs"— drugs that can start kids off on abuse and "open the gate" to more sustained and more serious addiction.

While many parents don't even consider alcohol a drug, it is in fact our most widely used and abused drug. Almost five million of our teenagers have drinking problems, and alcohol-related accidents (most of them drunk driving) are a leading cause of death for teenagers and young adults. The statistics for adult alcoholism are equally sobering (pun intended). Alcohol abuse is the fourth-largest health problem in this country, right up there with heart disease and cancer (both of which, incidentally, have important links to the abuse of alcohol).

Cigarettes have equally devastating effects on health. Smoking is a leading contributor to death among adults, most of whom started smoking as teenagers. Nicotine, the active ingredient in tobacco, is as addictive as heroin—as anyone who has ever tried to stop smoking can tell you. How many of us who are trying to stop smoking now fervently wish that we had never started smoking as kids?

And these days, kids don't wait until they're teenagers to experiment with smoking. School-age youngsters (ages ten to thirteen) are already at risk for nicotine addiction. Most children try cigarettes before they have reached high school. By the time these kids are in high school, almost one quarter of them have already become addicted smokers. Yet each and every cigarette pack carries a message that indicates that smoking is hazardous to your health! Why don't they pay attention? Why don't we?

Worse, smoking tobacco is not the only addiction that our kids are exposed to in early adolescence. For most of them (as for most of us when we were their age), marijuana is easily available and commonly used. Many youngsters even smoke pot in the mistaken notion that it's "healthier" for them than tobacco.

We have to keep in mind that children yearn to become

adults, and most youngsters get their first exposure to forbidden "adult pleasures" through teenage smoking and teenage drinking. Many of them will never develop a taste for either, some will develop a dependence on one or both that will last their entire lives, and others will go on to deepen and broaden their experimentation to include an exposure and addiction to much more dangerous drugs—drugs that will damage both their psychological and physiological development. The earlier the addiction, the more likely that a child will have later psychological and physical problems, including early death. As protective parents, then, we want to help our kids turn away from cigarettes and alcohol well before they become adolescents. How can we do that?

Prevention: Paving the Way to Protection

Just as we saw that sex education needs to begin in early childhood, so, too, that is the time to begin drug education. Unfortunately, many parents still believe that they don't have to deal with either sex or drugs until their kids become teenagers. That is too late! And even more important, adolescence is the *worst* time to begin to educate your kids. For one thing, we all know that teenagers are the least likely to listen to their parents and the most likely to be influenced by their peers. They're not being deliberately difficult; breaking away from your parents' influence is normal in adolescence. It helps adolescents to begin the extended and difficult separation from their families and prepares them to move out into the world. They have to make their own choices and their own mistakes at this age. That's why your basic attitudes and values must be transmitted to your children much earlier—in the years between three and twelve, when your children are still eager to learn from adults and still responsive to your direction. Drug education nowadays deserves the same attention you would give sex education, and it needs the same cumulative approach we've been discussing—an approach that calls for laying a foundation early on, and then sharing appropriate bits of information more and more as your child grows older.

Protective parents need to keep four basic principles of drug education in mind. You must:

- Begin early to educate your children to the dangers of drugs.
- Set down a foundation that can be built upon throughout childhood.
- Convey your values clearly to your children when they are still young enough to want to hear them.
- Set the example that you want your kids to follow.

So far, we've been talking about why you need to talk to your young kids about drugs. Now we need to see how and when you should begin these talks. This is where our understanding of the special stories we've been calling reparative narratives can be useful to you.

Think about the four C's: compassion, communication, comprehension, and competence. Remain interested and nonjudgmental if you want to keep the lines of communication open and have an effect on your kids. And be sure to use your understanding of the five basic fears to help you reach your child effectively. Drug abuse hurts your child's body and sense of self. It conjures up the fears of the unknown and it stimulates fears of the voice of conscience. You need to help your child to appreciate the dangers that lie ahead.

Begin by giving your kids information right at the beginning, and keep updating and expanding that knowledge as your child grows and can absorb and comprehend more. *Don't wait for your child to mention drugs.* Don't assume that because your kids don't talk or ask questions about drug use or abuse, it doesn't affect their lives. The media—ads, books, television, video, movies, and plays—and real life are filled with examples of alcoholism, smoking, and drug abuse. In fact, close to home, among your family and friends, there are probably several adults who are abusing drugs at this very moment. Some children *will* ask you questions about drug use or abuse. But if they don't, take the initiative and "jump start" the conversation with them. Here's how you can create a reparative narrative that could help draw your young child (four to eight years old) into a discussion of alcohol abuse. This mother is using an experience with a family member.

DEREK: Why is Uncle Roger so mean?

NARRATIVE	REPARATIVE ELEMENTS
MOTHER: I know you were really upset that Uncle Roger was so angry and bad-tempered when we all went out for dinner. That's because he has an alcohol problem. Did you notice that he had four or five drinks, while the rest of us only had one or none? Uncle Roger's an *alcoholic.*	COMPASSION: This mother begins with an empathic statement.
Alcoholism is a kind of disease where people drink too much but they can't stop themselves. What makes it worse is that many people who are alcoholics refuse to believe they have a drinking problem, so they won't get help. Aunt Anita is trying very hard to help Uncle Roger to get help.	COMMUNICATION: She offers her son information and confirms the reality of alcoholism for him. COMPETENCE: She tells her son about a possible outcome for the problem.
Alcoholics lose their tempers a lot, too, which is hard for everyone in Uncle Roger's family. Too much alcohol is very bad for your body. It not only makes you feel sick, it also makes you get sick.	COMPREHENSION: As she develops her narrative, she tries to help her child understand the situation better.

Here's another reparative narrative that could help you to jump start a conversation about teenage marijuana use with your child:

MIMI: Why was Nick's mom crying?

NARRATIVE	REPARATIVE ELEMENTS
DAD: She's really worried about Nicholas. He's been smoking marijuana a lot with his friends, and it's really ruining his life. He used to be a terrific basketball player, and he was a very good math student, too.	COMPASSION: This father opens the conversation with an empathic statement.
But marijuana can make people lose their interest and their energy. The more they smoke it, the less they want to do anything else. He's been cutting classes in school now and not coming home at night on time. Instead, he's been hanging out with his friends who also smoke marijuana. Because you smoke it like cigarettes, marijuana can also cause lung cancer and other diseases, so his mom is really worried about him.	COMMUNICATION: He offers his daughter more information about the event, and confirms the hard realities of drug abuse.
But it's hard to get Nicholas to listen to his parents because sometimes teenagers think they know everything. They think they can take care of themselves and they don't need their parents.	COMPREHENSION: He uses the reparative narrative to expand his daughter's understanding of the situation.

NARRATIVE	REPARATIVE ELEMENTS
Nicholas's mom is going to try to take him to a special center for kids who are addicted to drugs. She hopes they'll be able to help Nick.	COMPETENCE: The end of the narrative lets his daughter know there's a resolution for this drug problem that offers some hope for the future.

Remember, although young children are not yet ready (or interested in) a sophisticated assessment of drug use and abuse, they can still listen and learn a lot about life from narratives like the two I have just outlined. Try to base your narratives on real-life stories about real people that your children know—or if you can't do that, use public figures that they've heard about or seen on television. That makes it easier for them to get the message. (There will probably be no shortage of examples!)

In order to help your kids to make responsible decisions about drug use as they get older, you need to help them to make responsible decisions *now* about what they take into their bodies. Even very young children are called upon all the time to decide whether something is clean or dirty, safe or poisonous, or whether the person offering the food or drink is to be trusted. If you want your teenager to "say no to drugs," you've got to instill in your young child all along appropriate habits of caution about eating or drinking. Our understanding of the five basic fears tells us that very young children (two to four years old) are often afraid that something could happen to their bodies. So that's where your drug education for a young child needs to begin: with the body—by teaching your child what's safe to swallow and what's not.

You have probably already taught your kids to recognize and stay away from poisons in the house, such as bleach, cleaning fluid, furniture polish, and so on. At this age, you can use your child's normal fears about his body to help him make thoughtful decisions about what to swallow. The challenge is to be careful not to make him so worried that he becomes phobic and wary about food and drink. We already know that there's a big difference between protecting your kids and frightening them. Here's a mom who doesn't know the difference.

HEATHER: Can I buy some gummy bears from the man with the cart, Mommy?

MOM: Yuck! That candy looks disgusting, and it's been out there all day. Who knows how many people with filthy hands and terrible germs have touched it or breathed on it. Never, ever eat anything unless Mommy gets it. We can't tell what awful disease you could pick up.

This mom is trying to teach her child to be alert to the possible dangers of street food, but she's more likely to have scared than educated her child. The messages she's sending are too harsh: Don't trust anyone but Mom; people are filthy; food is filled with germs; you can get terrible diseases. Her child may pay too high an emotional price for what should have been an ordinary caution. This mom isn't being a protective parent, she's being an overprotective parent.

Here's another way to approach the same situation:

NOAH: Can I buy some gummy bears from the man with the cart, Mommy?

MOM: Let's see, honey. This candy doesn't look very fresh, does it? And look at the man's dirty hands. But I know you really want gummy bears. Let's go into the supermarket and see if we can find some in packages. They may not be exactly the same, but at least they'll be clean.

This mom is also trying to help her child be alert to the possible dangers of street food but, she's educating her child to make decisions on his own—to become self-reliant: Does the candy look fresh? Does the man have clean hands? She's creating an atmosphere of caution, not catastrophe.

Such a discussion helps children think about what they put into their bodies. Further, young children still listen to adults and look to them for help in making decisions. They can understand important distinctions like good and bad, safe and dangerous, clean and dirty. Helping them to make these distinctions now about food, helps them to make similar distinctions about drugs, later.

By the time your child is five to ten years old, he will spend most of his days in school. Now he's listening to other adults besides you and is beginning to be capable of "playing by the rules." This is the time to start talking about the difference between what's permitted for adults and what's permitted for children. It is also the best time to begin to raise questions of what's legal and what's illegal. Such conversations will be effective now, because a child of this age has developed a "conscience," and the fear of the voice of conscience is developmentally available to him. This is the age to try to help your five-to-ten-year-old become aware of what's right and what's wrong. Children this age can comprehend both keeping to and breaking the law. They are naturally curious and bolder than younger children and they are capable of both lying and keeping secrets—actions that indicate that they have begun to live a life separate from you and away from your direct supervision. All of these developmental accomplishments make your discussions about drug use and abuse more important than ever. Children need your help to consolidate the voice of conscience, so that they can act on their own behalf. They need you to shore up this inner voice in a steady and reasonable way.

Now is also a good time to emphasize the family's rules about behavior and to underscore what's permissible in your family and what's not. But remember that we want to encourage responsible autonomy—not blind obedience. Your children are going to need to feel strong enough and competent enough to make up their own minds when you're not there to help them. If you don't let them exercise their options to say no now, within the family circle—and have their decisions respected—they are unlikely to have the strength to say no later, in their circle of friends. A child trained to blind obedience within the family may later transfer that same blind obedience outside the family to a gang or a cult.

The next developmental stage, the preteen years (ten to twelve years old), are the most critical years for drug education. This is when smoking and drinking become linked to the forbidden pleasures of adult life—when it seems cool to be reckless and when the temptations and excitement of adolescence are just around the corner. Children of this age are already beginning to reject their parents' values, affection, and attention in favor of their peers, and studies have shown that they are at the greatest risk for drug abuse. Further, children who begin to smoke and drink at this early age remain at risk for more sustained drug abuse later on. At this stage everything is changing in your child's life—his body, his mind, his sense of self. Changes increase anxiety and anxiety interferes with functioning. If you're a kid who isn't functioning you don't feel good about yourself, and if you don't feel good about yourself you are more at risk for drug use and abuse. That's what makes this such a vulnerable time.

By the preteen years, your child is preoccupied with the new adolescent concerns about the self. He has become more capable of abstract reasoning and can observe and judge events and their consequences. This is a good time to talk about the *downside* of drug use. (He will have picked up the glamorous side from his friends, movies, television, advertisements, songs, books, and so on.) Now he needs to know more specific details about smoking, alcohol, and drug abuse: the names of all the drugs; their effects on the body; the short- and long-term consequences of use; and the profound toll that illegal drug abuse takes on our society, including its relationship to violent crime.

With preteens, pay attention to the relationship between drug abuse and car accidents, the damaging influence of substance abuse on school performance and sports achievement, and the possible fatal effects of combining drugs. Youngsters need to be particularly warned about the unpredictability of drugs bought on the streets and the idiosyncratic and dangerous reactions of each individual to drugs. (The unexpected drug deaths of young, famous personalities are relevant examples of this danger.)

Don't try to focus too much on the future with children this age. They have no interest in moral lectures and only a limited understanding of their own mortality. Instead, talk about the present—what's here and now. Talk about the potential for their loss of power and control over themselves; the interference with achievements they want; the effects upon their moods; the potential damage to the body's organs, including the brain; the accidental deaths.

Youngsters are particularly vulnerable to drug use in pre-adolescence and early adolescence because they ordinarily feel upset, disturbed, inadequate, shy, nervous, sad, worried, and so on a great deal of the time. Because the normal developmental tasks of adolescence (separation from parents, transformations of the body, hormonal changes with their attendant mood swings, and consolidation of psychological and sexual identity) are so difficult to manage, every adolescent is under emotional strain. Teenage drug use is often an attempt *to self-medicate against the pain of growing up.* Protective parents, alert to the ordinary blues of adolescence, can help prepare their kids to deal with this difficult phase of life without leaning on drugs to take the edge off their experience.

Can Kids "Just Say No"?

Many parents are so frightened of drugs that they refuse to face up to the fact that most teenagers in our culture will inevitably try tobacco, alcohol, or drugs—or all three. While blanket prohibitions of drugs, alcohol, and cigarettes may sound good in the media ("Just say no") they rarely deter youngsters from experimentation. This is because most drugs become dangerous (either psychologically or physiologically) over time, and their often profoundly destructive effects are initially hidden. Adolescents are good at not thinking about their future, anyway, and unless they've had a close encounter with danger through their own or a friend's experience, many tend to deny the dangers of drugs. But again, remember, there's a big difference between short-term experimentation with "gateway" drugs and shooting up with heroin. Parents need to take a firm line against drug use but not panic if they find out that their child has crossed it. The important thing is to prevent initial experimentation from becoming a habitual, chronic dependency. To do this, you've got to keep the lines of communication and connection open.

There are three kinds of drugs, both legal and illegal, that many of us depend on in our daily lives—drugs that help us feel *up* (stimulated, high, excited); drugs that help us come *down* (calm, chilled out, relaxed); and drugs that help us feel *different* (weird, far-out, altered). Many drugs fit into more than one category, or change categories with prolonged use. (For example, alcohol can start as an "upper" and become a "downer," and marijuana can both relax you and alter your consciousness.) The more you know and learn about the effects of the drugs that are available to your children, the better prepared you'll be to discuss their experiences with them and caution and counsel them.

While my focus is not on drugs themselves, but on how to talk to kids about drugs, I think it's important for you to know some of the most popular drugs, their street names, and their common effects. (See the table on page 224.)

In addition to these, illegal drugs called "Designer Drugs" are available on the street (ecstasy, essence, killer weed, angel dust, PCP, etc.).

Feeling Better or Getting Better?

We all want our children to feel good and to be happy all the time. But that's not real life. Real life is filled with ups *and* downs, pain *and* pleasure, success *and* failure. To be truly protective parents, we must help our children learn to face what life will bring them. If we have not prepared them to manage hard times as well as good times, we have not done our job. We need to help our kids to understand that, just as physical pain is the body's warning signal that something is wrong, emotional pain helps us to understand that something is wrong inside our minds. Yes, we can take a shot of novocaine and we won't feel the cavity in our tooth, but unless the cavity is filled the pain will return the minute the novocaine wears off. Similarly, we can smoke pot so we won't feel anxious at

STIMULANTS (to bring you *up* or make you feel high)	NARCOTICS (to bring you *down* or make you relax)	HALLUCINOGENS (to take you *out* or alter your consciousness)
1. *Amphetamines* (street names: ups, uppers, pep pills, speed, sleeping beauties, bumble bees, bennies)	1. *Opiates:* Heroin, Codeine, Morphine, Opium (street names: smack, horse, skag, sugar)	1. *Lysergic Acid Diethylamide* (street names: LSD, acid, white lightning, blue heaven, micro dot, sugar cubes)
2. *Methamphetamines* (street names: crystal, meth, crank)	2. *Barbiturates:* Nembutal, Seconal, Amytal, or *Tranquilizers:* Valium, Librium, Equanil, etc. (street names: downers, yellow jackets, barbs, ludes, tranks)	2. *Mescaline and Peyote* (street names: mesc, buttons)
3. *Cocaine* (street names: coke, snow, crack, nose candy, flake, blow, white, free base)		3. *Psilocybin* (street names: magic mushrooms, 'shrooms, blotters)
4. *Inhalants* (street names: poppers, rush, glue, snappers, whippets, rush, bolt)		4. *Cannabis: Marijuana* (street names: pot, grass, weed, Mary Jane, reefer) *Hashish* (street name: hash)

night, but unless we address those anxious thoughts, they'll return the next night to haunt us.

The idea of our children feeling pain is difficult for us. How many times have we wished we could shield them from fear or worry or sadness or even obliterate these experiences? This wish for oblivion—to feel no pain—lies at the base of a great deal of drug abuse. People who become addicts are often people who have never been helped to develop the strength to cope with pain of any kind—disappointment, frustration, anger, fear, insecurity, despair, sadness, rage. So when they feel any of these emotions, they look for a way to obliterate their feelings, rather than modify or master them.

Mastering pain, like anything else in life, takes practice, and you have to begin to practice early. Here's an example of a mom who is unable to let her seven-year-old child suffer, even in a small way, so that he can begin to learn and grow:

TODD (*crying*): I'm not going to school. I hate school. No one likes me. No one wants to play with me.

MOM: My poor sweetheart. It sounds like you're having a bad time. But I bet it's not so awful. Most of the time you like school, and I'm sure you have lots of friends. Stop crying, and I'll make you a chocolate milkshake.

While this mom is surely loving and may have helped her child to "cheer up" in the short run, she's also given her child some other messages:

- Don't address the real issues.
- Don't face your fears.
- Turn to food or drink to make you feel better.

Here's a protective parent helping her child to face the same issue—and develop some real strengths to deal with the real pain:

JAMAL (*crying*): I'm not going to school. I hate school! No one likes me. No one wants to play with me.

Mom: Some days it just seems as if everything's going wrong. Let's figure this out. Did something happen yesterday that makes you so unhappy today?

Jamal: We're learning baseball and no one wanted me on their team, because I stink.

Mom: I can understand why you wouldn't want to face the kids today. You're good at lots of other things, but baseball is what counts now. You know, if you really want to get better at sports, you have to work at it. Up to now, you haven't been too interested. But now it sounds as if you may be. I used to play baseball on my high school team. I could show you some things I know. We could play after school tomorrow and practice so you feel more confident.

What's the message this mom has given her child? When you're unhappy, it's important to:

- Address the real issue, instead of trying to obliterate it.
- Face your real fears and failures.
- Empower yourself.

Helping your child to bear what seems unbearable to him is one of the most important jobs a protective parent can accomplish. In the first example, the mom focused her energy on helping her child to *feel better;* in the second, the mom was able to help her child to *get better*—a far more important accomplishment. Building strength to deal with hard times will not only help your child to get through them; it will help him get through them without relying on drugs.

Drug use may be a moral issue in our society, but for protective parents, drug use is more importantly a psychological issue. Every time your son takes a drink to overcome his shyness at a school dance, he's learning to rely on alcohol as a "quick cure" for his problems; every time your daughter smokes pot before an exam, she's learning to rely on drugs to make her feel more competent. The kinds of drugs we use (or want to use) indicate what we are trying to change in our sense of ourselves. Youngsters who basically feel good about themselves are less likely to turn to drugs than youngsters who feel upset, disturbed, inadequate, enraged, or depressed.

Youngsters need to be told directly about the effects drugs are likely to have on their minds and bodies. Here's a narrative that a parent might use to discuss drug use with a pre-adolescent (ten to twelve years old) child:

NARRATIVE	REPARATIVE ELEMENTS
MOM: You know, you're getting old enough for us to be talking about all the different drugs you're likely to hear about or see kids using. We've already talked about our strong feelings about smoking and how bad it is for your body and yet kids do it anyway. Well, the same thing is true about drugs.	COMMUNICATION: This parent starts out confirming her son's reality, and offering information about her feelings.
Some kids will be asking you to drink or smoke dope, or maybe even to sniff cocaine or take pills. You know we feel strongly that drugs, particularly street drugs that are illegal, are very, very dangerous. They're not good for your body or for your mind. They can even be poison. Some kids die from bad drugs. We've encouraged you to make your own decisions and to trust yourself.	COMPREHENSION: She lets her son know she understands the situation he faces.

NARRATIVE	REPARATIVE ELEMENTS
We know you wouldn't risk your life on something as stupid as an illegal drug. But some kids will. They'll think it's cool to be reckless, or to break the law. If you're with someone like that, you'll need to be strong enough to resist the temptation to join in, even if it costs you his friendship.	COMPASSION: Here, she makes an empathic statement, while continuing to confirm reality.
If you can't resist, walk away from the group—and whatever you do, never be afraid to tell us about it. We're here to help you.	COMPETENCE: She opens up a possible outcome to her son and emphasizes a resolution that includes ongoing communication.

If your child's friends or his neighborhood offer a lot of temptations, you'll need to be especially protective. Talk with your kids about ways of refusing to participate that don't make him sound like a "goody-goody" or a "chicken." Most ten- to twelve-year-olds can still use their parents' rules and curfews as viable excuses to absent themselves from high-risk behavior ("I can't stay. I've got to get home by the time it's dark or my dad will kill me!" or "My mom freaks out if she smells smoke on my clothes!").

As your child grows up, he naturally grows away from you. His friends, his relatives, his teachers, books, television, movies may all expose him to perspectives that are different from yours. You want your child's life to be enriched by this exposure, but you also want your child to keep coming back to you to discuss confusing or contradictory information. That's why we've been emphasizing the importance of knowing what you should tell your kids all along. Remember, when it comes to drugs, what your child doesn't know can not only hurt him—it could actually kill him!

11

Tough Topics in Today's Times—AIDS, Homosexuality, Abuse, and Incest

When we were growing up, our parents may have bolstered their courage to talk to us about sex, but they didn't have to include incest, abuse, homosexuality, or AIDS in their conversation. Today our children inevitably see more, hear more, and know more about the ways of the world than we ever did, but their new knowledge can be overwhelming and difficult to absorb. Protective parents need to be particularly mindful of the meanings this kind of information can have for a child, and particularly alert to its impact on ongoing development. We need to make sure that we neither overprotect our children (depriving them of information they need) nor overexpose them (asking them to cope with information before they can understand it).

Talking About AIDS: A Matter of Life and Death

As your children grow older they will begin to ask questions about things they've heard about that seem "strange" or "dirty" to them. How can we begin to tell a ten-year-old about anal sex or sadomasochism? And what about the most fearful consequence of sexuality in today's times—AIDS? The worries we all had growing up (of pregnancy, or herpes, or even syphylis and gonorrhea) are dwarfed by the present fear of the sexual transmission of HIV infection and the possibility of contracting AIDS. For the first time, our children will grow up linking ordinary sexuality with the possibility of *death*. This single fact has irrevocably and completely changed all of our sexual attitudes. It has made our job as protective parents, particularly as parents of pre-adolescent children, much more crucial. And it has made talking to our kids about actual sexual practices literally a matter of life or death.

By the time your child has become school age, she will have been exposed to the deaths of famous personalities, a barrage of public service announcements about practicing safe sex, and school or community programs devoted to AIDS. She may even know someone who has died of AIDS among her friends or within her own family. She may have seen magazines, books, or plays that deal with AIDS. Nevertheless, it will still fall to you to help her to assimilate all of this disturbing information and to address her underlying concerns.

Your understanding of the five basic fears will tell you that AIDS draws on all of them. Fear of the unknown is heightened when we have an illness as deadly and as mysterious as AIDS. Fear of being alone is stimulated by the intense stigma associated with this virus and the phobic reactions of other people. Fears about the body are central to the physical devastation of AIDS. Fear of the voice of conscience is heightened by the popular association of the transmission of the virus with forbidden sexual practices—promiscuity, homosexuality—or drug abuse. And finally, of course, your child's fears about the self are underscored by the reality of the disease—living a life in which your sense of self is under constant siege by the persistent threat of illness or death.

Many parents feel that they can protect their children best by not talking to them about sex until they are old enough to have sex. They feel "ignorance is bliss." But this doesn't work. For one thing, adolescence is not limited to the teenage years (ages thirteen to nineteen). It is a complicated and extended phase of life accompanied by psychological and developmental changes that begin to take place much earlier: Children from nine to twelve years old are already enmeshed in the struggles and tasks of pre-adolescence. Love, sexuality, and AIDS have a special relevance for your older children because these themes have already directly touched their lives. Their bodies and their minds are already undergoing the transformations that will ultimately prepare them to move out into the world as loving, sexually mature people. If your child is nine or ten, now is the time to lay down a foundation that will make this possible.

But there's another reason why it is too late if you wait until adolescence to talk to your children about these modern dangers. Developmentally speaking, adolescents *need* to refute and rebel against their parents' wisdom. Otherwise, how do they learn to leave home? They are often quite willing to experiment with drugs, with sex, with pain, with aggression, with danger—and more important, they believe themselves invincible. They are, by nature, risk-takers. (That's why veteran military officers say that adolescent boys make the best soldiers.) Adolescents often don't stop and think; they don't look before they leap! So, early preventive education—at the time when your children are still young enough to take in what you say and make it part of their own thinking—is so important. Protective parenting dictates straight talk in these crucial years. You need to be prepared to discuss not only love and sex with your kids but also the psychological, moral, and ethical meaning of these experiences—and the medical risks. Your child's early absorption of your values will help her hold the line against the later dangers of adolescence.

With the emergence of AIDS, today's adolescents are facing more risk than ever before. Each unprotected sexual act exposes them not only to any viruses their partner may carry but also to the viruses carried by their partner's previous partners—the risk is manifold. Each time they engage in unsafe sex, they are playing a dangerous game of Russian roulette. It is hard to convey this sense of imminent danger to a teenager who thinks she's immortal. So the best time to begin is *now*—by starting to talk to your three-year-old about not going anywhere with strangers, by telling your five-year-old about the privacy of her body, by teaching your seven-year-old to discriminate between trustworthy and untrustworthy people, and by helping your nine-year-old to use all of this cumulative information to protect herself. Here's how a contemporary mother might talk to her eleven-year-old son about love, sex and AIDS:

NARRATIVE	REPARATIVE ELEMENTS
MOM: When you grow up and you're old enough to love someone and want to have sex with them, you'll need to be very careful to protect yourself from catching the AIDS virus.	COMMUNICATION: This mom is confirming an important reality.
JOSH: How do you get it?	
MOM: AIDS is a blood disease, and the AIDS virus is present in our bodily fluids, particularly our blood. That's why some people caught it by getting blood transfusions before we knew about it and could screen blood like we do now to make sure it isn't infected. That's why drug-users who share needles can catch AIDS, too. But the next easiest way to catch the virus is in seminal fluid. That's why it's so important for a man to use a condom, because the condom catches the semen in a little balloon which fits over the penis.	More COMMUNICATION and COMPREHENSION: Now she's offering her son important information. She also is helping him to understand the entire situation.
JOSH: That's so silly. All the kids laugh about condoms.	

NARRATIVE	REPARATIVE ELEMENTS
MOM: It does seem a little silly, but it has a serious purpose. When you use a condom, semen doesn't go into the woman's body. Condoms also prevent a woman from getting pregnant. And they protect the man, too, because women can have the virus, and the man can catch it from having unprotected intercourse.	COMPASSION and COMPETENCE: Here this mom empathizes with her son's feelings of awkwardness, while offering him a resolution that helps him feel more in control.

Talking About Homosexuality

The AIDS epidemic also raises questions about homosexuality for children because the media have emphasized that the gay community is at risk for infection. Unfortunately, the choice to love someone of your own sex is not a neutral choice in our culture. Homosexuals are subject to social prejudice; they are the subject of jokes; and now, as one of the high-risk populations affected by the AIDS epidemic, they are the focus of aggressive homophobic reactions. A ten- or eleven-year-old is aware of associations of AIDS with homosexuality. If anyone they know and love is gay, they may be particularly worried; if a parent is gay, they may become terrified. Because of the AIDS epidemic, a child is faced with fears of the unknown, the body, the conscience, and the self in a new way when a parent is gay.

But even if they don't know anyone who is gay, children can still ask questions like "Is homosexuality inherited?" or "Will I be homosexual?" or "Will I get AIDS?" When your child asks these kinds of questions, you have an opportunity to talk to her about different outcomes of development and different personal choices. Here's how a parent might discuss these issues with a nine- to eleven-year-old child:

RAMONA: How do you get to be a homosexual, Mommy? Can children be homosexual?

NARRATIVE	REPARATIVE ELEMENTS
MOM: Some people who are homosexual have always felt that they were different, even when they were children. Others may not realize they're homosexual until they're teenagers or adults. Some people believe homosexuality is inherited, like blue eyes or black hair, and others think that gay men and women learn to be gay as they grow up and choose to have sex with someone just like them.	COMMUNICATION and COMPREHENSION: Here this mother is confirming an important reality for her child and helping her to understand a complicated situation.

If a child asks about why gay men are at risk for AIDS, a contemporary father could reply:

NARRATIVE	REPARATIVE ELEMENTS
DAD: Men who are gay and infected with the virus can give the disease to each other through oral or anal intercourse. Anal intercourse is particularly dangerous because little blood vessels in the anus often break, and that's how many gay men became infected with the virus.	COMMUNICATION: Here, this father is explaining an important reality to his child.
MARCO: But only gay men get it, right?	

NARRATIVE	REPARATIVE ELEMENTS
DAD: No, anyone can get AIDS. That's why everyone talks about practicing *safe sex*, where men always use condoms. But it's really only *safer sex*, because the only way to be absolutely safe is not to have intercourse at all. That's why it's so important to know a lot about your partner before you ever decide to have a sexual relationship.	COMPREHENSION and COMPETENCE: Now he's enlarging his son's understanding of the situation, and helping him to find a resolution.
MARCO: I'm *never* going to have sex.	
DAD: I can see you're worried, but someday I hope you'll fall in love, and then you'll want to have a sexual relationship. That's an important decision. Having intercourse with someone means getting very, very close to them. You need to be careful about whom you get close to. You should love them and trust them before you decide to have sex with them.	COMPASSION: Here, this dad empathizes with his son's feelings, but again, offers hope for the future.

You may also want to reassure your child many times about the specific way people become infected with the HIV virus—particularly your younger child. There is still a lot of misinformation out there about the transmission of the disease. Here's a mom responding to her seven-year-old daughter's concerns:

CATHERINE: Can I catch AIDS, Mommy?

MOM: You know that we can all catch viruses that cause colds and flu through drinking from another person's glass or having someone sneeze or cough on us. Well, you can't catch the AIDS virus that way. You can only catch it through infected blood or through having sex with someone who has the virus.

It's important for modern youngsters to know that it has always been possible to catch diseases through sexual intercourse, but that the AIDS epidemic has brought a new dimension to our anxieties:

"When you let another person come inside your body—or when you come inside another person's body—you share bodily fluids with them, and you can catch whatever viruses they may have. We can catch herpes, warts, or syphilis through sex. But now, it's even more serious: We can catch AIDS. There's a big difference, because you can die from AIDS. We don't know how to cure the virus yet. That's why it's so important to keep your body safe."

Here are some important injunctions a protective parent would want to share with a pre-adolescent child:

- Wait to have sex until you're old enough to make important choices. You can get sick and even die if you make the wrong choice.
- Don't have sex with anyone you don't know or trust.
- Even if you know and trust your partner, find out as much as you can about their sexual experiences, and make sure they haven't used intravenous drugs, *before* you have sex.
- Use safe sex practices: Always, always use a condom, so that you're protected not only against pregnancy and diseases but against the HIV infection.
- If you have any doubts, *don't*!

If your older child asks you a question you are unable to answer ("How do birth control pills work?"), or something you haven't thought about ("Can children be gay?"), or something that you are embarrassed to answer ("How do women have sex with each other?"), you can always buy time to consider your reply by saying, "That's a very important question, but I don't know the answer. We'll need to find out." Or "I need to find out about it first, and then we'll talk." Or "That's an interesting and complicated question. I need some time to figure it out." Or "I'd like to think about that for a while before we talk some more." Also tell your children that sex is a very big topic, and people have a lot of different feelings about it. You're telling them what *you* think and feel, but other people may think and feel differently—kids and adults, too. Grandma may not even believe that kids should know anything about sex!

Remember, you don't have to talk about everything with your kids. You have a right to privacy, too. If a child asks a question about sex that you don't feel is appropriate to answer, like "Do you and Daddy have oral sex?" or "When do you and Mommy make love?" or "Have you ever had an affair?" you can reply, "My sexual life is private," or "I can try to answer all your questions about sex. But what I do and what Daddy does is our private business."

Similarly, you need to respect your child's need for privacy. Children should not be put under constant scrutiny, or relentlessly questioned, or exposed to experiences they do not choose for themselves. Sometimes it is hard for parents to know what to show a child and what should remain private. For example, while it is obvious that most children will see their parents nude in the course of ordinary family life, making a point of displaying your body to your child may not produce that wholesome acceptance you're aiming for. In fact, in some children, it can produce the opposite. One family of confirmed nudists were astonished to find their six-year-old son dressing and undressing in the closet—the only way he could establish a sense of separation and privacy for himself in his "let-it-all-hang-out family"!

A final way to address your child's developmental needs for information, yet shield him from overexposure, is to be alert to the signs that your child is "on overload"—glazed eyes, distracted attention, fidgety feet. When you see these signs, your child is signaling you that he's had it—that's enough conversation!

Private Parts, Secret Stories: Talking to Kids About Incest and Abuse

It is very hard to explain to a child how sex can be used to punish or hurt someone when we've been trying all along to link it with love and pleasure. But the frequency of sexual abuse is a constant reminder of how much damage and danger there is in ourselves and our world. As protective parents, we want to help our children to recognize the differences between people—between good and bad, kind and cruel, healthy and sick. We want to help our kids to make judgments about these differences that will keep them safe. This means preparing them to think for themselves when they are still very young.

Consequently, parents today often feel as if they're walking a tightrope between telling their kids too much and not enough, between teaching them to trust other people and teaching them to stay on guard, between helping them learn about love and helping them learn about fear. One of the first warnings that parents give to their children is about strangers. The need for caution around strangers is highlighted even in many of the stories and fairy tales we read and pass down from one generation to the next. Little Red Riding Hood, for example, is a cautionary tale about strangers.

In our new world, parents still need to reinforce this old message. We begin to warn our children about strangers when they are still very little. We tell our toddlers never to talk to or accept any food or drinks from strangers. We tell our school-age children never to go in a stranger's car. We say, "Not everyone you meet will be nice or kind. Some people may be mean or bad underneath. Because we can't tell if someone is safe right away, you must never go anywhere with anyone you don't know." We try to warn our older children about deceit and manipulation: "Don't listen if a stranger tells you to come with him, even if he says I sent him to get you. He would be lying—I would never ask a stranger to pick you up." These kinds of stories give your children proper warnings. They help protect them from the potential danger of sexual abuse.

What Should I Ask Myself?

Many of us have had upsetting sexual experiences as youngsters—the well-dressed man on the subway who exposed himself under his *Wall Street Journal,* the camp counselor who took nude showers with us, the teacher who became too familiar on school trips, the drunk uncle who caressed us on his lap, the teenager next door with whom we played "marriage." But some of us have had actual experiences of sexual abuse—experiences in which an adult has engaged us in satisfying their sexual needs through masturbation, fellatio, cunnilingus, or vaginal or anal intercourse.

These premature and profoundly disturbing experiences leave their marks on us—on our sense of our body and our sense of self. But these marks may not be visible. An adult woman can "forget" her abusive experiences, yet they can play an important ongoing role in her life. For instance, Arlene was bewildered by the repetitive play behavior of her six-year-old daughter, Gwen, who seemed to masturbate a lot, and often asked for lots of Band-Aids for all her girl dolls. As a single mother, Arlene had encouraged Gwen's friendship with her neighbor, an older man who seemed charmed by the little girl and devoted to her. One day, as Arlene was bathing Gwen and noticed some reddening of her vaginal area, she had a vivid memory of an incident from her own childhood: A gardener, working around her parent's house, had asked her to come into the shed with him and then had attempted to have intercourse with her. She had successfully run away, but not before he had shown her the large clipping shears and told her if she ever told anyone, he'd cut off her arms and legs. Suddenly, Arlene became convinced that Gwen, too, was being abused and was afraid to tell her about it. Now, aware of her own past experience, she realized she'd been missing her daughter's clues to her about what was going on—the hurt girl dolls who needed Band-Aids. Arlene was able to gently question Gwen, who tearfully revealed that this "devoted" neighbor was "hurting her tushy with his fingers." Once Arlene remembered her own sexually abusive experience, she was able to protect her daughter adequately.

Have you ever been sexually abused? Try to remember your earliest sexual experiences. Were they with kids your own age or adults? What did you feel about these experiences? Were they pleasurable? (Remember, children are capable of sexual pleasure, too.) Were you frightened? Were any of the sexual experiences you had painful? Were you ever abused or threatened by adults you trusted?

Sadly, not all sexual abuse is done by strangers; a great deal of the sexual abuse of children is done to them by people they know well and even love—babysitters, teachers, friends, and family. Explaining and warning against this kind of abuse needs a different story. To protect your child against this kind of abuse, you need to say, "If anyone tries to touch your body, particularly the private parts of your body, or kiss you or asks you to touch them, and you don't know if it's OK, come and tell me about it. It could even be someone you know and like, but be sure to tell me, and we'll figure out what to do together."

Incest: The Ultimate Betrayal

The hardest sexual abuse of all to talk about is incest, because incest is the sexual abuse of a child by his own parent. Some sort of explanation is important to help your child begin to comprehend this incomprehensible experience. Here's a possible reparative narrative about incest that a mother is constructing with her eight-year-old daughter:

JULIA: Mommy, what's incest?

NARRATIVE	REPARATIVE ELEMENTS
MOM: Sometimes very sick, disturbed adults try to have sex with girls or boys they know. The worst of all is when a parent tries to use a child this way. That's called incest.	COMMUNICATION: This parent starts out offering information and confirms an important reality for the child.

NARRATIVE	REPARATIVE ELEMENTS
JULIA: Why doesn't the child just say she won't do it if it's bad?	
MOM: Sometimes the child is too afraid to say no to a parent and too upset to talk to anyone about incest because, even though she might know it's wrong, she still loves him, and she's afraid he'll get in trouble.	COMPASSION: She follows the information with an empathic comment.
JULIA: But he's bad.	
MOM: You're right, but sometimes kids are afraid to tell anyone because they feel maybe it's *their* fault their parent is acting this way. But it's *never*, ever the child's fault when a grown-up sexually abuses them.	COMPREHENSION: In expanding her child's understanding of the situation she also makes sure to absolve the child of responsibility.
JULIA: Why doesn't she tell her mommy?	
MOM: You're right! Children *always*, always need to tell a grown-up they trust—their mommy or their teacher or their grandpa—about what's happening. Then they can get help to stop it.	COMPETENCE: Now, in her suggested resolution, she reinforces an outcome that can help keep her child safe.

The sexual use and abuse of children by adults is far more widespread than we would like to believe. While most of us are horrified at the idea of an adult taking sexual advantage of a child, we know that it is common enough for us to need laws against such things as pederasty, child molestation, statutory rape, exhibitionism, and voyeurism. Our laws are meant to limit sexuality to acts performed together by *consenting adults*—with equal emphasis on the "consenting" and the "adult." This is because we recognize the special vulnerability of the child's position, dependent on and under the control of the very adults who may abuse him. Adults need to preserve the generational boundaries necessary to ensure the health of children, but often they do not.

Men appear to have the most difficulty preserving these generational boundaries, and there is overwhelming statistical evidence that incest and sexual abuse are almost exclusively male crimes (most often enacted against girls). This is a striking phenomenon, demonstrating that with men, the incest taboo functions with much less power and certainty. This is probably due to several factors. First, there is the anatomical distinction between the sexes. (An adult male can have sexual intercourse with a sexually immature female, while it is not possible for an adult female to be sexually satisfied by a little boy.) Second, perhaps women have a stronger prohibition and horror about adult-child intercourse because of the fact that the child has been carried and nurtured in the woman's own body. And finally, many sexual crimes are crimes of violence as well, and men appear to master their aggressive impulses less effectively than women do. But mothers in abusive families play a part in the abuse, too. Too often, they deny or obliterate the clues they get from their kids about incest or sexual abuse. And sometimes they even punish the child for revealing the incest or blame the child for making it happen!

All families have secrets, like the money Papa won playing poker, Aunt Lydia's alcoholism, cousin Peggy's abortion. Incest and sexual abuse are family secrets, too—secrets that adults persuade children to keep. Sometimes a child will keep this secret out of *love* (for children, sadly, love the adults that abuse them), sometimes a child will keep this secret out of *fear* (for adults often threaten children with terrible consequences), and sometimes a child will keep this secret out of *shame* (because children believe that somehow whatever is happening to them is their fault). To be a protective parent in today's world, you must teach your kids that they can always come to you with anything that bothers or upsets them—even (or particularly) if someone has told them to keep it a secret.

Here's an example of a mom who cuts off communication, isn't able to comprehend the secret that lies beneath her son's behavior, and is unable to be compassionate or competent, because she is defended against hearing any bad news:

MOM: You're always so jumpy when Michael comes over. Relax, will you. You know you like him. He's a great guy, isn't he?

KIRK: Yes.

MOM: Then stop acting so hyper, and settle down.

Here's another Mom whose reaction to her son's secret is likely to increase rather than decrease its traumatic effect:

KIRK: Michael touched my penis and made me touch his penis. Then he tried to put his penis in my behind. He told me I'd better not tell anyone or he'll kill me.

MOM: Oh, my God, how disgusting. Michael is a sick, sick boy and he belongs in jail. My poor, poor honey. That was a horrible thing he made you do, and he'll be punished for it, don't you worry. He's an animal. We'll never leave you with another teenager again.

This mom's reactions are perfectly understandable. We can all identify with her horror, her wish to punish the boy who sexually abused her son, and her distrust of any teenager that she might employ again. But she has not been able to function as a protective parent and help her son master his traumatic experience. Let's look at what she has unwittingly accomplished:

- Her reaction of horror has *heightened her son's worry* about what has happened and his role in it.

- Her *pity* and *disgust* (rather than *compassion* and *empathy* for both Michael and her son) have deprived her son of acknowledging the full range of his feelings about the incident—particularly the most forbidden feelings, his own possible sexual excitement and pleasure.

- She has *increased her son's guilt and shame* for his participation, rather than helping him see that, even if he liked what happened, Michael was wrong to invite or coerce him to participate.

- She has *left no room for compassion* for the disturbed teenager. Her wish to see him put in jail can only increase her son's emotional burden and sense of responsibility for betraying Michael's secret.

- She has made it *unlikely that her son will share any other secrets with her* in the future.

Here's an example of a dad who has helped his nine-year-old son to share a dangerous secret through creating a reparative narrative.

NARRATIVE	REPARATIVE ELEMENTS
DAD: Maybe I'm worried for no good reason, but I've noticed that whenever Michael comes over to babysit, you seem nervous. Is there something that goes on between you and Michael that you need to let me know about?	COMMUNICATION: This father starts by confirming a reality he's observed. Then he asks for more information.
KIRK (*looking anxious*): No!	
DAD: You know, sometimes teenagers are interested in doing things or saying things to kids that may be OK for the teenagers but that aren't good for kids. Has Michael done anything or said anything to you that has upset you? Or has he done something that he's told you never to tell anyone about? A	COMPREHENSION: By exploring his child's understanding of the situation, he also absolves his child of responsibility in the event.

NARRATIVE	REPARATIVE ELEMENTS

secret that would upset
you should never be kept,
no matter what anyone
says.

KIRK (*upset and crying*):
Michael touched my penis and
made me touch his penis.
Then he tried to put his penis
in my behind, but I ran
downstairs. He told me I'd
better not tell anyone or he'd
kill me.

DAD: Now, I can see why you
get so nervous whenever
Michael comes over. It was
brave of you to tell me. You
did the right thing. You must
have had a lot of different
feelings when all of this was
going on.

COMPASSION: He offers empathy
for his son's predicament.

KIRK: I wanted Michael to like
me so I didn't mind the
touching part so much, but
then I was scared about my
behind.

DAD: Michael is doing
something wrong—something
that big boys shouldn't be
doing to little boys. Michael's
supposed to be taking care of
you, and instead he's abusing
you. We won't let him babysit
for you anymore.

More COMPREHENSION and
COMPETENCE: He suggests an
outcome or resolution for this
terrible problem that offers
his child hope for the future.

KIRK: But Michael will be mad
at me now. He told me not to
tell.

NARRATIVE	REPARATIVE ELEMENTS
DAD: I know you like Michael, but Michael has a problem. He doesn't know how to handle his sexual feelings. He's trying to have sex with children. I'm going to talk to his mother, to see that Michael gets help. This is Michael's problem, not yours. Even if you let Michael touch you—or even if you liked it—he's old enough to know that it's wrong to touch children or to ask them to touch his penis or to try to have sex with you.	More COMPASSION, more COMPREHENSION, and more COMPETENCE

This dad, acting as a protective parent, has accomplished a number of things that are crucial in the handling of this incident:

- He has been *alert to changes in his son's behavior* that could signal trouble.

- He has *invited and encouraged open communication* about these changes.

- He has *used empathy* to understand both his son's worry and Michael's inappropriate behavior.

- He has casually *acknowledged rather than condemned* the possible sexual pleasure that this incident could have afforded his son.

- He has *listened calmly* to this shocking story, without expressing horror or disgust—both of which would increase the trauma of the experience for his son, rather than decrease it. Staying calm also encourages future communication.

- He has *lifted the burden of guilt and responsibility* from his son's shoulders by placing the responsibility for the encounter with Michael.

Incest and abuse are adult crimes against children. Don't confuse them with ordinary childhood sexual exploration. It's normal for all children to experiment with sexuality. All of us have had experiences of playing doctor, or pretending to be married, or engaging with our friends in some form of mutual masturbatory games. Children are as naturally curious about their bodies and other peoples' bodies as they are about other aspects of their lives, and we don't want to interfere with this natural curiosity. But this play among peers is *not* the same as sexual encounters with teenagers or adults, where the child is prematurely stimulated by adult needs and the child's sexual development is placed at risk.

What do we, as protective parents, want to convey to our kids about sexual abuse? There are four basic principles that all children need to know:

- Sexual experiences with grown-ups are not good for kids.

- It's not your fault. Even if you wanted to—the grown-up should know better.

- Your body is private and belongs to you. Don't let other people touch your private parts and don't touch other people's private parts—even if they want you to.

- Never be afraid to tell your parents anything, particularly if someone threatens you and tells you to keep a secret.

Also, if your child has been sexually abused, you may want to consult with a mental health professional to determine the best way to help your child manage this experience. Be sure to choose someone who has child development training and background in this area. In some cases, you may be able to offer your child all the psychological support she needs; in others, your child will benefit from some psychotherapy to enable her to master this trauma and move on in development.

12

As the World Turns—How to Talk to Kids About Manmade and Natural Disasters

Natural and Unnatural Disasters

Every day, we hear dire predictions about life on our planet. The ozone layer is depleted, exposing us all to the damaging effects of the sun; industrial pollutants are spilling into our rivers and oceans, poisoning our waters; radioactive wastes are piling up, contaminating our earth; garbage incineration is spewing filth into our air. We read the newspapers, listen to the radio, and watch television in a state of apprehension. What's happening with the greenhouse effect? How bad is global warming? What can be done about acid rain? Every catastrophe in the news seems to underscore the perilousness of our existence. Even the products we use in our ordinary lives have frightening consequences for our bodies: The lead in the paint on our walls can cause brain damage in our children, pesticides in our fruit can cause cancer, smog from cars can cause respiratory disease. No one knows how to repair the damage that we have already done to ourselves and our world. No one is able to escape from the dreadful knowledge that the way we live might not preserve our planet but destroy it.

Our very existence on this Earth is the result of the environment into which we emerged—our planet's land, air, and water. In the normal course of things our impact on our environment would be relatively insignificant; after all, we're so small and our Earth is so large. But there has been a hitch in human affairs: The evolutionary development of our brains has made us too smart for our own good! Our ingenuity is not matched by our caution or consideration, for our world or for each other. Increasingly, we have become aware that our dangerous exploration and domination of our planet has changed the very nature of life itself, perhaps irrevocably. No one knows at this point if the tremendous efforts we are now beginning to mobilize to control the damage will be able to contain, let alone reverse, the damage we've already done.

Further, because these dangerous changes are manmade, they follow human timetables, and people are notoriously impatient and reckless—unlike Nature, who takes her time. Many of the most serious alterations in our Earth have come in the course of a few generations, not over millions of years. Only now, belatedly, are we beginning to appreciate the intricate diversification and exquisite balance of life on our planet, a life that has evolved slowly and that could be destroyed by us in a moment's time.

But even if we take better care of our home, the Earth, and we are able to avert these *unnatural*, manmade disasters, our planet is equally vulnerable to *natural* disasters that similarly and unpredictably devastate all of us. Earthquakes, droughts, hurricanes, tornadoes, floods, and volcanic eruptions all rearrange the shape of our world, and claim millions of lives in the process.

How can we help our children to deal with both natural and unnatural environmental threats, when we ourselves are so bewildered and anxious? How can we answer their questions in ways that help them to understand the dangers that lie about us, without making them feel even more frightened? How can we offer them our protection when we feel so at peril? What should we tell our kids?

Mother Earth

When we try to make sense of our existence through science, or religion, or myth, we inevitably look for meaning in what we know best—relationships in the human family. That's why even the gods we choose to worship are called "father" or "mother." It is in our nature to personalize the forces we feel. Thunder and lightning become the sky god's anger, waves and wind, the moods of the mermaids; "brother sun" and "sister moon" are worshipped by millions of people on our planet; and, of course, even in our westernized, industrialized country, we still refer to "Mother Nature" and "Mother Earth."

This kind of thinking, in which trees, clouds, rain, and stars are given human characteristics, is quite natural to children. It is called *magical thinking,* and it imbues inanimate objects with life. Little children need to take their teddy bear under the covers because "Otherwise he'll get cold"; they push their chair under the table "so it won't get lonely." They attribute the same feelings and thoughts that they themselves experience to the objects in their world. That's why the idea of a sick, diseased, poisoned, dirty, or contaminated world is particularly frightening to children—because these things are happening to *their* "Mother Earth."

If children feel that the Earth itself is not healthy, and that the adults around them are powerless to help keep them safe, they cannot possibly attain either the basic trust in others that is the necessary foundation on which their development takes place or a sense of confidence in themselves that makes it possible for them to take their place in the world. What should we tell our kids when they ask, "Will we get bombed?" "Will all the whales die?" "Will the earth burn up?" "Can't we wash the dirty air?" "Will there still be a world when I grow up?" Before you can help create a cushion of safety for your kids on your threatened planet, you have to know how *you* feel about your environment.

What Should I Ask Myself?

What's your feeling about the world you inhabit? Are you opposed to the use of chemicals in our food and pesticides in our crops? Or do you feel that all the fuss about the poisoning of our water and our air is hysterical? Are you optimistic about the future because you feel that human knowledge tends to stay ahead of human ignorance and any damage we incur we will also be able to repair? Or are you pessimistic about the human condition because you feel that our tendency to destroy ourselves and our world far outpaces our tendencies to preserve and create?

Do you currently do anything in your own life that helps to alleviate threats to our environment? Do you turn off lights to save energy when you can? Do you plant wildflowers to preserve them from destruction? Do you pick up litter? Do you recycle? Do you give money to environmental causes? Do you leave your grass cuttings on the ground to mulch the lawn? Do you own a fur coat? Do you buy organic produce? Do you carpool to save gas?

As we've discussed, children typically pay more attention to what we do than what we say, so it's important that as parents we act in accord with our beliefs—and give our children reason to hope. For instance, Jane and Marshall's daughter, Jill, has become very concerned about what she can do to save the Earth. Her class has been talking about threats to the environment in school, and each child is supposed to pick a project. Jill's project is conserving gasoline, and every time the family goes out, she pesters them about using too much. At first her parents were frustrated and exasperated by Jill's interference, but then they realized that she was learning how to be committed to a cause, and that they needed to take her concerns seriously. They held a family council meeting and decided to walk or bike one day a week instead of using the car, and Marshall and Jane also told Jill that they wouldn't drive faster than fifty miles per hour, which also conserves gasoline. Jill was able to feel that her concerns were important and attended to.

Is your environment particularly at risk? Do you live at the edge of the sea? or in an area of tornado activity? or over a major fault line, where earthquakes are likely? Do you live near a nuclear facility? or a chemical plant? or in a smog-filled city? Do you worry about your risk or *deny* it?

What about your childhood? Have you ever survived a catastrophe? Might it have been averted, or was there nothing that could have been done about it? Is there anything you learned from your catastrophic experience that you'd want your children to know, if they should have to face such a threat in their lives? Remember, being a protective parent with your kids means walking that fine line between overexposure (prematurely exposing them to experiences they cannot manage) and overprotection (inappropriately shielding them from realities about which they need to learn).

The fact that our environment is continually being threatened by events over which we have little or no control is a real problem in our real world. Creating a cushion of safety for your child does not mean denying or diminishing the very real threats that surround us. It does not mean encouraging our children to expect that there is a fairy godmother for our environment that can step in and make everything better. What it does mean is recognizing that terrible things happen in the world, and that while sometimes there's nothing we can do about them, other times there are things we can do. This means we need to help our children to feel empowered to act on their own behalf and on behalf of their world, whenever we can.

Manmade Disasters: Learning About Ourselves

As we move into the twenty-first century, the first thing we can do is to help our children to begin to think of this whole Earth as their home. They need to be exposed to the scientific knowledge we have that will enable us to take better care of our world, as well as the ethical knowledge that makes this care a moral responsibility.

All along, we've been talking about laying down an early

foundation for what we want our kids to know later on in their lives. When it comes to manmade threats to our environment, we also need to start early to alert our children to make efforts to keep our world safe. When children are still very young, it makes sense to focus on an area that they can understand, one that, even in a small way, they can do something about. For instance, even a young child can see the results of littering; even a three-year-old can be taught to pick up a candy wrapper that she's thrown on the floor. And a four- or five-year-old can easily be taught to recycle by throwing metal cans away in a special receptacle, or to save energy by shutting off the lights when he leaves the room. Children feel empowered and effective when they can actively participate in reducing the threats to our environment.

When you begin to talk to your children about our environment, follow the same rules we've been using throughout this book:

- Rely on the four C's (compassion, communication, comprehension, competence).
- Use words they know.
- Relate it to their experience.
- Address the five basic fears.

When it comes to unnatural disasters, children need to know our history and our role; they need to understand what *manmade* means. As children recognize that the adults around them have not been able to take good care of themselves or their world, they experience profound disappointment. Young children believe in your strength and judgment, but when bad things happen over which you have little or no control, they come to realize the limits of your power. If even the adults around them cannot stop pollution or hurricanes or fires, then children feel frightened and unprotected; they may even feel angry and betrayed by the adults that they love. Under these conditions, the five basic fears are heightened. Realizing that adults are not omnipotent, while a disillusioning experience, also brings children into contact with reality. They can understand that they must protect themselves, rather than relying on adults. They can begin to make their own observations about what's needed, and they can begin to see that some people help and others hurt our environment. As a protective parent, you can help your child to begin to see the difference and to know what makes a difference. But remember, your agenda is *psychological*, not *political*, so don't overwhelm your young child with sophisticated geopolitics.

Here's an example of a reparative narrative that could be constructed to help a four-year-old understand a manmade disaster that she's heard about in school:

RITA: Our teacher said men are killing the rain forest. Are they bad men? Will they kill us?

NARRATIVE	REPARATIVE ELEMENTS
MOM: No, they won't kill us, honey. It's not that kind of killing. Your teacher is talking about men who cut down trees and plants in the rain forest. In the forest, plants need each other to stay healthy and grow—just like people need each other. The men are only thinking of themselves and what they need, like room for their houses or roads. They don't think about the forest and that it could die if they keep cutting it down. I can understand that you'd be upset about all of this. I am, too.	COMMUNICATION: This mother is giving her child the information she needs, which clarifies and confirms reality. COMPASSION: She also, by making an empathic statement, lets her child know she understands how she feels.
RITA: Tell them to stop. Put the bad men in jail.	

NARRATIVE	REPARATIVE ELEMENTS
Mom: That's hard to do. Rain forests are in faraway countries, and sometimes the governments there let people cut the trees down. We have to show these men that the forest will help them if they let it grow. They may not know much about forests. Companies that make medicines are trying to find out all about special plants that can be used to make medicine. Then these companies would pay the men who live near the forest to find special forest plants and trees and grow them instead of cutting them down. That might work. Maybe by the time you grow up, the rain forests will still be alive and healthy.	COMPREHENSION: She's enlarging her child's understanding of the situation.
We can't stop the men ourselves, but we can give money to people who are trying to save the rain forests, and we can try to take care of our forests where we live, too.	COMPETENCE: Now, this mother offers her child a possible resolution. While not entirely reassuring, it offers some hope for the future.

Here's a more sophisticated narrative to use with an older child (ten years old) about another manmade disaster.

Ian: There was a big magazine article about lots of kids who lived near that Russian nuclear plant that exploded getting cancer. We live near a big factory and we always see black smoke coming out of all the chimneys. Could we die, too?

NARRATIVE	REPARATIVE ELEMENTS
MOM: I can see you're really worried about getting sick like the kids you read about. That was a terrible nuclear accident. It's really frightening to think that children could be dying now because people didn't realize how dangerous a nuclear accident can be.	COMPASSION: This mother addresses her child's fears with an empathic statement.
The factories near us are bad, too, but they're not nuclear facilities, and they haven't ever exploded, so none of the people in our town have gotten cancer. But all over the world now, more and more people are realizing that we've got to be much more careful, particularly about radiation. We have to try our best now, even though we've already done a lot of damage to our environment.	COMMUNICATION: Now, she's offering her child information and confirming the reality that her child is facing.
Daddy and I fought against a nuclear facility being opened near us two years ago. Even though nuclear energy can help our world a lot, we're all still worried about what we can do to control nuclear accidents.	COMPREHENSION: Here, she's expanding her child's understanding of the complexities of the situation.
IAN: How do we know that another accident won't happen?	
MOM: We don't, but we do know about the dangers in nuclear facilities and more about	More COMPASSION: She makes this empathic statement.

NARRATIVE	REPARATIVE ELEMENTS
safeguarding them. I know you think and worry a lot about all of this. People all over the world are worried just like you are. Scientists are trying to make nuclear energy safer for all of us, but we don't have all the answers we need yet.	
When I grew up, we were always worried about a nuclear war. Now countries are working toward worldwide nuclear disarmament, so things can get better. It's safer now than it used to be. Maybe if we all work together, we can find a way to control nuclear energy. I hope that happens by the time you're grown up, so things will be even better.	COMPETENCE: By drawing on her own childhood, this mother is offering her child a broader perspective on the problem, as well as a possible resolution or hopeful outcome.

The Developmental Advantages of Hope

Though we have been trying for centuries to see ahead of us, nobody can predict the future; the very nature of our world makes it subject only to probability or possibility. Therefore, as adults it is really our choice whether we decide to live with hope for the future or with despair. But what about the influence of our choice on our children? Hope offers children a developmental advantage. It enables them to grow and develop under conditions of psychic safety. Even if their lives are endangered, hope gives them an advantage over terror and despair. Children whose lives were in terrible peril from moment to moment, such as the hidden children of the

Holocaust, have left us heart-rending messages that are an enduring testament to the usefulness of hope for the survival of the human spirit, even under the darkest conditions of existence.

I began this book talking about the sanctuary of childhood. A sanctuary is a refuge, a safe house in which the spirit as well as the body can be protected from harm. It is your job, as a protective parent, to create this sanctuary for your children, even if you yourself have doubts about the future of our Earth, even if you yourself are filled with dread at each new scientific discovery that reveals how our world has been contaminated. Even if you yourself have no faith at all in the possibility of rescue or repair of the damage we've done to ourselves, your children deserve to be protected from your darkest thoughts.

Further, our world needs the energy of the next generation; we need them to try to clean up the mess we have made. If we do not protect the sanctuary of childhood for them, when our children reach adolescence, instead of mobilizing their energies to separate from us and build a new order, they will sink into lethargy, apathy, and depression. Children raised without hope have no desires for the future. Life, in the present, is too painful to bear. But how do children get to feel hopeful?

Hope is an ordinary psychic outcome of the oedipal phase of development (ages two to six years). During these years, parents help their children move out of the family circle and hold out for them the hope of love, a home, and a life of their own in the future. Children who feel prematurely endangered early in their lives, children whose parents are not able to help them maintain the sanctuary of childhood or protect them from overexposure to threats consistently experience an intensification of the five basic fears. When these fears are not adequately mastered as children grow, the fears distort and compromise the children's development and make them feel helpless and hopeless.

Natural Disasters: Learning About the World

We can try to help empower our children by helping them to realize that there is much they can do to alter the way they live in the world. We can help them realize that manmade disasters can be averted with proper understanding and commitment. But what about natural disasters? How can modern parents realistically protect their children from these uncontrollable and unpredictable events? What can we say about famine, floods, fires, volcanic eruptions, or hurricanes?

It's much harder to say soothing and convincing things in today's times because of our extensive exposure to them via the media. All of us are bombarded daily with traumatic visual images, and one picture is indeed worth a thousand words. What makes these images particularly disturbing is that, in their attempts to dramatize the devastation, photographers will frequently focus on the human face of pain: the mother searching in the rubble for her missing child, the father holding onto his son in the midst of a raging river, a child's doll shattered by the tornado that destroyed her home, the blank eyes and distended bellies of the starving children in a famine. This approach makes for good photojournalism; it gives disaster a human face and helps us all to identify with the suffering of others. But for young children, who are often unable to understand the transformations of time and space that help us to distance ourselves from these experiences, these visual images can be traumatic. They can hit "too close to home."

This is why protective parents need to be alert to the profound influence of the media on the lives of their children—newspapers, magazines, movies, and of course, the ever-present television. Children need to be protected from this intense visual bombardment because often they do not have adequate capacities for either comprehension or assimilation of traumatic experience. Remember, too, that ultimately children can only understand visual imagery by reference to their own bodies. Even adults, watching the news, can be haunted for years by the pictures of broken bodies. Imagine how children feel.

Protective parents, who are anxious to offer their children an understanding of the human condition, need to help their children understand four things about natural disasters:

- Unexpected, chaotic, destructive things can happen to anyone at any time.
- It's nobody's fault when disasters happen.
- People are strong and can survive even terrible events.
- Even when terrible things happen to us and our world, there's still hope for the future.

Home Is Where the Heart Is

The very first physical home that the baby inhabits is the mother's body. After we are born, the sense of safety and security that comes to mean home for us is extended to the surroundings inhabited by the mother and the baby. The maternal significance of home is represented in our dreams, where houses are often symbols for the female body; in children's games, where "home base" is set up to symbolize the safety of return to the mother; and in our literature, art, and music, where the concept of returning home is an enduring and poignant theme. As the child grows older, the home originally provided within the mother's body now extends to include the mother's room, the mother's house, the mother's neighborhood, and so on. The enormous nostalgia we often feel for the things of our past, (collectibles and antiques, the farms and houses of yesteryear) testifies to our lasting attachment to the concept of home, in all of its symbolic representations.

For very young children, under the age of three, the world is still bounded by their parents. As long as they have access to the people whom they love they can be psychologically centered, even if they have been physically uprooted from their homes and communities. But children over three years old have already begun to invest their surroundings with the same sort of attachment that they give to those they love. The loss of a favorite toy or one's cozy bed, the familiar rocking chair or a fuzzy rug, can be both disorienting and disturbing to young children. The loss of a child's familiar possessions undermines his ongoing assumption of safety and security.

The sense of security, safety, wholeness, and continuity, which are provided for the infant by protective parenting, becomes linked, by the time the child is three years old, with home. That's why we can say, "Home is where the heart is." That's why children who have lost their homes have lost something precious in their development. Children who have had the bad luck to be involved in natural catastrophes in which their homes were destroyed are particularly vulnerable to feelings of fragmentation. The loss of home, like the loss of a parent, puts the child at high developmental risk. It draws on all of the five basic fears that we have been trying to address in protective parenting—fear of the unknown ("What will happen to me now? Where will I live if my house is destroyed?"), fear of being alone, ("If an earthquake could kill my house, could it also kill my family? If there's a hurricane, will I get separated from everyone I know? Will the fire get my family and leave me alone?"), fears about the body (which are heightened in any circumstance that displays to a child the vulnerability of the body), fear of the voice of conscience (since children often feel that a natural disaster must be directed toward them as some sort of punishment for imagined wrongdoing), and last, fears about the self, which is always mobilized in any threat to the environment (since so much of a child's sense of self is tied up with the sense of bodily well-being and the welfare of those the child loves).

When a child has lost a home, through a natural or manmade catastrophe, the child's relationship to the parents must be immediately strengthened to counterbalance the loss of the child's surroundings. A child without home has lost the *symbolic surround* that enables parents to substitute other things for themselves, a process that begins in infancy with the teddy bear (offering the baby the solace of Mom without her presence) and moves on in childhood to include the child's room, toys, books, and belongings. Now, with everything wiped out by disaster, the child has nothing symbolic to cling to anymore. Now all that's left is the actual parent. The child's life has been stripped bare.

Children deprived of all that is familiar to them will naturally try to shield and console themselves by clinging to their parents. This new heightened dependency is a normal reaction to the massive losses that they have sustained. Children in these situations will display intense separation anxiety, with all of its accompanying symptoms—nightmares, fears and phobias, acute dread, crying, and whining, among others. Added to their terror is the realization that, if one's home can be swept away with such force and devastation, then surely one's parents could be similarly taken. This, too, increases children's need to keep the parents as close as possible.

A reparative narrative that can help a child who has lost his home feel less terrified, must take into account the five basic fears. Addressing these fears in a reparative narrative will help the child to begin to get his bearings in the aftermath of a disaster. Here's a reparative narrative that could be constructed after a family has survived a tornado in which their entire house has been destroyed. Both parents are trying to address the catastrophe with their two children, Rebecca, age seven, and Jon, age eleven.

JON: Why did this happen to us?

NARRATIVE	REPARATIVE ELEMENTS
DAD: There's no good reason for bad things happening. Even though this tornado has been the most awful thing we've ever had to face, what's most important is that we're all safe and we're all together! We'd like to blame someone, but we can't. We're alive and well, and now we can begin to plan what to do next.	COMPASSION: This father is letting his son know that he empathizes with him. COMMUNICATION: But he's also giving the children information and confirming the reality they need to face.
REBECCA: Where will I sleep, Daddy? Our house is smashed and I have no bed.	

NARRATIVE	REPARATIVE ELEMENTS
MOM: Tonight we're going to stay with the Browns next door. You're going to sleep in Edith's room, just like you always do when you two have a sleepover. Jon is going to sleep in Logan's room because he's away at college, and Daddy and I are going to sleep in the den, on their sofa-bed. We're going to stay with them as long as we need to, until we decide what we're going to do next. That way, you'll be able to get picked up by the school bus and see all your friends, like you always do.	COMPETENCE: The mother offers an immediate resolution to the family's crisis, taking charge of the situation and reassuring the child.
JON: But, what'll I do about my homework, Mom? All my books are gone!	
DAD: So are a lot of kids' books. When there's a tornado like this, everyone understands everything will be in a mess for a while. All your teachers know about the tornado. Maybe some of their houses were destroyed, too.	More COMPASSION: Now the empathic statement includes an understanding of people's reactions to the event.
REBECCA (crying): Will we ever get our house back?	
MOM: No, we'll never have our old house. It's gone and that's sad for all of us, but houses are insured, so we'll have money from the insurance agency to help us build a new	More COMPASSION: Another empathic statement about the loss is given.

NARRATIVE	REPARATIVE ELEMENTS
house. First, we have to see how much we can save of our old house, and we have to find someplace else to live while our new house is being built. Daddy will be trying to find a house for us to rent close to here.	COMPETENCE: Here, the mother suggests a resolution and predicts a possible outcome.
JON: Why did this have to happen to us? We're so unlucky!	
DAD: It is rotten luck that we were in the path of the tornado, but it's very good luck that none of us got hurt! Things happen in life that we have no control over, but it wasn't anyone's fault. We didn't do anything, and we're not being punished in any way. We just have to pick up and start over again, like lots of families when bad things like tornados, or floods, or hurricanes happen to them. But we've got each other, and that's what really counts, now.	More COMPASSION: In this empathic statement, the father also expands the child's comprehension of the situation and absolves the child and family of responsibility. More COMPETENCE: An outcome or resolution that bonds the family together is emphasized, offering hope for the future.

Here's a narrative that tries to address global warming with a very young child (three to five years old) who has heard about it on TV. In this case, the child has not understood the complexity of the situation and the program has frightened him into believing that the flooding of his city is imminent.

JUAN: Mommy, will we all die?

NARRATIVE	REPARATIVE ELEMENTS
MOM: Boy, that program sure sounded scary, didn't it? That was a science program about what could happen to cities that are on the coast near oceans after years and years and years of hot temperatures on the Earth. That's why it was called "Global Warming." It means that if we don't take better care of our Earth by not using aerosol sprays anymore, and by making sure companies don't burn their garbage in ways that hurt our air, and by using better fuel for our cars, then in a long, long time, the ice at the North Pole could begin to melt.	COMPASSION: This mother's empathic statement lets her child know she understands his fears. COMMUNICATION: She's offering the child more information and is confirming the reality of the situation.
JUAN: Is the ice melting now?	
MOM: This problem wasn't about right now. We would never, ever let anything bad happen to you. If we knew that the ocean was going to rise near us, we would move to a higher place to live, just like when we're at the beach, and the tide comes in, we pull our blankets further up on the beach, so we don't get wet."	COMPETENCE: This mother is helping her son understand that the frightening outcome is not imminent. She is trying to offer him a hopeful, more reassuring resolution to think about.

Any child or family who has experienced the physical dismantling and psychic upheaval of a natural disaster—the loss of a home to floodwaters, the destruction of an apartment by fire, the demolition of a town by a tornado's force, or the ravages visited on a community by a volcano or an earthquake—is aware of the devastating effects of anxiety and terror and the enduring consequences of loss. Coping with these strong assaults on the integrity of the self requires all the energies that we can muster on our own and our children's behalf. Remember, too, that once children have experienced a disaster, they are likely to be subject to "flashback fears," and may be extremely sensitive to any signs of reoccurrence. Be sure to emphasize that just because something bad has happened once, it doesn't mean it will happen again—not every strong wind is the first sign of a hurricane; not every rain causes flooding; lightning seldom strikes twice. In this way, protective parents help keep alive their children's hopes for the future.

13

Necessary Losses: Dealing with Helplessness and Hopelessness

Necessary Losses

In real life, pain is as present as pleasure, grief is as common as joy, disappointments follow fulfillment, and sadness as well as happiness mark our days and our children's days. We feel hopeless and helpless; we get headaches and backaches and stomachaches; we lose weight and gain weight; we sleep too much or we can't sleep at all; we catch colds and pick fights and get into accidents. What's the matter with us? We're depressed! Why are depressive reactions such a pervasive problem for all of us? What makes us feel depressed?

All depressed feelings are linked to *loss*. We feel grief-stricken when we've lost someone we love; we feel sad when we've lost something we value; we feel low when we've lost self-esteem; we feel despondent when we've lost our hopes and dreams. When we don't know which direction to take in our lives, we say "I'm at a *loss*"; when we get angry, we say, "I *lost* my temper"; when we fall apart under stress we say, "I *lost* it."

From the moment we're born and lose the comfort of our mother's womb to the moment we die and lose our lives, loss is an inevitable part of our lives—not only the profound developmental losses we must all sustain (relinquishing the breast or bottle, letting go of our childhood, leaving home), but also the smaller losses that are a part of our daily lives (the misplaced ring that belonged to your grandmother, the job you wanted and didn't get, the friend who never returned your call, the ruptured disk that prevents you from running). That's why we have so many words to describe our feelings about loss: We say we feel blue or black, desolate or melancholy, dejected or down in the dumps, dismal or moody, heartsick or disconsolate, gloomy, in the doldrums, or brokenhearted. Our capacity to feel sad when we lose something or someone we value testifies to our emotional depth, and defines us as human. That's why we call people who do not experience sadness "heartless," "alienated," "detached," "cold-blooded," or even "inhuman."

Sadness Versus Depression:
An Important Difference

While we often say we're depressed when we feel sad, there is an important difference: Sadness is a normal and healthy reaction to loss—from the loss of a beloved baby doll to the loss of a beloved grandmother. When we lose someone we love, we *mourn* them. Mourning is a process which includes a complex series of emotional reactions: *protest* that the person has died, *denial* and disbelief about our loss, *anger* that we could be abandoned by someone we love, and finally, *resignation* to our abiding grief. Some losses (like the baby doll) we "get over," but some losses (like our grandmother) are irrevocable; we will never get over them. We will just learn to live with them. Only time can diminish their claim on us.

Depression adds a new dimension to the normal sadness we all suffer. When we are depressed, in addition to feeling sad, we feel bad—we blame, attack, and devalue ourselves. We turn the anger we naturally feel at our loss ("Why did Grandma have to die now right now, when I'm the star of the school play?") against the self ("If I wasn't so busy rehearsing for the play maybe Grandma wouldn't have died. It's all my fault"). The more ambivalent we feel toward the person who has died, the more anger and guilt we are likely to experience during mourning, and the more extended the grieving process is likely to be. Depression makes it hard to sustain any good feelings about the self, and when our self-esteem plummets, we feel more depressed, setting up a vicious cycle that quickly spins out of control. Depression heightens all the five basic fears, but particularly fear of the voice of conscience and fears about the self.

When we feel depressed, even the way we think gets distorted. When we're feeling hopeless, we say things like, "It'll never get any better; it can only get worse. This is the beginning of the end." Or, "I've always been miserable; I always will be miserable; nothing ever changes." We also feel completely helpless to do anything about the way we feel. Our helplessness makes us feel exhausted, enervated, and overwhelmed by the demands of ordinary life.

Children get depressed, too, for reasons of their own. Babies grieve for their teddy bears, toddlers mourn for their absent mothers, school children cry when their friends are spiteful, teenagers are heartbroken when a love affair is over. Children's lives are touched and transformed by loss—the birth of a sibling, the move from a familiar apartment, the loss of a favorite babysitter, the breakup of a family. Each loss provides a challenge to the child's emerging sense of self and requires psychological effort to repair. Children ask themselves, "If I was good enough, why would my parents need to have another child?" or "If Mommy and Daddy really loved me, they wouldn't make me move away from my house," or "If my babysitter cared about me, why did she go away?" or "How can Daddy move out and leave me behind?"

Even infants can feel sad and dejected, but because depression draws on dark feelings about the self, children cannot truly be depressed until the sense of self has begun to be crystallized (between three and four years old). By then, children are able to sustain and appreciate enduring relationships and to appreciate their value. Once this ability to sustain relationships is established, children also have the capacity to suffer depression in the absence of these relationships. Depression depends as well on the consolidation of the voice of conscience (the fourth basic fear). Once this takes place (between three and six years old), children are vulnerable to guilt. Now, in addition to feeling sad, they can also feel bad. These bad feelings are at the core of many depressive reactions.

A young child's depression can be observed directly in a sad facial expression, lack of energy, moodiness, slowed reactions, fatigue, apathy, and self-statements, particularly statements about death or dying. But children who are depressed can also reveal their depressed feelings indirectly— in what professionals call *depressive equivalents*. They may fail to thrive, refuse to eat, have trouble sleeping, or even show problems growing at normal rates. They may also engage in hidden acts of self-destruction. For example, a child may misjudge dangerous situations, or appear to act recklessly, without appropriate caution. Childhood depression can be revealed as well in the school setting, where it can interfere with your child's ability to concentrate and achieve. At home, too, your depressed child may have trouble listening or paying attention.

Childhood depression can be triggered by any significant loss, so be particularly alert to such common events in your child's life as a change in school or caretaker, moving from one home to another, the birth of a sibling, or the illness of a parent.

As a protective parent, you will want to provide your kids with that important cushion of safety against the developmental impact of significant loss. You will also want to be alert to the presence of the fourth basic fear, fear of the voice of conscience, in order to protect your child against damaging guilt and relentless self-punishment. Understanding how the five basic fears are heightened during the necessary and unnecessary losses of childhood, and knowing how to build a reparative narrative to heal hard times, will help you to help your child. Here's a parent talking to a four-year-old child about her recent separation from her babysitter, who has just gone away to college.

NARRATIVE	REPARATIVE ELEMENTS
Mom: It was hard to say goodbye to Adria. She was one of your favorite babysitters, wasn't she?	COMPASSION: The mother starts the conversation by offering her child empathy for her feelings.
Sharon: I like Adria. Why did she leave us?	
Mom: She's old enough now to go away to school. She doesn't live at home anymore, so she can't babysit for you.	COMMUNICATION: Now the mother offers information to her child and confirms the reality that the child is facing.
Sharon: Why couldn't she go to school here with me?	
Mom: Because the school she wanted to go to is far away. When you're big like Adria is, you'll go away to college, too. I can see that you really miss her and wish that she was still here with us. I do, too.	More COMMUNICATION and more COMPASSION
Sharon *(crying):* I don't care about her, anyway.	
Mom: You're angry with her because she left, and you think she didn't care about you. But she misses you, too, and she's going to come and visit you when she comes home for Christmas vacation. Meanwhile, we could call her, if you want. Or you could make a drawing and send it to her. I bet she'd be happy to get something from you. I bet she's lonely, too. She's never been away from home before.	COMPREHENSION: Explaining the child's emotional reactions to her and linking her anger to her defensive reaction ("I don't care!") helps this child to understand the situation better. It also offers the mom a chance to be competent and come up with a resolution which can affect the outcome of this experience for her child.

NARRATIVE	REPARATIVE ELEMENTS
SHARON: I spilled milk on her new boots and she yelled at me.	More COMMUNICATION (from child): Because her child feels understood, she's opening up, offering her parent more information about her guilty fears (fear of the voice of conscience) and worries about the self (fears about the self).
MOM: I didn't realize you were worried about that. Adria was angry with you, but that was just for the moment. That has nothing to do with her leaving for college. She was going to college way before you spilled the milk on her boots. You didn't do anything to make her go away.	More COMPREHENSION: Now, the parent is able to understand how her young child has (typically) distorted the cause and effect of her babysitter's leaving. She is able, with this information, to absolve her child of any responsibility in the event.
SHARON: Maybe I can draw a picture of her boots and send it to her.	CHILD'S COMPETENCE: Here, the child offers her own resolution to the situation, creating a reparative outcome.
MOM: That's a great idea. It will make her laugh!	

Bearing Unbearable Feelings

It's very painful for us to see our children suffer, but part of our job as protective parents is to help our children bear unbearable feelings. Because we are so anxious to protect them, however, we can actually wind up depriving them of the opportunity to experience things deeply. In our loving attempts to shield our kids from emotional pain and distress, we can actually prevent them from developing strength. But children develop "psychological immunities" in the same way they develop physical immunities—by being exposed to small doses of upsetting experiences, coping with them, and mastering them. That's why it's important for us to permit our children to struggle, with our support. These developmental struggles increase their endurance and resilience, creating a kind of psychological immune system. In our attempts to cope with our own anxieties, we can make some important mistakes as parents. Here are some common ones:

- We can detach ourselves from our child's inner thoughts and feelings.
- We can diminish, obliterate, or deny our child's pain.
- We can abruptly cut off communication with our children.
- We can prematurely take charge of our children's experiences, without letting our kids struggle through and master their feelings.

You cannot help your child manage life's trials unless you're willing to let your child experience some of life's tribulations. This means recognizing, accepting, expressing, and enduring upsetting feelings. Every time you support your child's efforts to cope, you help to strengthen her resilience. Giving this kind of support while your child is young helps her to rehearse for the hard times that are bound to come later on as she gets older.

Here's a parent who cannot bear to see his ten-year-old child suffer, so he's trying to diminish the importance of her depressed feelings:

FATHER: You're so gloomy. What's the matter?

VERONICA: Nothing. Leave me alone.

FATHER: I'd like to, but you're always going around the house with a long face. Can't you ever smile for me anymore? What happened to my sunny girl?

VERONICA *(crying):* I feel so unhappy.

FATHER: Don't be ridiculous! You should be ashamed of yourself. You have everything you need in life to be happy. Stop being silly! Why don't we go to the movies? That will take your mind off these gloomy thoughts. What do you want to see?

This father is unable to listen to what his daughter is trying to express. Instead, he's trying to obliterate her pain, deflect her feelings, and distract her thoughts. He may believe he's trying to cheer her up, but he's really letting her down, because he's not able to fulfill his protective function to help her bear unbearable feelings.

Here's a reparative narrative that's been created by a more alert protective parent facing the same situation:

NARRATIVE	REPARATIVE ELEMENTS
FATHER: You're so gloomy. What's the matter?	
VERONICA: Nothing. Leave me alone.	
FATHER: I've been trying to leave you alone for weeks now, honey, but it isn't working. You seem so sad; I want to try to help you.	COMMUNICATION: This parent is reaching out to help his child, trying to get information, confirming the child's reality and encouraging dialogue between them.
VERONICA: I feel so unhappy.	
FATHER: This is really serious. These must be very important worries. Can you tell me about them?	COMMUNICATION and COMPASSION: Here, the parent offers his child empathy and tries to help her reveal her upsetting feelings.
VERONICA: No, and besides it wouldn't matter. You can't do anything.	

NARRATIVE	REPARATIVE ELEMENTS
FATHER: Well, we can try together. But you're right; I can't do anything to help if you don't let me know what the problem is. If you can't talk to me, maybe you can talk to Mommy. Or maybe if it's something embarrassing or upsetting, you could write us a letter. We've got to find some way to help you with these feelings.	More COMMUNICATION and attempts at both COMPREHENSION and COMPETENCE: Now, this parent tries to expand his child's understanding of the situation, as well as offer a possible outcome or resolution.
VERONICA: I wrote a poem about how I feel, and you can read it after I go to bed.	Child responds with more COMMUNICATION.

We've talked about walking that fine line between overexposing your child to upsetting events and overprotecting them from these same events. Protective parents need to find the right balance for their kids, as they struggle to deal with ordinary sadness and loss, as well as the extraordinary helplessness and hopelessness of depression. But how can we know when our kids are just sad, and when they've become depressed?

Evaluating Childhood Depression

There are three kinds of depression that we all experience, even as young children: *transient depression* (momentary or fleeting feelings); *reactive depression* (responses to a major situational or developmental loss); and *chronic depression* (when helpless and hopeless feelings have crystallized into an emotional attitude).

Transient depressive thoughts and feelings usually require no intervention from us beyond a pep talk or a hug. These are just the fleeting feelings of sadness and badness that we all experience in the ups and downs of the day.

Reactive depressive thoughts require thoughtful attention. They often reflect children's profound responses to real problems in the real world—illness, divorce, death, threats to the environment, and the like. Reactive depression can usually be helped by addressing the five basic fears with children, and using the four C's to help them construct a reparative narrative. If the depression is clearly linked to a recent event, the child should begin to feel better within a short time (a few days to a few months).

Chronic depressive feelings are helpless and hopeless feelings that are not going away. You or your child may have started out feeling sad in response to an *external* situation or crisis, but by now the depression has become part of an *internal* experience; it has crystallized into a chronic pattern that may require professional help.

How can a protective parent know when a child's transient or reactive depressive feelings have become chronic? Look for these eight warning signs:

- A sad, dejected mood and facial expression
- Feelings of helplessness and vulnerability
- Feelings of pessimism and hopelessness
- Tearfulness and crying
- Irritability and oversensitivity
- Loss of interest and investment in life (a lack of motivation or enthusiasm)
- Lack of self-esteem or a loss of self-regard
- *Persistence of all of the above over several months*

The bad news is that depression is often not even diagnosed, let alone treated, in children. This is because depressed feelings can be expressed in so many different areas of your child's life and because the symptoms of depression can be so easily confused with other problems. For example, let's think about a four-year-old child who feels listless and apathetic, who's not interested in eating, and who is sleeping poorly. Is she depressed, or is she coming down with a virus? What about a seven-year-old child who's irritable and cranky at home, inattentive in class, and who reports consistent feelings of worthlessness? He could be depressed, or struggling with undetected learning disabilities. And what about an eleven-year-old child who's melancholy, sleeping a lot, and gaining weight steadily? She could be depressed, or beginning to enter puberty.

The good news is that many children who appear depressed will get better within six months with appropriate attention from their protective parents, the kind of attention I'm talking about in this book.

To evaluate your child's potential for depression, first think about your child's *mood.* Is she sad? gloomy? blue? melancholy? Does she cry easily? or overreact to what you say to her? Do you feel that you're always "walking on eggs" around her?

Next, look at your child's *thoughts.* Does she always assume the worst? Is she generally pessimistic and negativistic? Does she seem to feel helpless to do anything about it? Does she always see the glass half empty instead of half full?

Then, look at your child's *behavior.* Does she always seem to fall or cut herself? Would you describe her as accident-prone? Has there been a change in her eating or sleeping habits? in the way she cares for herself or her body?

And last, *listen to your child.* Depressed children often express suicidal thoughts directly—the wish to be dead, or the feeling that life is not worth living. Any child who states, "I wish I could die" or "I hate myself; I want to die" or "I would be better off dead" or "I don't want to live" is communicating a serious struggle with depression. Statements of this sort need to be taken seriously and addressed immediately. There is no such thing as a child who says she wants to die just "to get attention." If a child sets out to get attention by threatening death, you need to *pay attention fast!*

Here's a parent who's unable to help an older depressed child who's expressing some suicidal thoughts because of her own anxious denial of her child's feelings.

MOM: How did you do on that big test you were worried about?

DEAN: I failed. I only got a 63 and everyone else did better. I'm no good. I'm stupid. It doesn't matter what I do, it always turns out wrong.

MOM: Don't be ridiculous! You're getting yourself all upset over one test. Who cares?

DEAN: I always screw up. I'd be better off dead. Then I'd never have to worry. I wish I were dead!

MOM: Now that really *is* a stupid exaggeration. I never want to hear you say such a thing! You ought to be ashamed of yourself.

DEAN: You never understand.

Here's a protective parent struggling to address the same serious issues with her child:

NARRATIVE	REPARATIVE ELEMENTS
MOM: How did you do on that big test you were worried about?	COMMUNICATION: This question opens up a dialogue about an event in her son's life that the mom has kept in mind. She's asking him for information.
DEAN: I failed. I only got a 63 and everyone else did better. I'm no good. I'm stupid. It doesn't matter what I do, it always turns out wrong.	
MOM: You're really disappointed and down on yourself because you failed. It sounds like you feel there's no use trying. It's too discouraging.	COMPASSION: Because her child is expressing strong feelings of self-denigration, this mother offers empathic support for the failure, without criticizing. (Her child is already overly self-critical, and his self-esteem has been severely undermined.)

NARRATIVE	**REPARATIVE ELEMENTS**
DEAN: I always screw up. I'd be better off dead. Then I'd never have to worry. I wish I were dead!	
MOM: When you fail a test, you feel like things will never change. No wonder you'd like to be dead and rid of these worries. But there's got to be a much better way for us to help you. We'd never let you hurt yourself.	COMPREHENSION: Now this mom is trying to expand her child's understanding of the situation. By linking his feelings of hopelessness to his suicidal thoughts, she helps her child see that the wish to be dead is really a wish to be rescued from the pain of failing. She also reassures him about parental protection ("We'd never let you hurt yourself").
DEAN: Nothing helps. I'm just stupid.	
MOM: Well, I know you studied hard, and I know you've been having a hard time with school this year. Maybe we need to find out more about this. It could turn out that you need some special tutoring to make things easier, or you need to learn or study differently. One thing I do know is that you're not stupid!	More COMPASSION, more COMPREHENSION, and COMPETENCE: Offering some hope for the future can help this child to feel less helpless and hopeless. The solution the parent presents confirms the reality of the problem without confirming the child's overly harsh self-perception.

The Pre-Pubertal Blues

Sometimes kids just feel blue. They don't know why and we don't why. Sometimes the reasons may be buried too deeply for us to unearth. But often their blue feelings simply reflect the bodily or hormonal changes of pre-adolescence, which may begin several years before your child reaches puberty. (These blue feelings can be particularly common in nine- to eleven-year-old boys and girls.) In pre-adolescence, both boys and girls begin the long psychic struggle to separate from their parents and their childhood. This process makes them sad because of all they are about to lose. It stimulates the five basic fears in new ways: fear of the unknown adolescent life that is ahead, fear about being alone and separated from the loved parents, fears about the body with all its bewildering changes, fear of the voice of conscience related to guilt about emerging sexuality, and fears about the self in connection with questions about social identity. In these pre-adolescent years, at the very end point of childhood, protective parents need to remain emotionally steady in the face of their child's ups and downs. They need to let their child know that these blue feelings are natural, that they will eventually go away, and that they are linked to normal development and the enormous changes of adolescence.

Here's a mother trying to console her twelve-year-old daughter about feeling blue:

NARRATIVE	REPARATIVE ELEMENTS
MOM: You seem really gloomy today. Is there anything I can do to help?	COMMUNICATION: She's confirming her child's reality and asking for more information.
ANNA: I don't know. I feel so sad and I don't know why. *(bursts into tears)* I've tried to think, but there's nothing.	
MOM: Well, maybe you don't have to try so hard. Maybe today is just a blue day for you. That's OK. Everyone has days when they feel down. Sometimes you figure it out and sometimes you can't.	COMPASSION: This mother's letting her child know her feelings are respected. She's making an empathic statement.

NARRATIVE	REPARATIVE ELEMENTS
ANNA: I just feel like crying all the time.	
MOM: Maybe this just means you're growing up. Sometimes before girls get their periods and become teenagers, they feel blue like this. It could be because your body is changing and also because your life will be changing, too. I remember I used to read sad poetry and cry and cry when I was eleven.	COMPREHENSION and COMPETENCE: Now this mother offers her daughter more understanding of the situation. She also offers her an outcome and hope for the future.

As parents, we try to become attuned to our children's thoughts and feelings, but our children become attuned to *our* thoughts and feelings, too. In thinking about depression, it's particularly important to think about yourself. That's because depression can run in families. Both mothers and fathers need to know their own family history.

What Should I Ask Myself?

Was your mother or father depressed a lot of the time when you were growing up? Do you remember either of your parents being constantly irritable? glum? moody? overly excitable? Did anyone in your family have an eating problem? a drinking problem? a sleeping problem? Did anyone in your family take medication for depression? Were either of your parents ever hospitalized? If you've answered yes to any of these questions, then you have already felt some of the developmental consequences of having a depressed parent. You may have taken over the role of caretaker in the family— filling in for your depressed mother; you may remember how abandoned and angry you felt when your father was "out of it"; or you may recall your anxiety and confusion about your parent's unpredictable mood swings. We call caretaking children who assume these kinds of premature responsibilities "parentified" children, and often when they become parents themselves, they are extra sensitive to their own kids' moods and extra anxious to "fix" them, rather than to help their kids to work things out on their own.

Did you have a happy childhood? Do photos of you show a pleasant, smiling youngster or do you look sad or sullen? How were sad feelings handled in your family? Did your parents try to "jolly" you out of them? distract you? ignore you? punish you for not being a cheerful camper? Did they say things like "Put on a happy face," or "Smile and the world smiles with you"?

Adult depression not only compromises our personal lives, it also compromises our lives as parents. Children require an enormous amount of effort under the best circumstances. Under the worst circumstances, when parents are depressed, they may be unable to take financial, emotional, or even physical care of their children. All of us will feel depressed at some point in our lives, but some of us may be particularly vulnerable to depression because of our early experiences.

What about your life right now? How do you feel? Do you find it hard to get up in the morning? Do you feel reluctant to get out of bed? Do you overeat compulsively? Is it hard to eat at all? Are you exhausted and depleted a lot of the time? Do you suffer with insomnia? Have you been feeling unmotivated and uninterested in anyone or anything? Have you stopped taking physical care of yourself? Is it hard for you to make the effort to take care of your children?

Answering yes to any one of these questions may mean you're feeling depressed right now; you may need to consult with a mental health professional.

Remember, a depressed parent cannot be a protective parent. Not only are you suffering if you're depressed—your children are suffering, too. So by getting professional help for yourself when you need it, you're also helping your kids.

Surviving childhood is no easy matter. Many children must endure emotional pain at a time when their psychological resources are just barely consolidating. Protective parenting can help children to master early experiences of hopelessness and helplessness, build up their psychological resilience, and strengthen them to face the challenges of adolescent life that lie ahead.

14

Beyond This Book:
When You or Your Child
Needs Help

There may be times in your efforts to protect your children properly when you need to rely on professional help to get things back on the right developmental track. But parents can have a hard time deciding when a child's problem is a normal part of the ups and downs of development and when it is an abnormal reaction that requires professional intervention.

Most of us are aware of how to get the right kind of professional help for *physical* symptoms in our kids: If a child doesn't see the blackboard, we whisk him off to the eye doctor for glasses; if a child has a fever, we immediately call the pediatrician; if a child fractures a bone, we know that X rays and a cast are necessary to the healing process. But we are not so alert or informed about *emotional* symptoms, nor do we so easily seek out the right kind of professional treatment.

In this last chapter, I hope to help you understand and respond to the special needs that you and your child may have, and to know when problems in your life exceed your ability to cope with them. Sometimes, these problems may be within you and you may need *individual psychotherapy*, sometimes the problem may lie between you and your partner, and *couples* or *marital therapy* may be indicated; sometimes *parent guidance* is needed to help you find a way to be a more effective parent; sometimes the problem may lie within the dynamics of the entire family, and *family therapy* may be the best solution; and sometimes your child may need to work on problems in his own life that are compromising his psychological growth. In this case, *child therapy* can help him.

Parents face many difficulties in their daily attempts to care for and protect their children—difficulties that may be hard to evaluate. Suppose a child wakes up screaming four nights in a row? Is he having nightmares? or night terrors? Is he in pain? Is there some undetected medical problem? Should you take him to the pediatrician? Is there something that's frightening him? Should you take him to a child therapist?

Or, suppose your child seems to stumble and fall often, or gets into a lot of accidents. Is he just clumsy, like you used to be as a kid? Is there an undetected orthopedic or neurological problem? Is his balance disturbed by a middle-ear infection? Or is he a depressed child, whose self-destructive feelings are causing him to become accident-prone? How can a parent tell?

What about a child that seems to be having problems in school? Is the teacher the source of the difficulties? Is your child in the right school for him? Is he beginning to reveal signs of learning difficulties or learning disabilities? Should he be evaluated? Should he be tutored? Or are underlying emotional conflicts draining your child's energies and compromising his academic performance?

And what about trauma? If a child's mother is dying, should he be taken for therapy immediately as a preventive measure? Or should he be left to work out his grief with his family and friends and not taken for any help unless he begins to show symptoms? What kinds of symptoms would indicate that a child who's in mourning needs professional help?

Taking a Chance on Love

At the beginning of this book I warned you that "the life of a parent is the life of a gambler." No matter how much we try to cushion and shield and protect our children, we still can't predict the hand our kids will be dealt, or control how they will play their cards. Every parent who raises a child takes a chance on love, but unfortunately, love is not enough. Even with all the love in the world, a lot can go wrong in life. A mother can become severely depressed; a child can be born with a grave disease; a father can be suddenly killed in a car accident.

And even if we are lucky, even if nothing goes so terribly wrong in our lives, the very influence of our own personalities on our children is unpredictable. We can't even tell if our influence will fall within normal bounds, or push beyond into abnormal responses. For instance, a daughter's early experience of her father's obsessive neatness can influence her to become a landscape architect (a normal outcome helping her to bring order to the unruly forces of nature), or an avant-garde artist (another normal outcome that enables her to confront disorder), or a compulsive young woman who needs to wash her hands twenty times a day (an abnormal outcome). A son's early exposure to an emotional, histrionic mother can go on to influence him to become an actor (a normal outcome enabling him to use his emotions), or a behavioral scientist (another normal outcome that helps him detach from his emotions), or a neurotic young man paralyzed by panic reactions (an abnormal outcome). That's why it is so very important for all of us to become aware of who we are as well as who our kids are; that's why it's so crucial for us to try to distinguish between what we actually do to our kids, and what we think we're doing. Often these distinctions will determine whether our kids are able to develop in normal or abnormal ways.

The Parent-Child Connection: Identification/Disidentification

Becoming a parent is a new kind of growing up for adults. It requires new understanding, new capacities, and new responses. But where do we learn them? We aren't taught how to be parents in high school or in college; it isn't tucked in somewhere between trigonometry and the War of 1812. Without formal education to break through and broaden our horizons, we fall back upon the only experience we have—being the child of our own parents. Even when we have few conscious memories of our own childhoods, these early experiences of family life are so enduring that it is extremely difficult for us to evade or escape their impression. We know, for instance, that children who are physically beaten by their parents frequently grow up to abuse their own children, and that children of alcoholics frequently grow up to abuse alcohol. But we are influenced by our parents in much more subtle ways, as well. How many of us swore we would never, ever tell our kids "You do that right this minute because I said so!" or insist, "Children should be seen and not heard," or say, "I'm counting to ten and then you'll be sorry!" How many of us were sure we'd never, ever make a fuss about grades, or care whether our children kept their rooms clean, or worry about their manners, or ask them to sing or dance for company?

When we take on the characteristics of our parents, which is a normal aspect of all development, we call it *identification* with them. When we refute or rebel against their characteristics, which is also normal, we call is *disidentification*. The same is true for our kids. Both identification and disidentification are ordinary outcomes of parent-child connections. Children both consciously and unconsciously absorb aspects of their parents' personalities in forming their own. Who else could they use as models? We are the people they see and hear, day in and day out. Parents are the people we all love and learn from.

From the first moments of your baby's birth, your baby is listening and learning from you. (In fact, there is even evidence that this happens *before* his birth.) What makes us such extraordinary creatures is this very ability to learn and to keep on learning throughout our lives. These early patterns serve as a kind of first draft for later editions of ourselves that are yet to come. But we can rewrite this early draft all along the way, as long as we're aware of its parameters. As we become freed from our dependency on our parents we can decide to emulate aspects of their personalities or reject them. A mother can decide she'll never leave plastic covers on the furniture in the living room (as her own mother did); a father can decide he'll never smoke (because his father smoked three packs a day all of his life and got emphysema). We are not compelled to repeat our parents' mistakes if we can become conscious of who they were and thoughtful about their failings. For protective parents, this kind of knowledge is power.

A father who won't let his son learn how to use a hammer unless he does it "exactly the right way" may have no idea that his need for control could be eroding his son's confidence. But if he remembers how angry he was as a child at his own father's overly scrupulous standards, he can find a better way to initiate his son into the principles of carpentry. A mother who is aware of how much she hated being compelled to take dancing lessons can permit her own daughter to take squash lessons, instead—or no lessons at all. She can decide to let her daughter spend her afternoons reading.

One of the most important things we need to do when we're parents is to recognize the difference between our needs or desires and our children's needs or desires. All parents have trouble with this difference because it's normal for us to want our kids to be like us. But sometimes they're only somewhat like us, and sometimes they don't seem to be like us at all, and that needs to be all right, too. Protective parents understand that a child is a separate individual with his own thoughts and feelings, not just a smaller version of his parents. Most parents love their kids, but not all parents realize that their love must also leave room for the child's unique individuality to become established. Often, when we act out of love, what we think we're doing for our children and what we're actually doing to them may turn out to be two separate experiences. The following are some examples of parents who are not mindful of this gap:

WHAT WE THINK WE'RE DOING

DAD: My father was a stickler for discipline. He was a tough guy to grow up with, but I admire him now, because eventually I learned standards that have lasted me all my life. Most kids today are soft and spoiled. I don't want my son,

Gary, to be a lazy slob, so I made sure he's learned standards right from the beginning.

WHAT WE MAY BE DOING

GARY: I'd really like to please my Dad and live up to his standards, but it's no use. My Dad makes everything into a big deal, and he criticizes everything I do. No matter how hard I try, I'm never able to do things the way he wants. It's easier to just give up and not do anything at all.

WHAT WE THINK WE'RE DOING

MOM: My mother never taught me how to dress. She was always too busy for me, and I had to take care of myself. All the girls used to make fun of my color combinations. I'm going to make sure my daughter, Dorrie, is never embarrassed like I was. I'm going to choose her clothes myself, and make sure she always wears the right thing.

WHAT WE MAY BE DOING

DORRIE: Sometimes it feels like my Mom cares more about what I *wear* than about *me*. She never lets me choose my clothes for myself. She thinks she knows everything and I know nothing. She's so picky about everything, too. She makes me feel stupid.

Why Love Is Not Enough: The Parent's Contribution

Most mothers and fathers do not set out to ruin their children's lives. Even mothers and fathers who physically abuse their children may believe they're "doing the right thing," or that they're punishing their children "for their own good." And it's easy to wind up interfering with a child's own developmental course without even realizing it. The mother who picks out her daughter's clothes each night so that "everything will match" is acting out of love, not understanding that she could be undermining her little girl's ability to make choices. The father who wants his son to grow up with standards is also acting out of love. He wants his son to have "the right stuff," not to turn off or turn away from life's challenges.

Most of us make all kinds of mistakes in the name of love. We try to give our children what we didn't have, so we insist that they take piano lessons (whether they want to or not). We try to give our children what we wish we had, so we send them to competitive schools (without regard for their ability to cope with the pressure). We try to give our children what we want for ourselves, so we press a daughter to become a doctor or a son to play baseball (without leaving them room for their own choices). In all of these cases, love is not enough.

Why Love Is Not Enough: The Child's Contribution

So far we've been talking about our children's reactions to growing up with us, but each child also brings his own temperament and character to bear on the parent-child connection, as well. Each baby comes into the world with a particular genetic inheritance that includes intellectual and emotional characteristics as well as physical ones, like blue eyes or red hair. These characteristics include things like intelligence, artistic or musical talents, physical restlessness, emotional sensitivity or resilience, assertiveness and shyness, and muscular agility, among others. They will go on to play their part in your child's personality growth, creating the continuities of development we all recognize when we say things like "She was always a little dynamo—even as a baby she was into everything," or "He's always been musical; he used to hum along with the stereo in his crib."

Sometimes, these characteristics are accepted by us and acceptable to us—we recognize and admire them. But sometimes these characteristics are difficult to accept or unacceptable to us—and we may criticize or condemn them. Then, even our language will change as we describe the characteristic:

A DESCRIPTION OF A CHILD BY AN ACCEPTING PARENT	A DESCRIPTION OF THE SAME CHILD BY AN UNACCEPTING PARENT
She's really got a mind of her own. It's remarkable that such a little baby has such a strong will. Nobody's going to push *her* around when she grows up!	She's impossible to manage. She's stubborn and difficult already, and she's only a baby. I don't know how I'm going to control her when she gets older.

It's clear to see that one mom will be able to help her baby daughter to develop her strong will as a *positive* characteristic. She's already creating room for her daughter's unique needs. But the other mom is already gearing up to do battle with her strong-willed baby. She is distressed and disturbed by what she feels are her daughter's *negative* characteristics. She and her daughter are already headed for trouble.

Getting the Help You Need

Every love relationship hits some hard times, and the loving relationship between parents and their children is no exception. Most of the time, I hope you will be able to use the information in this book to help you to understand and cope with the ordinary problems of family life. But sometimes, you may find that you have come to the end of your resources for dealing with a problem your child is experiencing. Then, I hope this chapter will help you to make the decision to seek out professional help.

All along in these chapters, I've been emphasizing how important it is to address problems in your child's development as they come up, with all the resources you can muster. This is particularly important when we're talking about recognizing psychological problems that require professional intervention. Being a protective parent means recognizing the problem when it appears, addressing it directly if you can, and getting the finest professional help if you can't.

DEVELOPMENTAL TASKS/DEVELOPMENTAL OUTCOMES: HOW TO KNOW WHEN THINGS GO WRONG

There are physical milestones that help us to know when to expect our kids to master certain capacities—walking, talking, holding a pencil, throwing a ball, and so on. So, too, there are certain psychological milestones that alert us to the tasks that our kids need to master as they grow and develop. In order to know when things may not be going well for our kids, we have to understand these ordinary milestones. Following is a brief survey of the developmental course of an ordinary child's life:

From Birth to One Year

When a baby is born, he and his mother must try together to work out a "fit" in both physical and psychological rhythms that will help her to supply the baby with what he needs (for example, to be fed every three hours), while still permitting his mother to get what she needs (a decent night's sleep). The mother-infant partnership is based on working this out to the advantage of the baby, so that he may thrive. Protective parents realize, when they decide to have a child, that their needs must often be sacrificed in favor of the needs of the baby. (That's why it's a good idea to get many of your own needs met before you have a baby.) We already know that in the first year of a baby's life, mothers gradually build their confidence, so that they can "read" their baby, and the baby gradually builds his confidence in his parents to fulfill his needs. Psychologically, this mother-infant "attunement" translates into the beginnings of a sense of trust—in his parents and his world. Disruptions of this trust and difficulties within the mother-infant pair will reveal themselves in the baby's ability (or lack of ability) to attach to his parents appropriately and to make use of their love and care for him. The baby's most basic needs will provide the first opportunity for mothers and babies to struggle toward "attunement," so, naturally, problems around eating and sleeping are common in the first year of life. How well the subsequent years will go has a great deal to do with (but is not wholly determined by) how well the first year of life has gone. This is because in human growth, psychological development accumulates in layers, with each new phase of growth building on the accomplishments (or lack of accomplishments) of the previous experiences. If trust and confidence and attachment have been adequately established, then the next challenges of separation, growing autonomy, and independence will begin to become the focus of development. If they have not been managed, then these deficits in development will be carried over into the next phase.

From One to Three Years

In the second year of life, babies talk and walk and begin to define themselves apart from their parents in new and exciting ways. Problem areas now have expanded beyond feeding and sleeping and attachment difficulties. Now, you will be able to note a new willfulness, the emergence of self-regard and self-reliance, and problems with self-control—control over one's own body ("Mommy, I can do it myself!"), control over one's own aggression ("No, no, no!"), and control over one's own desires ("Give me that pail with the big red shovel"). The reason that parents often refer to this phase as "the terrible two's" is this very emergence of the toddler's will, an important developmental accomplishment. The modulation and transformation of will, then, becomes an important milestone at this age, and children who are unable to master their assertive/aggressive impulses will begin to show behavioral symptoms of their struggle which, unless addressed, will cause them great difficulties in their lives.

From Three to Six Years

The nursery school years reveal the accelerated growth of your child's mind. Your child has now left the comfort of the family circle for the challenges of the world at large. (Remember our discussion of the resolution of the oedipus complex in chapter 4, and how it helps your child grow up and move on?) Psychological problems that emerge at this phase will most likely cluster around your child's growing capacities for symbolization (which is often accompanied by heightened fears, anxieties, and phobias—fears of the dark, of witches, of alligators, of vampires, and so on), problems around separating from you in more substantial ways (with accompanying sleep disturbances and anxieties), and problems in relating and adjusting to the new peer group life that is now required of him in school. Here, too, leftover problems with trust, attachment, and self-control will persist if they have never been adequately resolved. When a child is still working on old developmental tasks and has little energy for new age-appropriate challenges, we describe him as emotionally immature. A child like this is likely to stand out in his school setting, already claiming the special attention of his teachers.

Remember, *struggling* with these problems is normal, and you can expect to see conflicts in these areas appear and reappear in these early years. Most children under six still have some problems with separation, self-control, aggression, and anxiety, but their difficulties are usually transient, and your child's overall functioning is not compromised. (Even though he may protest, your son will eventually accommodate to staying at school without you; even though your daughter is afraid of the dark, she will eventually fall asleep with a night-light.)

But sometimes, these difficulties are not transient; sometimes it seems as if your child's concerns may appear to overwhelm his ability to function; sometimes, he may develop behavioral systems which will persist for months without change. When there has been a significant change in your child's mood or personality, or he displays new behavior that troubles you, and it does not seem to go away within a few months, then professional consultation may be indicated.

Since children are always growing, the earlier you intervene, and the more quickly the problem can be addressed, the less effect your child's problems are likely to have on his ongoing development. Another good reason to help young children is that the younger the child the easier it is for help to make a real difference. Three- to six-year-old children, for instance, have only just developed the maladaptive behaviors that they're revealing. Their personalities have not yet fully crystallized, and this means that they are still fluid enough to make significant changes. It's a whole lot easier to help a three-year-old change than to help a thirty-year-old!

Since each subsequent developmental phase builds on the strengths (and weaknesses) of the previous phases, another good reason to intervene early is that it enables your child to remove obstacles to his ongoing growth as they happen. This makes it possible for him to make fuller use of his capacities as he grows, without the accumulated distortions and deficits that conflict imposes on development.

From Six to Eight Years

By the time your child is six or seven years old, he has developed a more cohesive sense of self, a more formed sense of conscience, and a more consolidated sense of sexual identity. If you are concerned about whether or not your child knows the difference between right and wrong, or observe that he or she is still struggling against accepting their gender role ("I don't want to be a boy" "I wish I wasn't a girl") then, again, this may be a time to seek out professional consultation. You will need to determine whether this sexual conflict (for instance, effeminacy in a young boy) is something that your child will "outgrow," or something that your child will need help to resolve. Again, persistent odd or maladaptive behavior that consistently sets your child apart from his peers needs to be evaluated (a little boy who always gets into fights with his peers, for example, or a little girl who cannot stop herself from masturbating).

From Eight to Ten Years

Eight- to ten-year-old children are school-age and school-centered. At this age, many of the problems your child struggles with will be based on his ability (or lack of ability) to make his way in his school world. This is also the age when learning differences and learning difficulties are most likely to be detected, as your child is now faced with specific academic expectations. If your child is having learning problems, a full neuropsychological evaluation can help you to discover whether he is struggling with internal psychological conflicts that interfere with his concentration, constrain his motivation, and impede his performance, or with undetected learning disabilities. Most of the time, both psychological and neurological factors are involved. It is rare to find a child who has a learning problem with no psychological consequences. This means that even if your child is diagnosed with a neurologically based learning disability, psychotherapy may be as important to help him repair his damaged sense of self as tutoring is to help him remediate his failing school performance.

By this age, children have the capacity to suffer with a whole array of thoughts and feelings that are all too familiar to us.

They are capable of anxiety and panic, obsession and compulsion, rebellion and opposition, and apathy and depression. Any one of these internal states, and its accompanying symptoms, is worthy of professional attention, if the behavioral manifestations do not abate within a few months. But remember, a *chronic* behavioral reaction is very different from an *acute* behavioral reaction. Obviously, a child who feels panicky when he goes off to camp for the first time is displaying a different (and more normal) picture than a child that panics each and every time he has a playdate. In addition to analyzing whether the behavior is chronic or acute, you also need to evaluate how much your child's conflict interferes with his life. A child who must count to five hundred and turn around ten times every time he leaves his room is going to be more compromised in his life than a child who is just obsessively neat about his dresser drawers. And a child who pulls the hair of his eyebrows off needs more attention than a nail-biter.

Wise guys and class clowns, children who goof off or who constantly disappoint, under- or overachievers, children who antagonize their parents or their teachers all are asking for help by demonstrating their negative and self-destructive impulses. Protective parents need to respond to their pleas and get them the right kind of attention.

Last, and very important, any child who talks about or writes about suicide, who expresses a feeling that life isn't worth living, who states that he wishes he were dead, or who is consistently accident-prone, needs immediate professional attention. As I discussed in chapter 13, "Necessary Losses: Dealing with Helplessness and Hopelessness," childhood depression is a serious matter, and signs of its occurrence are increasing in our society, as today's children face our troubled times.

Protective parents pay attention to their children's behavior, and recognize the early warning signs of psychic distress. Your child's external behavioral symptoms are a signal that your child's internal emotional resources are overwhelmed.

The Five Mental Health Myths

Parents who would fly to the ends of the earth to track down the most skilled doctor for a physical problem their child had will think nothing of delaying or avoiding consultation with a mental health professional about an emotional problem. Why? I have found that there are five major myths about mental health consultation that usually prevent parents, even relatively sophisticated protective parents, from seeking out such help when it is needed.

"He'll Outgrow It!"

Children are always in the process of growing, and their moods, thoughts, and behaviors change all the time. That's why it's so easy to tell ourselves that if we do nothing, our child will simply outgrow the problem. Some of the time, this attitude may in fact be appropriate to the situation, particularly if the child's disturbed behavior is a *reaction* to a recent event (like the death of a grandparent, or an illness, or a mugging, or a divorce—in fact, to any of the events we have been exploring in the chapters you have just read). But—and here's the important distinction—if your child's behavioral reactions seem to have "hardened," and if his reactions have persisted over time, unchanging without modulation, then he is demonstrating that he does not have the internal resources to master this recent experience, nor to move on in his life. Then your child's reactions have created an obstacle to his ongoing development. In these cases, he is no more likely to outgrow this emotional "fracture" to his sense of self than he would be able to outgrow a fracture to his arm. Seeking out a mental health professional to help him heal his distress is as essential as seeking out an orthopedist in the latter situation. An orthopedist will set your child's fractured bone so that it will grow in the right direction, reducing interference with the arm's function, as your child develops. Similarly, a mental health professional can help your child to heal the fractures in his mind. A child therapist can help reduce the obstacles to your child's growth, reducing the interference with the mind's natural course of development.

"You Have to Be Really Crazy to Wind Up in Therapy!"

Just as the practice of pediatrics is often referred to as "well-baby care," so the practice of child therapy is primarily work with children who are *not* severely disturbed* but have come up against a developmental obstacle, either internally (within their own minds) or externally (within the dynamics of their relationship to their parents and their family). Most of these children are struggling with psychological issues that can be effectively eased by psychotherapeutic treatment—issues like phobias, nightmares, lack of confidence, problems in learning, overaggressive or oppositional behavior, low self-esteem, lack of self-control, childhood depression, and others. Many of the parents of these children can also be helped to alter their understanding and their approach to their children in order to lighten their emotional burden. Most important, seeking out psychological support *early* in the onset of the problem prevents it from worsening and permits new patterns of behavior for both you and your child to take hold.

"Therapy Is a Crutch—My Child Needs to Stand on His Own Two Feet!"

Very often when parents first consult with me, one of their greatest fears is that they and/or their child will become dependent on the very process that they are hoping will make

---

*There is a small (fairly constant) percentage of children who suffer with severe mental disabilities, just as there is a small percentage of children who suffer with severe physical disabilities. In childhood, these illnesses encompass autism (a bewildering syndrome of behaviors with an early onset, in infancy or toddlerhood), childhood schizophrenia (another grave mental disturbance, where the distinction between reality and fantasy is blurred), and specific developmental and psychoneurological disabilities (where the ability of the child to learn and grow at normal rates is severely compromised.) This chapter is not meant to address these specific disorders, as an understanding and approach to them lie outside the scope of this book. Parents who are deeply concerned about their child's development need to consult their pediatrician, family practitioner, local hospital, or mental health agency, to locate a child development center in their area that will help them to diagnose and treat their youngster's condition.

them independent. They will frequently say, "I don't want therapy to become a crutch." I often reply, "Why not?" A crutch, after all, is something you use to lean on when you're not yet strong enough to support your own weight. As your body heals, you use your crutch less and less until, one day, you naturally throw your crutch away and stand unaided. When you make the decision to take your child to see a therapist, it is because your child is dealing with something that he is not strong enough to master on his own. He needs the support of a therapist. Through therapy, the child's mind is strengthened, and as he is strengthened, he takes over more and more of the therapeutic process on his own. One day, when he is strong enough and has understood enough, your child will be ready to terminate his therapy. It will no longer be necessary to his development and the treatment will stop. He will now be ready to throw away his crutch and stand on his own two feet. What's wrong with that?

"Therapy Will Open Up a Can of Worms!"

Every family has its struggles. Sometimes, one of the members of a family becomes emotionally overwhelmed and can no longer manage. When this happens to an adult, sometimes we say that she has suffered a "nervous breakdown." This has become a socially acceptable way of indicating that things have gotten to be too much to handle. But breakdowns can happen to children, too. They can begin to have trouble eating or sleeping, learning or playing, or listening. They can become hard to manage, listless, hostile, fearful, or nervous. They can be unable to manage at school or at home, or be unable to leave their room, or even their bed.

When this happens to your child, you had better "open up the can of worms," because that's the only way to let them out. Otherwise, both you and your child are trapped inside. Every family has its wormy side, but keeping things in the dark only encourages more worms to grow. Shedding some light on the issue enables you to see things as they are. The most important thing a protective parent can do when things go wrong, is to get help to get better. To do this, translate the four C's into effective therapeutic action:

> *Compassion:* Understand who your child is.
> *Communication:* Address his problems quickly.
> *Comprehension:* Recognize the signs of trouble.
> *Competence:* Get help if you need it.

"It's All My Fault!"

Bringing your child to a therapist is much harder than bringing your child to any other kind of doctor. Most of the time if a child gets a virus, we don't think, "It's my fault." But, because we are so intimately connected to and responsible for our children's emotional lives, we often feel guilty and ashamed, as well as anxious and upset, if something goes wrong. We become reluctant to expose our pain and our failure to a professional, who (we're afraid) will judge us and (we're sure) will find us lacking.

I compared the life of a parent to the life of a gambler in order to help you appreciate that even if you are devoted, attuned, and sensitive, all kinds of unexpected problems can arise which might still need special attention (even as the healthiest child can still fall ill with a virus). If you feel that the therapist you consult is judging you, rather than helping you explore and understand—find another therapist!

Choosing a Therapist

Picking a professional who can work with you and your child is understandably confusing to most parents. First, because mental health practitioners come from so many different backgrounds, and second, because it's hard to know what to look for. Because child therapists are drawn from psychiatry, psychology, social work, and nursing, you will need to inquire directly about the training of any therapist you consult. Always ask the therapist whether he or she has had specialized training to work with children and parents. Without this training, a practitioner is less likely to be aware of and alert to the special developmental needs of children and less likely to be able to address those needs therapeutically. And you are much less likely to get the kind of empathic parent guidance that will help you to understand and alter your relationship with your child.

Each of the mental health disciplines brings its own unique perspective to the treatment of children. For example, psychiatry is the only discipline at this point licensed to prescribe drugs, and psychiatrists are therefore most familiar with the extensive advances in psychopharmacology and with the effects (both positive and negative) of psychotropic medications. In contrast, many psychologists and social workers with advanced child training have extensive experience with the kinds of psychological difficulties that enmesh children and their parents, and both of these disciplines may be able to offer understanding and the therapeutic interventions that will effectively address these issues without resorting to drugs. Nurse practitioners (nurses with psychiatric training) are also licensed to provide private child therapy in some states. In addition, psychologists are specially trained in the administering of psychological tests, which are often crucial to the evaluation and diagnosis of many psychological disturbances in childhood.

As with all professional referrals, a satisfied customer is your best resource. Ask your friends and relatives if they've had any good personal experiences with mental health practitioners, or if they've heard of anyone excellent "through the grapevine." Schools are often a fine source for professional referrals, as well, since they need to make recommendations to parents when children have problems, and often maintain a referral list. Your pediatrician or family doctor may also be a good person to ask for a referral—but keep in mind that you are more likely to be sent to a psychiatrist or child psychiatrist by your doctor, since doctors often feel most comfortable recommending colleagues who share their medical background. In many cities and large towns there may be local mental health organizations that you can call for referrals.

Over and above the standard discipline training (Ph.D., C.S.W., D.S.W., R.N., M.D.), some mental health practitioners go on for postdegree specialty training in psychoanalytic therapy, family therapy, behavioral therapy, cognitive therapy, or the like. All of these represent different approaches to psychological problems, and any of these approaches might help you and your child.

The approach used in this book is *developmentally based* and *psychoanalytically informed.* It is an approach that I have practiced with confidence for more than twenty years. Don't be afraid to ask any therapists you interview to tell you about their education, training, and approach. Don't be afraid to ask about the therapists' clinical experience, either. Has the therapist treated many children? Many children the same age as your child? Many children with problems similar to your child's problems?

Remember that, above all, therapy is a relationship—a special kind of relationship that makes the expression, exploration, and understanding of your child's emotional struggles possible. It is also an extended relationship, very different from one that comes down to "Take two aspirin and call me in the morning." The very first questions to ask yourself are: Do I like and trust this therapist? Is this someone that I would want my child to get to know? Do I think this person is smart and thoughtful? Someone I can talk easily and in-depth to? Do I sense the capacity to help me and my child? You should be able to have a positive feeling about the therapist you select before you entrust your child to his or her care. Find out, too, if your child's therapist will meet periodically or regularly with *you.* Is parent guidance work a part of the therapist's normal method of working? If not, will you be seeing another therapist?

Take your time to decide. You can consult with a therapist several times before making your decision. Your child should *not* be included in these initial consultations and should not be given a choice of therapists. This is too great a burden for a young child to assume, particularly because children do not have any sense of the appropriate criteria for making this decision. If an older child (ten to twelve years old) insists upon being involved in the decision-making process, or wants to decide between seeing a man and a woman, be sure to limit the choices to no more than two people, and make sure you're comfortable with either choice of therapist that you present to your child. (If, for some good reason, your child doesn't feel comfortable with, or doesn't like the therapist you've chosen, the child should still be encouraged to see the therapist a few times before you present a second choice. Picking a therapist for a child, like picking any other doctor, is an adult responsibility.)

How to Prepare Your Child for Psychological Treatment

Say that you've realized that your child needs help above and beyond what you can provide. And you understand that in today's times, seeking out the help of a professional child therapist to address your child's emotional problems is no more (and no less) appropriate than seeking out the help of your pediatrician to address your child's physical problems. You're also aware that the earlier you diagnose and intervene, the greater your chances will be of avoiding more serious consequences for you and your child. Now you are ready to approach your child and help prepare him to see a professional. But what should you say? No matter what the age of your child there are three important elements to include as you create your reparative narrative:

- A description of your child's symptoms. (COMMUNICATION)

- A statement that expresses your concern about your child's struggles and conflicts. (COMPASSION/COMPREHENSION)

- A portrayal of who a child therapist is and what such a person does. (COMPETENCE)

Here's a mother talking to a young child (three to six years old) about going to see a child therapist.

NARRATIVE	REPARATIVE ELEMENTS
MOM: You know how you've been waking up almost every night, and you're so afraid that you can't go back to sleep? I've also noticed that you're getting more and more scared about things like witches and vampires—even though we've talked about them and we know they're not real.	COMMUNICATION: This mother is describing her daughter's symptoms in order to confirm their reality for the child.
DIANA: I hate witches. I'm scared of witches.	
MOM: But it's not just witches. You're having a lot of trouble with scary feelings. Daddy and I have noticed that it's getting harder and harder for you to go to nursery school.	COMPREHENSION: She's also linking the symptoms with changes in behavior, enlarging the child's understanding of the situation.
DIANA: I'm scared the witches will get me at school, too.	
MOM: You cry every morning and don't want to leave the house. We don't want you to be so scared. We need to find a way to help you.	
DIANA: Can you make the witches go away?	

NARRATIVE	REPARATIVE ELEMENTS
MOM: No, sweetie, but we've found someone who can help make them go away. Her name is Dr. Sarah Gabriel and she's a special children's "worry doctor." She helps children to understand their thoughts and their feelings and to deal with their worries by talking and playing. Daddy and I went to see her last week to make sure that she was someone you'd like. She's very nice, with long blond hair and a soft voice, and she has lots of interesting things to look at and play with in her office. We're going to take you to visit her next week, so you can see her for yourself, and begin to get some help to take away your worries.	COMPASSION: Here, she's expressing empathy for her daughter. More COMMUNICATION: The mother includes a description of the child therapist and therapy in order to expand her child's information. COMPETENCE: She offers her child a possible resolution to the present difficulties.

Here's a *reparative narrative* created by a father who's talking with his older son (eight to ten years old) about therapy:

NARRATIVE	REPARATIVE ELEMENTS
DAD: Mommy and I have been really worried about you lately. You've been down in the dumps, and there doesn't seem to be anything we can do to help you feel better. First, we thought it was just changing schools, and you needed some time to get adjusted, but things don't really seem to be getting	COMMUNICATION: This father lets his son know he's thought about this problem. He also is trying to confirm its reality for his son.

NARRATIVE	REPARATIVE ELEMENTS
any better. I know it's been hard to make friends and you feel lonely.	COMPASSION: He also expresses concern and empathy.
EVAN: I don't feel lonely. I don't need stupid friends.	
DAD: I found this note you wrote in your wastebasket, where you said you wished you could die, and you drew a boy with a noose around his neck. I know you didn't intend me to see your private note, but I'm glad I found it, because it helped us to know how unhappy you really are.	COMPREHENSION: By linking his son's feelings with his behavior and describing symptoms, he's enlarging the child's understanding of the situation.
EVAN: Leave me alone.	
DAD: We wouldn't be taking good care of you if we let you suffer alone without doing something about it. When kids feel really depressed, like you do, there are special children's therapists that they can go to.	COMPETENCE: Now, he's expressing a possible resolution in a compassionate way.
EVAN: I'm not going to any dumb doctor.	
DAD: We went to see a few last week and we picked someone we feel you could really trust with your problems. His name is Bob Morris, and he's young and really nice and easy to talk to. He helps kids with problems like yours, by talking to them and playing with them. He's even got some good games in his office.	More COMPETENCE: This narrative gives the child a positive description of the therapist and of therapy to think about. Hope for the future is offered as an outcome.

NARRATIVE	REPARATIVE ELEMENTS
We've made an appointment for you to see him next week, so you can get to the bottom of these bad feelings and get rid of them.	

But suppose you've said all of that, and instead of your child eagerly awaiting his appointment, he protests and refuses to go? What if, instead of a cooperative, compliant, relieved child, you have a screaming, squirming, resistant one?

Once you've decided that your child needs professional help, you must *stick to your decision.* This is part of what being a protective parent means. You wouldn't give your child the option to take his antibiotic for his strep throat, or let him decide if he wants to get a polio vaccine. Similarly, you can't give your child the option to decide about whether or not he'll go to therapy for his depression, or whether he should be evaluated for his academic failures. This decision is up to you and you alone. It's best if he understands that therapy is in his best interest, but treatment is not impossible if he doesn't. (In fact, part of every child therapist's training deals with handling resistant children, as well as resistant parents!)

Most of the time, for all of us, it's our fear and anxiety that stands in the way of treatment. When that's addressed, the resistance falls away. Here's a possible way of handling a young child's protest:

PAULA *(crying):* I don't want to go. I don't want to see anyone, Mommy. I don't want to see the lady. Please let me stay home with you.

MOM: I know it worries you even to see someone who could help, but I'll come with you and I won't leave you until you feel comfortable. You can start by telling her how nervous you feel going to see her. That's her job—helping kids to feel less afraid. But you need to go, honey, if we're going to help you feel better.

Here's a narrative that may offer a way of handling your older child's objections:

DEREK *(angry):* Forget it! No way! I'm not crazy, and I'm not going to see any stupid shrink!

MOM: Of course, you're not crazy, but you *are* sad and upset, and maybe even angry about things that you can't talk to us about. Lots of kids and lots of adults talk to shrinks when they're having problems, just like they go to doctors when there's a problem with their bodies. Remember when Adam's parents were getting a divorce and he told us that he was seeing a therapist? And what about last year, when your cousin Judith was doing so poorly in school, and she was tested and then went to see that psychologist who helped her with her learning difficulties? You know and I know that these feelings aren't going away or getting better. You need help and you owe it to yourself to at least try it. We'll meet with him next week. You can either see him alone or with us, and then we'll discuss it again.

Remember, you're not alone in helping your child to accept therapy. The therapist is there to provide you with support, as well. If you are having a particularly difficult time persuading your child to come for an appointment and none of the approaches that I've outlined in this chapter seem to help, call your new therapist. Now, it's his or her problem, too!

And don't forget that when one child in your family goes for therapy, it affects the other kids in the family, too. Siblings' reactions can range from envy and exclusion ("How come Dana gets to play with and talk with someone and I don't? You always give her everything she wants!") to shame and humiliation ("If someone finds out my brother goes to a psychologist, they'll think our family's strange").

Here's a reparative narrative that a mother has developed to help her ten-year-old son accept his seven-year-old brother's therapy without feeling so threatened:

VINCENT: Why does Kenny have to go to therapy? That's so weird. Everyone will think he's crazy!

NARRATIVE	REPARATIVE ELEMENTS
MOM: You sound worried that people will think Kenny's crazy, and maybe you're worried that they'll think you're crazy too.	COMPASSION and COMPREHENSION: This mother begins by letting her son know she can empathize with his feelings. She also tries to expand his understanding of why he's upset.
VINCENT *(defensive):* I'm not crazy, and Kenny isn't either.	
MOM: That's right! Kenny is just going to talk to a therapist about his problems with his bed-wetting—just like if he had a sore throat we'd take him to see Dr. Hirsch. There are doctors who help us with physical problems and doctors who can help us with emotional problems. There's nothing weird about that.	COMPREHENSION and COMPETENCE: Now this mother is offering more understanding of the situation for her older son and helping him reach a resolution of his feelings, "normalizing" the experience.

HOW CAN YOU TELL WHEN YOU OR YOUR CHILD NEEDS HELP?

In order to help you get a sense about when you or your child might need to seek out professional attention, I've created two Psychological Checklists of some of the most common problems parents and kids can face:

A Psychological Checklist for You

1. Do you find yourself depleted and overwhelmed around your kids most of the time?

2. Do you and your partner disagree or fight primarily about the children?
3. Do you feel your children are not living up to your expectations or turning out the way you imagined?
4. Most of the time, do you feel that being a parent is a joyless or thankless task?
5. Do you find yourself losing your temper when you're around your children? Do you scream at them or hit them?
6. Do you look for every opportunity to spend time *away* from your kids?
7. Do you feel anxious when you're with your children and imagine all the bad things that could happen to them? Do you feel this way most of the time when you're not with them, too?
8. Are you and your partner struggling with your relationship and contemplating a separation? Have you just separated or divorced your partner?
9. Do you have a major drug or alcohol problem? Does your partner?
10. Are you or your partner seriously ill, or are most of your emotional and physical energies mobilized by the serious illness of someone who is very close to you?

A Psychological Checklist for Your Child

1. Does your child have a serious and consistent problem with eating or sleeping?
2. Has there been any substantial change for the worse in your child's behavior?
3. Has your child's mood seemed consistently sad, blue, or melancholy?
4. Has your child seemed anxious, nervous, fearful, or phobic for some time?
5. Is your child repeatedly waking up with nightmares? night terrors?
6. Has your child's school performance consistently deteriorated? Does your child appear to be struggling or frustrated?
7. Has your child had a number of bewildering and disturbing accidents over a short period of time?

8. Is your child consistently reporting having no friends, and that no one likes him or her. Is your child very shy socially or "a loner"?

9. Has your child ever reported not wanting to live, or wishing to be dead, or discussed his or her own death in specific detail?

If you've answered yes to any of these questions, then a professional consultation may be useful to both you and your child.

You've just spent a lot of time carefully reading these fourteen chapters, now it may be necessary to get the help you need beyond this book. From one parent to another, Good luck!

INDEX